Literary Insinuations

Literary Insinuations

Sorting Out Sinyavsky's Irreverence

Walter F. Kolonosky

LEXINGTON BOOKS
Lanham • Boulder • New York • Oxford

LEXINGTON BOOKS

Published in the United States of America
by Lexington Books
A Member of the Rowman & Littlefield Publishing Group
4501 Forbes Boulevard, Suite 200, Lanham, Maryland 20706

PO Box 317
Oxford
OX2 9RU, UK

British Library Cataloguing in Publication Information Available

Library of Congress Cataloging-in-Publication Data

Kolonosky, Walter F., 1938–
Literary insinuations : sorting out Sinyavsky's irreverence / Walter F. Kolonosky.
p. cm.
Includes bibliographical references and index.
ISBN 0-7391-0488-8 (alk. paper)
1. Sinëìavskiæi, A. (Andreæi), 1925—Criticism and interpretation. I. Title.
PG3476 .S539Z74 2003
891. 7844'09—dc21

2002156789

Printed in the United States of America

∞™ The paper used in this publication meets the minimum requirements of American National Standard for Information Sciences—Permanence of Paper for Printed Library Materials, ANSI/NISO Z39.48-1992.

To Trish

Contents

Acknowledgments

I would like to thank the Graduate School and the President's Office at Kansas State University for the grants that supported my visits to Andrei Sinyavsky. These visits were invaluable to my research, and especially to my acquaintance with the man behind his writing. I hasten to add that I will never forget the warmth and hospitality that Andrei Donatovich and Mariya Vasilevna extended to me and my wife, Trish. I also want to express my gratitude to my friends and colleagues who shared their insights into literature as well as their experiences in scholarly publishing. Above all, I want to say a special word of thanks to Trish, to whom this book is dedicated, for she stood by me through both good and bad days. Finally, I am grateful to the *Slavic and East European Journal* for permission to republish a version of an article on "*Pkhents*" and on Andrei Sinyavsky's dissertation.

TRANSLITERATION AND TRANSLATION

Russian words are transliterated according to the Library of Congress system with modifications such as "ya" rather than "ia." Hard signs are represented by "; soft signs by '. Soft signs, which are ubiquitous in Russian, are omitted in well-known Russian names and titles in the body of the text, for example, Yeltsin, Gogol, Menshutin. Moreover, English versions of names are provided wherever possible, as in the case of "Dostoevsky" and "Sinyavsky." Translations into English, with few exceptions, are mine.

Chapter One

Introduction

Andrei Sinyavsky (1925–1997) is a well-known writer and literary critic who has been translated into several languages and around whom there has been considerable scholarship and press coverage, not to mention controversies. Arguably, he is one of the leading Russian intellectuals of the twentieth century. Three monographs have been published about him to date (Dalton, Lourie, and Nepomnyashchy), but none of them have theorized about the playful and provocative disposition of his writing. The study that you are about to read carefully considers this disposition, weighing, in particular, its strong ties with traditional modes of satire, as well as with modernist practices that are designed to delight and disturb the reader. Clearly, Sinyavsky is at odds with his era, but he is an intellectual rather than a political agitator, questioning, for example, the administration of a single "purposefulness" and "usefulness" in art and public policy. In his literary criticism he speaks directly, attacking what he considers to be a specific set of abuses and follies; in his fiction he speaks indirectly, turning to allegory, parody, and irony like any other satirist. Before arguing that Sinyavsky's fiction and literary criticism are a part of the same fabric of blistering assaults and tactical buffoonery, let us first get acquainted with some of the details of his biography.

Sinyavsky was born in Moscow on October 8, 1925, eight years after the Revolution. His mother was a simple Russian woman; his father was born into a noble family, but renounced his heritage when he joined the Socialist Revolutionaries in 1909. Sinyavsky's father paid dearly for his pre-revolutionary ties. Suspicion turned into harassment and blacklisting, and finally into arrest in 1951 when the last of the former Socialist

Revolutionaries were rounded up. Sinyavsky grew up in the shadow of his father's problems, seeing them eventually as a shared territory. Because of his father's past, Sinyavsky found himself in a communal apartment for forty years where a lightbulb or garbage pail became an issue and space for a kettle on the stove became an obsession (*Soviet Civilization* 168). He grew up during World War II, facing evacuation from Moscow in 1941 and then military service between 1943 and 1945. After the war, Sinyavsky abandoned his training as a radio technician and entered the University of Moscow to study literature, unaware that his undergraduate days would coincide with the mass persecution of scholars and scientists (Heller and Nekrich 491). He graduated in 1949, having completed his senior thesis (*diplomnaya rabota*) on Mayakovsky. The following year he enrolled in graduate school to continue his study of literature. In 1951, while he was writing his dissertation, his father was arrested and exiled to Rameno, the place of his birth, where he was forced to remain for five years. In spite of these distressing circumstances, Sinyavsky finished his 400-page dissertation on Maksim Gorky's novel *The Life of Klim Samgin* (*Zhizn' Klima Samgina*). The following year he received his *kandidat* degree, which, in the United States, is comparable to the Ph.D.

Sinyavsky is a product of Stalin's Russia. His childhood, boyhood, and youth coincide with Stalin's rise to power, highlighted by collectivization, industrialization, mobilization of the arts, and the purges. But when Sinyavsky was twenty-eight, Stalin died. For Russia a turning point seemed inevitable. For Sinyavsky a turning point took place before Stalin's death. In 1947, he befriended Hélène Peltier, the daughter of a French naval attaché, who was taking courses at the University of Moscow. The following year the KGB pressured him to start a romantic liaison with her in order to compromise her father. This pressure, which did not abate until 1952, turned Sinyavsky against the Soviet system (*Sobranie sochinenii* 2:590).[1] Before the "thaw," dramatically ushered in by Khrushchev's denunciation of Stalin's crimes at the twentieth party congress in 1956, Sinyavsky had at least two manuscripts ready for publication, *Chto takoe sotsialisticheskii realism (What Is Socialist Realism*) and *Sud idet* (*The Trial Begins*).[2] In December of that year, after much soul searching, he gave them to Hélène Peltier to smuggle to the West in order to find a publisher, insisting that she avoid anti-Soviet presses at all costs. Knowing that both works sharply satirized the Soviet system, he used a pseudonym, "Abram Terts." They appeared in France and the United States in 1959 and 1960, not long after *Doktor Zhivago*, causing another sensation.[3]

Speculation immediately began regarding the identity of Terts. In fact, it continued for six years. During these years Sinyavsky led two lives: one as Terts, completing two short novels, six short stories, and a collection of aphorisms; the other as a scholar and literary critic, completing twenty-nine essays, several of which he coauthored with A. Menshutin.[4] Actually, Sinyavsky already established himself as a scholar in the late 1950s, his essays on Gorky and Bagritsky having appeared in the prestigious *History of Soviet Literature* (*Istoriya sovetskoi literatury*) and his entries on A. Voloshin and Acmeism in the *Short Literary Encyclopedia* (*Kratkaya literaturnaya entsiklopediya*). With an enormous capacity for work, he not only finished project after project, but he also made time for excursions with his wife to Pereslavl-Zalessky in the lake region of northern Russia to photograph examples of old architecture and to collect folk art and icons (Dalton 15). Together with Igor Golomshtok he coauthored a book on Pablo Picasso in 1960, which was the first study of this artist to be made available in Russia for public consumption.[5] The following year he became a member of the Union of Soviet Writers. In 1964, he and A. Menshutin finished a major monograph, *The Poetry of the First Years of the Revolution* (*Poeziya pervykh let revolyutsii*), which the *London Times* called the best foreign language publication of the year.[6] The following year, which was the year of Sinyavsky's arrest, his well-known introductory essay to Pasternak's collection of poetry, "*Stikhotvoreniya i poemy*" ("Poetry and Narrative Poems"), appeared.[7] It turned out to be a part of a body of evidence of important scholarship, embarrassing in no small way to authorities. That same year, Aleksandr Tvardovsky, the editor of *Novyi mir (The New World)*, to which Sinyavsky was a regular contributor, named Sinyavsky as one of the most talented up-and-coming literary critics.[8]

In spite of the attention that has been paid to Sinyavsky's fiction, his scholarship occupies an equal place among his contributions. After all, he has written about a host of authors, including Pushkin, Gogol, Dostoevsky, Rozanov, Gorky, Mayakovsky, Evtushenko, Pasternak, Voznesensky, Babel, Bagritsky, Berggolts, Remizov, Akhmatova, and Zoshchenko. He was comfortable in nineteenth and twentieth-century literature, in poetry and prose, ancient and modern art, folklore, philosophy, and history. It appeared easy for him to write a survey of the literature of the Great Patriotic War (World War II) or to review a book on the poetry of Robert Frost. Beginning in 1959 his literary criticism vaunts careful arguments regarding the need for "*lichnaya intonatsiya*" (personal intonation) and "*novatorstvo*" (innovation) as well as a large measure of perspicacity and wit. At a time when ideology was often a substitute for talent, Sinyavsky held writers to high standards. He never hesitated to address a writer's shortcomings in the most candid way, or to ridicule the efforts of those who made a literary career by virtue of their political connections. Needless to say, Sinyavsky made enemies, his acerbic reviews and articles inciting one of the major polemics in the early 1960s.

Publishing abroad as Terts, Sinyavsky was free to follow his Muse. As a result, he hoisted up his modernist flag, mixing fantastic stories with Russian history.[9] He wrote in layers, incorporating events from his own life, images of Stalin and the KGB, philosophical disputation, and make-believe. He became a master at orchestrating a game of cat and mouse in his fiction, not just between characters, but between the narrator and the reader. This game was an important part of Sinyavsky's discursive practice, a practice whereby the reader became a major participant. There was no doubt that Sinyavsky was writing satire, that he cultivated humor and wit, playfully exploring the most forbidden topics in a society that was shaped by security and censorship. Most intriguing, Sinyavsky predicted that he would not get away with his satire. Again and again in his fiction he hinted at surveillance, at searches, at two plainclothesmen coming to make an arrest. In the epilogue to *Sud idet* (*The Trial Begins*), Sinyavsky's very first work of fiction, the narrator-author explains that his rough drafts were retrieved from a trap in the toilet. He goes on to say: "I was accused of slander, pornography and giving away state secrets" (*Sobranie sochinenii* 1:309). His words were prophetic. In *Lyubimov* (*The Makepeace Experiment*) the narrator also exclaims: "I warn you in advance. If terrible judges summon me to court, if they put me in irons, I will disavow everything" (*Sobranie sochinenii* 1:18).

Sinyavsky and another writer, Yuli Daniel, were arrested in September of 1965 and held for almost five months in Lyubyanka and Lefortovo prisons.[10] Before, during, and after the trial the press had a field day on both sides of the ocean.[11] The coverage and analysis on the part of journalists, scholars, and political *intriguers*, together with the trial transcript, as well as numerous documents, made up the raw material for a John LeCarré spy novel. Needless to say, the furnaces of international tension were rigorously stoked. Any measure of justice was threatened by the high drama of this "scandal." At the end of the four-day trial in February 1966, Sinyavsky and Daniel were charged with disseminating anti-Soviet propaganda under Section 1, Article 70 of the Criminal Code of the Russian Socialist Federal Soviet Republic (RSFSR).[12] It was the first time in the history of Russia that an author's fiction was used as evidence of criminal intent. Sinyavsky was sentenced to seven years hard labor (the maximum); Daniel—five.

According to Sinyavsky, a number of people knew that he was Terts. He sensed that he was under suspicion for some time and under close surveillance for seven or eight months before his arrest. The question remains: how did authorities find out about his double identity? In *Time* (February 9, 1987) Evgeny Evtushenko alleges that during a visit to the United States in 1966 he managed to get to see Robert Kennedy. According to Evtushenko, while locked in the bathroom of Kennedy's hotel suite with the water running full blast, he learned that the CIA revealed the identity of Terts to the KGB. In *Spokoinoi nochi* (*Goodnight!*) Sinyavsky claims:

> A well-informed individual swore to us that when he was in the U.S. he had heard a certain senator say that the KGB had been informed of Terts's real identity by American intelligence in exchange for data on a new Soviet submarine. (*Sobranie sochinenii* 2:417)

Donald Jameson, a former CIA official, maintained that the CIA did not discover the double identity of Terts until Sinyavsky had been arrested in September of 1965 ("What Yevgeny Knew" 40).

While Russian prisons in the nineteenth century became a place for revolutionaries and prophets to put their thoughts into writing, their *gulag* counterparts were places that were not conducive to writing of any sort. What with strict censorship and a lack of paper, even personal correspondence became a problem. But in spite of censorship and unspeakable conditions, Sinyavsky managed to complete the rough drafts of two-and-a-half books. Rather than prison-camp literature between the lines, Sinyavsky wrote down the exchanges of fellow prisoners together with fragmented observations on history, art, philosophy, literature, and the passage of time. He called this peculiar record *Golos iz khora* (*Voice from the Chorus*), which he published in 1973, right after his release from prison.[13] He also wrote a scholarly book, *Progulki s Pushkinym* (*Strolls with Pushkin*), which appeared in 1975, the same year as *V teni Gogolya* (*In the Shadow of Gogol*), only part of which was written in prison. It was not until 1984, with the publication of *Spokoinoi nochi* (*Goodnight!*), that Sinyavsky shared his thoughts regarding his years of imprisonment.

Although Sinyavsky's remarks about his ordeal are not free of writerly expression, there is in *Spokoinoi nochi* (*Goodnight!*) a glimpse of a man taking stock of where destiny has led him as a writer. Speaking as if from prison, he admits:

> In general I am myself here. Not simply as a person who has grown accustomed to life around him, but as a writer who has finally found himself in his work. It is sweet to slither into this garden of torture filled with wonders that elongate, in a strange way, my capricious thoughts, my own lengthy, slippery, serpentine traces. Who could have foreseen that my place is here. I could! The continuation of a path previously conceived at a rudimentary level. I am happy that I am in prison. (*Sobranie sochinenii* 2:440)

In spite of the hardships, including dragging and lifting heavy shipments in and out of the prison warehouse, Sinyavsky reveled in his discoveries about what he felt and saw, discoveries that he put down on paper. In many ways he announced to one and all: to live is to write, in spite of and because of where it may lead. Sinyavsky was released from prison in 1971, fifteen months before the end of his sentence.[14] Back in Moscow, he was under surveillance again, especially when he contacted editorial offices. Recognizing that he had no future as a writer in Moscow, he requested permission to emigrate under the alleged open-door policy of *détente*. Given Sinyavsky's notorious past as a writer and critic, his request was seen as an opportunity to be rid of him once and for all, yet make a gesture toward *détente*. In 1973, Sinyavsky, his wife, Mariya Vasilevna, and his son, Yegor, emigrated to France, moving into a house in a suburb of Paris. Shortly thereafter, Sinyavsky took up his new position in Russian literature at the Sorbonne (The University of Paris IV), resuming his life as a teacher and scholar. In 1978, Mariya Vasilevna founded a publishing house for a journal called *Sintaksis* (*Syntax*) in which a good part of her husband's writing was published. Through her efforts, for example, his notes from lectures were organized into books such as "*Opavshie list'ya*" *V. V. Rozanova* ('*Fallen Leaves*,' *of V. V. Rozanov* 1982), *Soviet Civilization* (1988), and *Ivan-Durak: Ocherk russkoi narodnoi very* (*Ivan the Fool: An Essay about Russian Popular Beliefs* 1991) and published under the *Sintaksis* label. While Sinyavsky resumed writing fiction with the novella *Kroshka Tsores* (*Little Jinx* 1980) and the novel *Spokoinoi nochi* (*Goodnight!* 1984), he spent much of his twenty-six years in France writing literary and social criticism, stirring up controversy in the process first in the émigré community and then in Moscow.

Immediately after Sinyavsky was released from prison in 1971 there were rumors that he collaborated with the KGB to ease his incarceration and obtain a speedy exit to the West for himself and his family.[15] This misinformation was well orchestrated, for it persisted, reverberating in wider and wider circles. In 1986, claims to discredit Sinyavsky were echoed in an interview with Mark Azbel' and Nina and Aleksandr Voronel' which was published in the journal *Dvadtsat' dva* (*Twenty-Two*), the same year that Sinyavsky restated and further delineated his differences with Maksimov, the editor of *Continent* (*Kontinent*).[16] Five years later, Maksimov, with whom Sinyavsky had a serious falling-out in 1976, reprinted excerpts from the interview in *Twenty-Two* together with an editorial avowal regarding Sinyavsky's and his wife's links with the KGB.[17] Sinyavsky and his wife immediately threatened to sue the journal for slander. When Maksimov did not retract his statements, Sinyavsky and his wife took legal action against him and the journal *Continent*. There must have been a settlement and perhaps a reconciliation, for the following year Sinyavsky and Maksimov went public together, co-signing a letter that called for Yeltsin's resignation shortly after the shelling of the Russian White House.[18]

While Sinyavsky got into many controversies, none would compare with the one that was sparked by his unorthodox book on Pushkin's poetry, *Progulki s Pushkinym* (*Strolls with Pushkin*). Although the angry response to this "*fantasticheskii literaturovedenie*" (fantastic literary scholarship) was slow and sporadic at first, it reached a high point in 1989—just when Sinyavsky's work as Terts started appearing in Moscow. That same year Sinyavsky visited Moscow—his first visit since he migrated to France in 1973.[19] There is no doubt that several interviews with this former-Russian-citizen-turned-professor-at-the-Sorbonne helped to fuel both old and new controversies. But sparks flew namely over Sinyavsky's playful assessment of Russia's most revered poet. Sinyavsky's clearly stated admiration for Pushkin notwithstanding, his animated and fanciful analysis caused outrage. Igor Shafarevich went so far as to compare Sinyavsky's "blasphemy" with that of Salman Rushdie ("*Rusofobiya*" 185). He was unwittingly drawn deeper and deeper into a storm of claims and counterclaims with writers and critics in Moscow and the émigré community, including Shafarevich, Roman Gul, and Aleksandr Solzhenitsyn.[20] But the storm subsided. In 1990, Sinyavsky was reinstated as a Russian citizen and invited to participate in a conference under the auspices of the Writers' Union to commemorate the thirtieth anniversary of Pasternak's death.

After his retirement from the Sorbonne in 1994, Sinyavsky continued to write. While he traveled to Russia several times, lectured at universities and read papers at conferences, he mainly devoted himself to his projects. Up until his death on February 25, 1997, he was working on a scholarly book about Mayakovsky and a novel called *Koshkin dom* (*The House of the Cat*). Perhaps other manuscripts will also be found hidden away in his upstairs study.

In 1978, the *Hudson Review* presented him with the Bennett Award for his significant achievements as a writer. Arguably, he should have been nominated for the Nobel Prize for Literature. But Sinyavsky, very much like Vasily Rozanov, never set out to exalt himself, to distinguish himself as a great writer, or be recognized as a prophet. He was clearly against the notion of an author pursuing a great purpose. He did, however, see his life as that of a man of letters, taking up a playful as well as provocative position in his texts. Moreover, in his writing he sensed a bond with what was forbidden and therefore a bond with prisoners. In his autobiographical novel, *Spokoinoi nochi* (*Goodnight!*), he shares his amazement when prisoners recognize him in a large communal cell. But this amazement turns to joy when they express respect for his writing, his openness, his defiance. In their eyes the abuse that was heaped on him in the press signaled honor. He is especially moved when a prisoner calls out to him: "You really gave it to them didn't you" (*Sobranie sochinenie* 2:399). Taken aback by this unexpected acceptance in these unexpected circumstances, he declares, "I have never experienced such fame before and I never will again. And I will never deserve and never hear any better criticism of my work" (*Sobranie sochinenii* 2:399).

In the following chapters let us consider the nature of Sinyavsky's playful and provocative stance in a detailed way, discussing its satirical connections in both his scholarship and his fiction. Let us proceed as follows. After reconsidering Sinyavsky's sensational trial, we will focus in on his first period (1959–1965), examining the roots of his satire, his scholarship of praise and blame, his brandishment of Vladimir Mayakovsky, his early polemics and his underground fiction, then his writing from his prison period (1966–1971), which was subsequently published in emigration. In addition to analyzing his postprison essays and works of fiction, we will pause to discuss his "fantastic scholarship," his wit, his metafictional ploys, his ludic use of folklore and his celebration of Vasily Rozanov, and finally his condemnation of the Russian intelligentsia under Yeltsin.

NOTES

1. Sinyavsky speaks about "the most serious turning point in his life" in regard to his decision to alert Hélène Peltier about a KGB plot to entrap her. After this

decision, he felt it was impossible to maintain any moral and political bonds with the Soviet system. Whenever I cite *Sobranie sochinenii* in the body of the text, it refers to Sinyavsky's *Collected Works* (*Sobranie sochinenii v dvukh tomakh*), which were published in Moscow in 1992. Needless to say, not all of his writing is included in this collection.

2. According to the trial transcript, in a search by the police a manuscript called "A Point of Departure" (*Tochka otscheta*) was also found (Ginzburg 248). Alfreda Aucouturier points to another manuscript called "Heaven and Earth," which was alleged to be an analysis of ancient Russian art, with special attention devoted to icons (Ginzburg 340).

3. Written by Boris Pasternak, *Doctor Zhivago*, was first published in 1957 in Italy, after it had been rejected by the censors in Moscow. The following year Pasternak was named as a recipient of the Nobel Prize for Literature, but he was forced to withdraw his name. In the climate of the cold war this novel became an issue. Pasternak was hailed in the West and vilified in Moscow.

4. A. N. Menshutin was one of Sinyavsky's colleagues at the Gorky Institute of World Literature. He collaborated with Sinyavsky on a number of projects, including polemical essays for *The New World* (*Novyi mir*). After Sinyavsky's arrest and trial, he lost his position at the Institute.

5. After examining the manuscript on Picasso, the Central Committee confiscated it, delaying its publication for years (*Goodnight!* 185).

6. *London Times Literary Supplement*, September 30, 1965, 884.

7. In 1958, Sinyavsky publicly defended Boris Pasternak when he was under attack for publishing *Doktor Zhivago*. He and Yuli Daniel were pallbearers for Pasternak's funeral in May of 1960.

8. See Tvardovsky's comments in "Po sluchaiyu yubileiya," 17.

9. There are many confirmations of Sinyavsky's modernism. In "Andrey Sinyavsky on the Eve of his Arrest," *On Trial: The Case of Sinyavsky (Tertz) and Daniel (Arzhak)*, Alfreda Aucouturier claims: "When Sinyavsky learned that the wrapper of the Italian edition of *The Makepeace Experiment* carried a picture by Chagall, he was moved to realize that he had been so well understood" (343).

10. Yuly Daniel was born in 1925, the same year as Sinyavsky. They became acquainted in the 1950s. Through Sinyavsky's connections (Hélène Peltier), several of his short stories were smuggled to the West and published under the pseudonym of Nikolai Arzhak: "*Ruki*" ("Hands"), "*Govorit Moskva*" ("This Is Moscow Speaking"), "*Chelovek iz MINAPa*" ("The Man from MINAP"), and "*Iskuplenie*" ("Atonement"). He was sentenced to five years of hard labor under Section 1, Article 70 of the Soviet Criminal Code. He died in Moscow on December 30, 1988.

11. For a discussion of the trial see chapter 1 in Catharine Nepomnyashchy's *Abram Tertz and the Poetics of Crime*; for a collection of documents and a transcript of the trial see Ginzburg, *Belaya kniga*; Galina Belaya, "Da budet vedemo

vsem . . ." in Eremina, *Tsena metafory*; Max Hayward, ed., *On Trial: The Case of Sinyavsky (Tertz) and Daniel (Arzhak),* and Murav, "Sinyavsky's Trial."

12. "Agitation or propaganda carried out with the purpose of subverting or weakening the Soviet regime or in order to commit particularly dangerous crimes against the state, the dissemination with a similar purpose of slanderous inventions denigrating the Soviet state and social system, also the dissemination, production or harboring for said purposes of literature of similar content, is punishable by imprisonment for a period of from six months to seven years, with or without exile for a further period of two to five years." *Ugolovnyi kodeks RSFSR*, Moscow, 1962, 47–48.

13. Hélène Peltier said that its original title was "Voice from the Heart" ("Andrey Sinyavsky Arrives in Paris," 65).

14. Daniel finished his prison sentence, returning to Moscow in 1970 in poor health.

15. For a discussion of these accusations see Sinyavsky's wife, Mariya Rozanova. "Abram da Mar'ya," 5.

16. It should be recalled that both Mark Azbel' and Aleksandr Voronel', who, in this interview, accused Sinyavsky of collaborating with the KGB, provided testimony to the prosecution at the trial of Sinyavsky and Daniel in February 1966. From the trial proceedings it appears that Azbel' was present at readings of "underground" works both in Sinyavsky's and Daniel's apartment in Moscow. "Dvadtsat' let spustya," *Dvadtsat' dva*, no. 46 (January–March 1986): 132–77. For Sinyavsky's comments on Maksimov, see John Glad's interview, "Antipadnichestvo," *Vremya I my* 88 (1986): 145–67, as well as "Emigre," *Encounter* 51, no. 3 (September 1978): 79–80.

17. "Spetsial'noe prilozhenie," *Kontinent* no. 71 (1992): 307–50.

18. "Pod sen' nadezhnuyu zakona . . ." *Nezavisimaya gazeta* (16 October 1993).

19. When Daniel was at death's door, Sinyavsky immediately applied for a visa. It was not issued, however, until after the funeral. Sinyavsky and his wife arrived in Moscow in January 1989.

20. Roman Gul', "Progulki khama s Pushkinym," *Novyi zhurnal* 24 (1976): 129; Igor' Shafarevich, "Russofobiya," *Nash sovremennik*, no. 6 (1989): 167–92; "Fenomen emigratsii," *Literaturnaya Rossiya*, no. 36 (8 September 1989): 4–5; Solzhenitsyn, "Koleblet tvoi trenozhnik," *Vestnik russkogo khristianskogo dvizheniya*, no. 142 (1984): 133–52; "Otvetnoe slovo na prisuzhdenie literaturnoi nagrady amerikanskogo natsional'nogo kluba iskusstv, N'yu-Iork, 19 yanvarya 1993," *Novyi mir*, no. 4 (1993): 3–6; "Nashi pluralisty," *Vestnik russkogo khristianskogo dvizheniya*, no. 139 (1993): 133–60.

Chapter Two

Satirists on Trial

On September 13, 1965, two writers, Andrei Sinyavsky and Yuli Daniel, were arrested in Moscow. At their trial, which took place February 10–14, 1966, the prosecution argued that the "blasphemous" opinions in their literary works were tantamount to treason.[1] In fact, Sinyavsky and Daniel were charged with criminal activity under Article 70 of the Criminal Code. The content of their writing was deemed to be a mode of agitation and a means for propaganda that maligned the USSR. At the symbolic level, this trial, which was widely covered in the press, sent a message that the Brezhnev era was beginning and that the Khrushchev era, with its intermittent liberal policies, was at an end. Meanwhile, it sent a message that justice in Soviet Russia was an open and public process, replacing the practices of the 1930s, including summary executions for "traitors" such as Sinyavsky and Daniel. But not unlike the infamous trials of the late 1930s, this one was truly for show. According to Sinyavsky's Lieutenant Colonel Pakhomov in *Spokoinoi nochi* (*Goodnight!*), "Our trial was supposed to be a present to the party from the KGB on the occasion of the Twenty Third Congress. A model trial served up with an eye to the West on a crisp snow-white napkin." (*Sobranie sochinenii* 2:391–92). In fact this trial was so important that it was conducted at the level of the Supreme Court of the RSFSR and presided over by L. N. Smirnov, one of the nation's most distinguished judges.[2] In the verdict a shift in cultural policy was unmistakable: Sinyavsky was given the maximum sentence—seven years of hard labor; Daniel—five. In the following chapter let us discuss the legal and literary issues of this trial, including the way it was conducted as well as the way it was reported.

Before turning to the trial itself, however, a few words are in order about the perilous path of Russian writers who express irreverence for privileged institutions. While it is widely known that many outspoken Russian writers have faced imprisonment and execution during the Soviet period, such consequences together with a system of censorship were in place before the Bolshevik revolution. Even the leading Russian writers in the nineteenth century did not escape the scrutiny of the censor and the police. It was not surprising that the well-known satirist, Saltykov-Shchedrin, was exiled. But Pushkin and Lermontov were also exiled. The poet Kondraty Ryleyev was one of five who was executed following the Decembrist revolt. Dostoevsky, who was originally condemned to death for his participation in the Petrashevsky circle, served ten years in a Siberian prison. Turgenev was put under house arrest and then exiled for sixteen months. Herzen, Korolenko, and Chernyshevsky also faced arrest and exile and Tolstoy was excommunicated by the Russian Orthodox Church. In the eighteenth century, when modern Russian literature was born, the hazards of written irreverence were punctuated by the arrests of Novikov and Radishchev. It was Catherine the Great, "the daughter of the enlightenment," who ordered the arrests and who added government censorship to church censorship for all publications, ushering in an era of heightened literary control, which lasted until the fall of the Soviet Union. In the struggle against "blasphemy," such measures were, of course, not uncommon. Satirists everywhere were at risk. Erasmus was attacked by the Roman Catholic Church; Thomas More was silenced; Juvenal lived under threat of exile; Lord Rochester was banished from court and Donne was called a "political outsider" (Griffin 140, 144–45).

It looked suspicious to authorities when a Russian author circumvented censorship by publishing abroad—especially under an assumed name. Early in 1960 there was anxiety if not alarm regarding the identity of Abram Terts and Nikolai Arzhak, the respective pseudonyms that Sinyavsky and Daniel used to designate the authorship of their satire published in the West.[3] One can only imagine that the KGB got involved in an all-out investigation, especially as time passed and more satire appeared under these names.[4] It was only in January of 1962 that the works of Terts, which were previously dismissed as "bourgeois falsifications" (*burzhuaznye fal'shivki*), received critical attention in a Russian publication.[5] At this time B. Ryurikov suggested that Terts was a follower of Peter Demets, a White Russian émigré who was living in Paris. In October of 1965, the mystery surrounding Terts and Arzhak entered a new phase. "Unofficial sources" reported that a certain Andrei Sinyavsky and Yuli

Daniel had been arrested during the second week of September in connection with disseminating anti-Soviet propaganda under assumed names.[6] At a Paris press conference in November, Aleksei Surkov, secretary of the Union of Soviet Writers, admitted that the arrest was official and that a trial would be conducted to consider the charges. The mystery that once surrounded the name of Terts and Arzhak was now attached to Sinyavsky and Daniel. A news blackout helped to sustain this mystery and underscore the possibility of a larger unknown.[7] From September 1965 to February of 1966, while the accused were held in Lyubyanka prison, no details about the arrest or charges were disclosed. Ironically, it was during this period that Mikhail Sholokhov received the Nobel Prize for Literature and Valery Tarsis, a militant antiestablishment writer, was permitted to leave the USSR.[8]

The trial turned out to be a theatrical production with the leading roles written for the prosecution, carefully chosen witnesses, and a courtroom audience that was favorable to a guilty verdict before the trial began. In addition to outbursts, there was booing, hissing, laughter, and thunderous applause.[9] Sinyavsky could not believe that those present in the courtroom actually cheered when the final verdict was read. There were, of course, several dramatic moments. At one point, someone shouted in regard to Remezov's testimony, "He is worried about his own skin. The witness has a noose around his neck" (Ginzburg 255).[10] Above all, there were accusations of "blasphemy," (*koshchunstvennoe vyskazyvanie*), "slander" (*kleveta*), "treason" (*izmena*), "profanity" *maternnaya bran'*), and "pornography" (*pornografiya*); Sinyavsky and Daniel were called "internal emigrés" (*vnutrennye emigranty*), "enemies of the Soviet Union" (*vragi Sovetskogo Soyuza*), "Anti-Soviet" (*antisovetchiki*). But it was Sinyavsky who was presented as the principal offender, for he was not only charged with producing, harboring, and disseminating his works, but also acting as an intermediary in smuggling Daniel's works abroad.

According to Sinyavsky, his lawyer, E. M. Kogan, coached him to refrain from making outbursts and especially from arguing with Judge Smirnov, whom he considered a liberal, a man not out of touch with the West. Kogan thought that Smirnov would try to play to the West to avoid any comparison with a run-of-the-mill Stalinist hangman (*Sobranie sochinenii* 2:363). Sinyavsky felt from the start that his soft-spoken lawyer had to walk a tightrope, that is, he was not in a position to argue forcefully for his "client's" innocence or to challenge the literary analysis of the prosecution. During periods when the court was in recess, he told Sinyavsky that he was aiming for four years—five at the maximum, adding that in

1967, the fiftieth anniversary of the Bolshevik revolution, there would be an amnesty for prisoners with a sentence of less than five years (*Sobranie sochinenii* 2:366). To Sinyavsky, it seemed that Kogan carried on a polemic with himself as to whether his "client" did or did not intend to send his works abroad. The judge and the prosecutor ignored this polemic as well as the expert opinion of a psychiatrist who drew attention to Sinyavsky's "peculiar fantasies." But in looking back to February 1966, what troubled Sinyavsky was that Kogan never told him about the smear campaign in the press that was going on outside the courtroom.

The stakes in this trial were raised as high as possible. The state prosecutor, O. P. Temushkin, went so far as to accuse Sinyavsky and Daniel of activities directed against the state, claiming that under the guise of literature they wrote filthy lampoons calling for the overthrow of the system (Ginzburg 295). Through the testimony of Garbuzenko, Khazanov, Azbel', Petrov, Remezov, and Dokukina it was established that Sinyvasky had sent his works abroad through Hélène Peltier and that he, moreover, had helped to smuggle out Daniel's fiction too. But proof regarding the alleged agitational and propagandistic nature of his works was not easy to establish. What was offered for evidence was never the character of his works of literature (satire), but isolated lines that could be interpreted as derision of the Soviet system, Russian culture, Russian leaders, Marxism, motherhood, and the Russian people. In his final plea, Sinyavsky objected to such "evidence," pointing out that it is difficult to find any leading satirist who has not had anti-Soviet ideas read into him. Everyone, he maintains, especially if he or she writes satire, has been suspected of anti-Soviet intentions, including Zoshchenko, Ilf and Petrov, and Demyan Bedny (Ginzburg 305).

In his defense, Sinyavsky puts himself in the company of Russian satirists, arguing that satire is an easy target for accusations. He could have made a case for the importance of satire in the development of the Russian intelligentsia and the unmasking of hostile forces in society during the formative years of socialism. But he took a different route, explaining that juridical standards have little to do with literature. Actually in the politically charged atmosphere that hovered over this trial, only Sinyavsky raised the issue of fiction, of characters with different voices, of conventions and words on paper. What with Western journalists and scholars making Sinyavsky into an anti-Sovieteer, his comments about the nature of literature fell on deaf ears. As Sinyavsky points out in his final plea, the prosecutor referred to the anti-Soviet readings of the foreign press as if they and not Soviet statutes were "the highest standard of truth" (*vysshii kriterii istinnosti*) (Ginzburg 304).

The outcome of this trial was crucial both as a policy-making statement and as a test of Smirnov whose enemies were not eager to see him advance to a permanent seat on the Supreme Soviet Court. Justice had to be swift; liberties had to be taken with the letter of the law regarding the connection between "blasphemy" and agitation and propaganda. Moreover, in linking criminal charges with sending manuscripts abroad, an unwritten law had to be assumed, for other Russian writers, such as Evtushenko, Tarsis, and Remezov, who had sent their works to the West, were not criminally tried.[11] Although transparent in design, the attacks on Sinyavsky and Daniel in the press before, during, and after the trial went as far as possible to dispel any doubts about the merits of the case against them. Meanwhile, in the courtroom Judge Smirnov permitted the defense to call only one witness, Professor Duvakin from Moscow University, who was immediately interrupted and dismissed when he praised Sinyavsky and his work. But Smirnov's rudeness was not limited to this incident. Throughout the trial he intervened with harsh comments and insinuations, cutting off explanations on the part of the defendants and their council. Soon after the trial, at a reception for writers and members of the KGB, Smirnov summed up the trial, boasting how, as chairman of the court, he helped the prosecution in its contest with two well-educated men (*Sobranie sochinenii* 2:367).

What especially puts a cloud over this trial is the attempt to interpret literature in a legal sense. To this end, opinions, which the prosecution considered as agitational and propagandistic, were attributed not to characters, but to Sinyavsky, even in the case of Karlinsky in *Sud idet* (*The Trial Begins*) who is clearly a negative character. On the other hand, opinions which the defense considered a reflection of faith in the Revolution or respect for the values of old Russian culture were excluded from the proceedings. Above all, all words were taken literally without any regard for the irony, which, in the writing of a satirist, is fundamental to a reader's understanding of the text. In the search for agitation and propaganda, no thought was given to literature as fiction, as fabrication with, as Sinyavsky insists, the important ingredients of hyperbole and fantasy. In his final plea, Sinyavsky argues that authors are not liable for the opinions or the behavior of their characters. He reminds the court that the underground man in *Zapiski iz podpol'ya* (*Notes from the Underground*) is not Dostoevsky, that Klim Samgin in *Zhizn' Klima Samgina* (*The Life of Klim Samgin*) is not Gorky and that Yudushka in *Gospoda Golovevy* (*The Golovev Family*) is not Saltykov-Shchedrin (Ginzburg 303).

The prosecution turned to V. V. Vinogradov, a well-established scholar at the University of Moscow, for an expert literary "analysis" of Sinyavsky's works.[12] According to Vinogradov:

> All the works are characterized by pretentiousness, affectation, the exploitation of dreams and hallucinations for literary effect, and by an obsession with demented states of mind. The typical ideas expressed in these works range from Freudianism through anti-Semitism and sex to 'God-Seeking.' (Ginzburg 289–90)

Although this expert opinion was built upon isolated statements from fiction, the state prosecutor, O. Temushkin, concluded that it established "clearly and without any doubt" that Sinyavsky's works were not only political, but also written with the intention of expressing an anti-Soviet message. According to Varlam Shalamov, Smirnov needed expert testimony to give the proceedings a sophisticated air—with even a measure of "literary" discourse (*Tsena metafory* 522–30). After all, the International Association of Lawyers was following the proceedings. Above all, Smirnov wanted to show that this trial had a scholarly side—a genuine seminar with material for testing aspiring lawyers. Meanwhile, he left no doubt that the burden of proof rested not so much on his shoulders, but on the shoulders of the literary experts.

In his final plea, Sinyavsky attempted to discuss some fundamental notions about what constituted a literary work, but he stopped short, explaining that it was futile under such circumstances. It was as futile as his argument that literature in the Soviet Union may not only be viewed as pro-Soviet or anti-Soviet, but also as un-Soviet. It is doubtful that Sinyavsky's eloquent summary of the mitigating circumstances in this case had any impact at all in the courtroom—except to irritate L. N. Smirnov, the judge with alleged liberal tendencies and a reputation to uphold in the West.

What must be considered in the disposition of this trial is the enthusiastic way in which Sinyavsky's "underground" works were greeted in the West.[13] *Sud idet* (*The Trial Begins*), after all, was translated into twenty-four languages (Ginzburg 171). Moreover, the reviews of *Sud idet* as well as *Chto takoe sotsialisticheskii realism* (*What Is Socialist Realism*) were not only filled with praise, but also with cold war gloating over the *succès de scandale* of Terts, who was thought to be a writer with pro-Western inclinations. Anti-Soviet sentiment did not simply surface here and there; it persisted in what seemed to be a large number of reviews.[14]

In the *Manchester Guardian*, for example, Michael Frayn declared:

> To anyone accustomed to the worthless rubbish that officially constitutes modern Soviet literature, this book [*The Trial Begins*] comes as a flash of lightning no less illuminating in its way than Pasternak's *Doctor Zhivago.* (29 April 1960: 11)

In the *New York Herald Tribune* Merle Fainsod brazenly suggested the intentions of Sinyavsky: "It is difficult to imagine a tale [*The Trial Begins*] more calculated to outrage the guardians of Soviet orthodoxy" (11 September 1960: 7). In the *New York Times Book Review* Harry Schwartz claimed:

> This little book [*The Trial Begins*] in short, tells more about the essence of Soviet life than a dozen reporters and experts who have never, as has Terts, penetrated to the soul of the modern Russian. (16 October 1960: 4)

In the *Saturday Review* Ivar Spector spoke about *The Trial Begins* in a manner that strangely foreshadowed a point-by-point accusation of Sinyavsky at the trial:

> In the first place . . . this novel has no positive characters. Second, the novel sharply disparages the Soviet regime, its institutions and communist bureaucrats. Third, the naked portrayal of sex alone would serve to ban the book in the Soviet Union. (5 November 1960: 32)

Eagerness in the West for an exposé of Stalinist Russia or a direct attack on Soviet literary policy was indicated by the overwhelming interest with which *The Trial Begins* and *What Is Socialist Realism* were received. When Sinyavsky's *Fantasticheskie povesti* (*Fantastic Stories*) appeared, however, there were mixed reviews and little patience for complicated stories with metafictional connections.[15] It was not until the allegorical *Lyubimov* (*The Makepeace Experiment*) appeared in translation that the same zeal that surrounded Sinyavsky's initial works reached another peak. Since this peak occurred late in 1965, concurrent with Sinyavsky's arrest, critics and Kremlinologists formed a chorus, suggesting further theories about Sinyavsky and Soviet "reality." But reviews of the-novel-that-upset-the-Kremlin variety, which speculated that Sinyavsky was an agent provocateur as well as the greatest living writer in the Soviet Union, only revealed the reality of the cold war. *Time* went so far as to call *The Trial Begins* "the most remarkable novel to have come out of the Soviet Union since the revolution"

(3 October 1960: 27). With issues such as smuggled manuscripts, charges of blasphemy, a six-year investigation, an arrest, a trial, and a potential cold war triumph, Sinyavsky had inadvertently stumbled into the territory of sensationalism. His initial fears about his writing falling into anti-Soviet hands were not unwarranted.

Although Western reporters did not get into the courtroom, there was a vast body of trial commentary in the West, including that which was published in *Problems of Communism*, a CIA-funded journal.[16] Besides a critique of the trial, there was an attempt to make Sinyavsky into a maverick or a dissenter, to speak about him in the same breath with Gumilev, Pilnyak, Mandelshtam, Meyerhold, Babel, Akhmatova, Zoshchenko, and Pasternak. The dearth of information about Sinyavsky actually permitted such uncontested and highly charged analogies. In the absence of facts, a context was supplied for Sinyavsky with allusions to twentieth-century Russian writers who had been sent to jail, exiled, committed to psychiatric hospitals, executed, or expelled from the Writers' Union. As Sinyavsky was linked to a broad category of writers, so his writing was linked to a broad category of influence, including that of E. T. A. Hoffmann, Gogol, Kafka, Leskov, Dostoevsky, Sologub, Saltykov-Shchedrin, Zamyatin, Olesha, Erenburg, Orwell, and Henry Miller. When confronted in the courtroom with such opinions from Western publications, Sinyavsky declared: "I have a strong impression that bourgeois propaganda indulges in wishful thinking" (Ginzburg 244). He goes on to say: "In the West they print rumors that I am from a family of Old Believers, that I am a close friend of Pasternak, etc. Anything is possible to be printed about me over there" (Ginzburg 244).

Western indignation for legal intervention against Sinyavsky and Daniel was not unlike Soviet indignation for underground satire aimed at socialism. Of course, without considering the enormous gulf between justice in the West and justice in Soviet Russia, facile criticism of the Soviet criminal code was inevitable. Moreover, without looking back into history, it was not possible to get a sense for changes in the Soviet legal code, a code, which, according to Harold J. Berman, had been liberalized.[17] Amidst claims that the world was witnessing another show trial and a return to Stalinist methods, there emerged historical analogy without historical perspective. Under Stalin, Sinyavsky could have been classified as a counterrevolutionary and silenced quickly. A trial, especially without a confession of guilt, would have been out of the question.

Newspapers such as the *London Times* and the *New York Times* followed the arrest and trial of Sinyavsky and Daniel with bold-faced headings and perspicacity in old-fashioned Kremlinology. Max Hayward's article in the *London Times* about "awkward voices" underscored the use of coercion to silence not only Sinyavsky and Daniel, but also Esenin-Volpin, Valery Tarsis, Yosif Brodsky, and a group of intellectuals who were arrested in the summer of 1965 (1 February 1966: 11). The issue became not Sinyavsky or his art, but the Soviet system, which created a lineup of literary personae non grata with little in common. In the *New York Times* Peter Grose clearly characterized how Western news agencies reported the course of this arrest and trial:

> The writings of Tertz attracted the attention of bourgeois propaganda agencies by their anti-Soviet content and were exploited in the ideological struggle against the Soviet Union. (15 February 1966: 8)

Ironically, a similar characterization appeared in *Pravda*:

> Unfortunately, the campaign organized on an unprecedented scale in the West in defense of the two subversive agents in literature has misled some honest people. Some progressive representatives in the West got alarmed, apparently not having enough information and taking at face value the writings of the bourgeois press. (22 February 1966: 2)

News journals such as *Time*, *Newsweek*, and *U.S. News & World Report* also were vigilant in focusing on the explosive side of this story. Shortly after Sinyavsky's arrest *Time* allowed the following statement to be printed: "Tertz has made his mark as a bitter, bedrock enemy of Communism, while Sinyavsky merely mocks its Stalinist aspects" (29 October 1965: 37). This very statement, together with Boris Filippov's anti-Soviet introduction to Terts in *Fantasticheskii mir Abrama Tertsa* (*The Fantastic World of Abram Terts*), was used later as evidence of Sinyavsky's malignment of the USSR. Such careless conjecture about Sinyavsky's intent belongs to the category of yellow journalism, the same kind of journalism that was echoed in *Izvestiya*, *Pravda*, *Literaturnaya gazeta*, *Sovetskaya Rossiya*, *Komsomol'skaya pravda,* and *Oktyabr'* before, during, and after the trial.

Details about the charges against Sinyavsky, as well as commentary about Sinyavsky's fiction, did not appear in the Soviet press until January of 1966. On January 13 *Izvestiya* carried a lengthy editorial on page six by Dmitry Eremin who had previously distinguished himself by receiving a Stalin prize (1952), as well as by denouncing Dudintsev's *Ni khlebom edinom* (*Not by Bread Alone*) and Solzhenitsyn's *Odin Den' Ivana Denisovicha*

(*One Day in the Life of Ivan Denisovich*). This editorial, entitled "*Perevertyshi*" (Turncoats), became the first installment of a pretrial attack upon the accused. It is in this editorial, twenty-six days before the trial, that Eremin displayed the characteristically caustic style of Marxist-Leninist criticism, accusing Sinyavsky and Daniel of vileness in all matters, calling them "*vragi kommunizma*" (enemies of communism), "*antisovetchiki*" (anti-Sovieteers), "*perebezhchiki*" (renegades), "*pisaki*" (scribblers), "*vnutrennie emigranty*" (internal émigrés), "*politicheskie vyrodki*" (political degenerates), and "*podonki*" (scum). Five days later *Izvestiya* published three letters of protest against Sinyavsky and Daniel, the contents of which were no surprise (18 January 1966: 4). It is such pretrial judgments in the media that A. Gorkin, chairman of the Supreme Court, warned against earlier in *Izvestiya* (2 December 1964: 4).

Izvestiya's courtroom correspondent, Yury Feofanov, described the cross-examination with venomous asides, declaring that there was no doubt about the defendants' guilt. Shortly after the trial *Izvestiya* printed another letter signed by six Uzbek writers who expressed contempt for the "vile slander" in the writing of Sinyavsky and Daniel (23 February 1966: 3). Two months after the trial *Izvestiya* printed an attack on Radio Liberty for publicizing the works of such "double-dealers," accusing the CIA of financially supporting its programs (14 April 1966: 2). While the court was in session *Pravda* provided only brief TASS agency reports. Toward the end of the trial it carried a lengthy summary of the proceedings by T. Petrov (15 February 1966: 4). Although this summary was by no means objective, it was free of the vindictive tone that characterized Eremin's editorials in *Izvestiya*. It appears that *Pravda*'s official ideological pronouncement concerning Sinyavsky and Daniel was printed seven days after the trial by way of a rejoinder to Communists in the West who raised questions about making opinion a crime (22 February 1966: 2).[18] After clarifying that Sinyavsky and Daniel were not tried for what they had written, but for crimes against the Revolution and the Soviet state, this editorial restated the tenets of socialist realism and the argument of the prosecution.

Literaturnaya gazeta, the official publication of the Union of Soviet Writers, printed a pretrial literary critique of Sinyavsky's and Daniel's work by Zoya Kedrina, who had been a colleague of Sinyavsky at the Institute of World Literature (22 January 1966: 2, 4).[19] She entitled her critique "*Nasledniki Smerdyakova*" (Heirs of Smerdyakov), linking Sinyavsky and Daniel with the illegitimate son of Fedor in Dostoevsky's *Brat'ya Karama-*

zovy (*The Brothers Karamazov*) who kills his father. Her literary analysis was more like an exercise in the vilification of the accused through quotes from their works. After the trial, *Literaturnaya gazeta* issued two official proclamations from the secretariat of the Writers' Union (19 February 1966: 4; 22 February 1966: 2). The first proclamation was written in response to irate Western writers.[20] The second was an excerpt from the meeting of the Moscow section of the Union of Writers at which Sinyavsky was denounced and expelled. Two days later *Literaturnaya gazeta* printed an article that took issue with Western opposition to the severity of the sentence (24 February 1966: 2). In response to the protest of sixty-two writers in Moscow, Mikhail Sholokhov attacked Sinyavsky and Daniel at the Twenty-third Party Congress.[21] Sounding like a diatribe from Zhdanov rather than lofty words from the fresh recipient of the Nobel Prize for Literature, Sholokhov claimed that the sentences were too lenient, that in the 1920s these blasphemers would have gotten their just deserts in compliance with "revolutionary justice" (Ginzburg 389).

During the trial *Sovetskaya Rossiya* published two spirited essays by M. Ilyin and I. Kotenko (11 February 1966: 4). While Ilyin recounted literary interpretations that were incriminating to Sinyavsky and Daniel, for example, the interpretations of Boris Filippov, Kotenko mocked their fantastic elements, using Zoya Kedrina's analysis to suggest an example of poor writing as well as plagiarism. *Komsomol'skaya Pravda* also contributed to this enormous volume of mudslinging. The first two installments were submitted by S. Mikhailov, the chairman of the State Committee for the Press. In addition to quoting single-minded eyewitness accounts of the trial, Mikhailov warned that a full measure of justice would be administered in all future cases of literary "hooliganism" (12 February 1966: 3; 15 February 1966: 3). The second installments were submitted by S. Golyadkov who attacked the U.S. Information Agency, the Voice of America, Radio Free Europe, and especially the *Posev* publishing house (*Grani*) as well as the editorial staff of *Kultura* in Paris for marketing underground literature (17 March 1966: 3; 18 March 1966: 3). In *Oktyabr'* the editor, V. Kochetov, reviewed *The Alpha Team* and *Death Is My Business*. But he was not interested in the literary merit of these novels. In fact he wrote a classic exposé of spy operations. Not only did he disclose the activities of American special forces and undercover agents in the tone of someone entrusted with classified or top secret information, but he managed to ramp up the idea that Sinyavsky and Daniel may also have been involved in espionage (March 1966: 212–18).[22]

In "Reporting the Tertz Affair" Philippe Radley draws our attention to the gossip, the inaccuracies, and the political character of the coverage in the *London Times*, the *New York Times*, and the *New Republic* (11–12). Given such carelessness and less-than-professional reportage, this story, in his opinion, reads at times like a comedy of errors. If we take the uneven translations of Sinyavsky's writing into consideration, there would even be a linguistic side to this comedy (Hugh McLean 434–40). But any notion of a comedy should be dispelled by the serious consequences here. Politically expedient scandal mongering in the West evoked a corresponding response in Moscow. What must be admitted is that on both sides of the cold war Sinyavsky and Daniel were seen largely in political terms. At the very start of their careers, they were denied a legitimate place among men of letters who comment with humor and wit on the frailty of our institutions. They were among the many victims of the ideological point and counterpoint of the day.

NOTES

1. For a transcript of the trial see Ginzburg, *Belaya kniga po delu A. Sinyavskogo i Yu. Danelya*; for a version in English see Max Hayward, *On Trial: The Soviet State versus "Abram Tertz" and "Nikolai Arzhak*." The initial trial proceedings were published under the auspices of Posev publishers, *"Sud nad A.D. Sinyavskim i Yu. Danielem."* "It should be noted that Aleksandr Ginzburg was tried and sentenced for publishing the underground journals *Feniks (Phoenix)* and *Sintaksis* (*Syntax)* as well as for making a transcript of the trial available to Posev Publishers in Germany. Up until his arrest, Sinyavsky had smuggled thirteen works abroad: an essay, *Chto takoe sotsialisticheskii realizm* (*What Is Socialist Realism)*, two novellas, *Sud idet* (*The Trial Begins*) and *Lyubimov* (*The Makepeace Experiment)*, six short stories, "*V tsirke*" ("At the Circus"), "*Ty i ya*" ("You and I"), "*Kvartiranty*" ("Tenants"), "*Grafomany*" ("Graphomaniacs"), "*Gololeditsa"* ("Icy Conditions"), and "*Pkhents*" ("Pkhents") and a collection of aphorisms, *Mysly vrasplokh* (Thoughts Unaware). At the trial, he was only indicted for his essay and his two novellas. Daniel, however, was indicted for all of the works that he had sent abroad through Sinyavsky, namely, four short stories: "*Govorit Moskva*" ("This Is Moscow Speaking"), "*Ruki*" ("Hands"), "*Iskuplenie*" ("Atonement"), and "*Chelovek iz MINAPa*" ("The Man from MINAP").

2. Sinyavsky felt that it was ironic that the first name and patronymic of Judge L. N. Smirnov was the same as that of L. N. Tolstoy: Lev Nikolaevich (*Sobranie sochinenii* 2:367).

3. Both authors wrote short stories, but Sinyavsky also wrote two novellas, *Sud idet* (*The Trial Begins*) and *Lyubimov* (*The Makepeace Experiment*), as well as an essay *Chto takoe sotsialisticheskii realism* (*What Is Socialist Realism*). Most of Sinyavsky's works from this period will be discussed in chapter seven.

4. See Andrew Field's comments on the theories about Terts's age and identity in "Abram Tertz's Ordeal by Mirror," 9.

5. B. Ryurikov, "Sotsialisticheskii realism i ego nisprovergateli," 195.

6. See John Renshaw, "The Elusive Abram Tertz," 52, and Max Hayward, "The Case of Tertz-Sinyavsky," 88.

7. See Deming Brown, "Moscow: The Defense Does Not Rest," 44. An editorial in the *New York Times* (21 February 1966, 3) disclosed that A. S. Yesenin-Volpin was the leader of a demonstration on December 5th in Pushkin Square. The demonstrators, which numbered over two hundred, gathered to protest the news blackout and to demand a public trial for the accused.

8. Valery Tarsis was permitted to leave the country in order to lecture in London. There he sought and received political asylum.

9. During the trials at the end of the 1930s that highlighted the purges, Stalin was most concerned with theater. He insisted that coffee and newspapers be available to defendants in the courtroom—props for a "congenial" atmosphere.

10. Andrei Remezov, an academic who worked at the Library of Foreign Literature, published several works abroad as Ivanov, among which was "Est' li zhizn' na Marse" ("Is There Life on Mars"). He alleged that he sent his works abroad through Sinyavsky. Kogan, counsel for the defense, claimed that Remezov made up this story. He raised serious questions about Remezov's credibility, insisting that this liar should have appeared as a defendant rather than a witness, for he too was guilty of publishing abroad under a pseudonym. Making what he considered to be an important distinction, Kogan pointed out that Remezov's works not only contained satire, but also political satire.

11. In his plea, Sinyavsky alludes to Remezov who was not indicted for sending manuscripts abroad under a pseudonym. He, of course, was given immunity for turning State's evidence (Ginzburg 305–6). See Harold J. Berman's discussion of Soviet laws in "The Writer and the Law" (13–16).

12. The trial transcript did not indicate who supplied this expert analysis. Sinyavsky names Vinogradov in a footnote in *V teni Gogolya* (*In the Shadow of Gogol*) (*Sobranie sochinenii* 2:317). Varlam Shalamov names Vinogradov as well as Prokhorov, Dymshits, and Kostomarov (*Tsena metafory* 523).

13. The smuggled manuscripts were taken to Paris and acquired by J. M. Domenach, the editor of *Esprit*, and Jerzy Giedreyc, the editor of *Kultura*. They were translated into French and Polish and initially appeared in the journals *Esprit* and *Kultura*. Shortly thereafter, they appeared in the United States in Russian and English.

14. Abel, "Art while Being Ruled: Tertz, Brecht, and Calderon," 405–12; William Barrett, review of *On Socialist Realism*, 97; Phoebe Adams, review of

The Trial Begins, 123; Adams, review of *The Makepeace Experiment,* 151; George Adelman, review of *Fantastic Stories*, 1905; Michel Aucouturier, review of *Lyubimov,* 271–76; Stefan Bergholz, "On Reading Tertz," 145–50; David Boroff, review of *Fantastic Stories*, 28; Ronald Bryden, review of *The Trial Begins,* 634; Guy Davenport, review of *The Makepeace Experiment*, 734; Merle Fainsod, review of *The Trial Begins,* 7; George Feifer, review of *The Makepeace Experiment,* 4; Andrew Field, review of *On Socialist Realism,* 28–29; Ludmila Foster, review of *Lyubimov,* 106–7; Michael Frayn, review of *The Trial Begins,* 11; Roman Gul', review of "Mysli vrasplokh," 276–79; Pawel Hostowiec, "Abram Terc," 3–7; Irving Howe, review of *Fantastic Stories,* 20; Oleg Ivsky, review of *The Makepeace Experiment,* 3074; Elizabeth Janeway, review of *On Socialist Realism,* 2; Stephen Hugh-Jones, review of *The Makepeace Experiment,* 82; Georges Kaniewicz, "Un anonym: Abram Tertz," 86–88; Martin Levin, review of *The Makepeace Experiment,* 40; Richard McLaughlin, review of *On Socialist Realism* 4D; McLaughlin, review of *The Trial Begins* 10C; Robert A. Maguire, review of *On Socialist Realism,* 193–95; Richard Mayne, review of *The Makepeace Experiment*, 619; Jean Bloch-Michel, "Sinyavsky et Daniel," 76–78; Helen Muchnic, review of *The Makepeace Experiment*, 33; *Newsweek*, review of *The Makepeace Experiment,* 94; S. K. Oberbeck, review of *The Makepeace Experiment,* 58; R. M. Ohmann, review of *On Socialist Realism,* 391; J. C. Pine, review of *The Trial Begins,* 4008; E. S. Pisko, review of *On Socialist Realism,* 9; Joel Porte, review of *The Makepeace Experiment*, 7; John Randolph, review of *The Trial Begins,* 10; F. D. Reeve, review of *Fantastic Stories,* 743–47; H. L. Roberts, review of *On Socialist Realism,* 10; H. E. Salisbury, review of *Fantastic Stories,* 35; Herman Singer, review of *The Trial Begins,* 19; Ivar Spector, review of *The Trial Begins,* 32; Maxiene Steinman, review of *Fantastic Stories,* 54–56; Harry Schwartz, review of *On Socialist Realism,* 26; Schwartz, review of *The Trial Begins,* 4; *Times*, review of *Fantastic Stories,* 31; *Times*, review of *The Trial Begins,* 84; *Times*, review of *The Makepeace Experiment,* 69; *Times* [London] *Literary Supplement*, review of *The Trial Begins,* 269; *Times*, review of *The Makepeace Experiment,* 324; Peter Viereck, review of *The Makepeace Experiment,* 45; Anthony West, review of *Fantastic Stories,* 186; Paul West, review of *The Trial Begins,* 642; Alan Moray Williams, "Ces contents d'Abram Tertz sont-ils de faux ou de nouveaux 'Kafka,'" 4.

15. In comparison with Sinyavsky's other works published under the name of Terts, *Fantastic Stories* received a small number of reviews. The following scholars show little enthusiasm for these stories: Victor Erlich, "Post-Stalinist Trends in Russian Literature," 415–16; Irving Howe, "Predicaments of Soviet Writing," 20; Howe, review of *Fantastic Stories,* 20; F. D. Reeve, review of *Fantastic Stories,* 743–47; David Boroff, review of *Fantastic Stories,* 28.

16. George Bailey, "The Trial of Two Soviet Writers," 34–38; Deming Brown, "Moscow: The Defense Does Not Rest," 43–45; Abraham Brumberg, "Socialist Legality on Trial," 34–36; Brumberg, "In Quest of Justice," 1–5;

Brumberg, "Traitors in the Dock," 70–78; Andrew Field, ""The Arrest of Andrey Sinyavsky," 10–11; Theodore Frankel, "Art, Politics, and the Soviet Writer," 52–59; Michael Frayn, "Writers on Trial," 80–88; Claude Frioux, "Sinyavsky et Daniel et la conscience politique," 227–34; Michael Glenny, "Sinyavsky and Daniel on Trial," 145–50; Max Hayward, "The Case of Tertz-Sinyavsky," 88–91; Hayward, "The Moscow Trial," 228–39; Max Hayward and Leopold Labedz, "Writers and the Police," 84–88; Leopold Labedz, "The Trial in Moscow," 82–91; Jeri Laber, "The Trial Ends," 26–29; Sidney Monas, "In Defense of Socialist Realism," 44–56; Richard Pipes, "The Soviet Jacobins," 9–11; Ernest Simmons, "The Trial Begins for Soviet Literature," 714–24; Stephen Weiner, "Socialist Legality on Trial," 6–12; "Breve chronology de l'affaire Sinyavsky-Daniel," 235–38; "Protestations d'ecrivans russes," 239–57; "The Writer and the Law," 13–16; "Echoes of the Tertz Affair," 17–18; "The Trial in Moscow," 598; "The West Registers Shock at the Soviet Writers' Punishment," 151–52.

17. This code, established in 1926, was revised after Stalin's death in 1953 and revised further in 1960. In the *New York Times* Berman claimed that the trial was a legal gain because the defendants were allowed to plead not guilty (26 February 1966: 3).

18. *Time* reported that the Communist newspapers of Norway, Sweden, Finland, Denmark, Great Britain, France, Austria, and Italy condemned the decision to prosecute Sinyavsky and Daniel (25 February 1966: 34). Deming Brown claims that the Soviet authorities became so sensitive to this condemnation that Western Communist newspapers were withheld from subscribers and removed from newsstands until an official rebuttal could be printed in *Pravda* ("Moscow: The Defense Does Not Rest," 45).

19. Like Zoya Kedrina, Arkady Vasil'ev, one of the prosecutors at the trial, had also been a colleague of Sinyavsky at the Gorky Institute of World Literature. Moreover, it appears that Vasil'ev had worked on this case in an investigative capacity, for he had detailed background information about Sinyavsky and a rather thorough analysis of Sinyavsky's texts. Leopold Labedz maintains that Vasil'ev plagiarized from Sinyavsky's *The Trial Begins* in his writing of a film script which appeared in *Moskva* 6, no. 12 (1962): 5–38. Labedz points out that such plagiarism is ironic as well as punishable by imprisonment for up to one year or a fine of 500 rubles ("The Trial in Moscow," 86).

20. The *London Times* printed a letter of protest from David Carver, secretary of the International PEN Club and Gian Carlo Vigorelli, secretary of COMES, addressed to Aleksei Surkov, secretary of the Union of Soviet Writers (22 November 1965: 9). It also printed a letter of protest signed by forty-nine of the leading writers in France, Germany, England, Italy, and the United States (31 January 1966: 9). Among the distinguished protestors were François Mauriac, Günter Grass, Ignazio Silone, Alberto Moravia, W. H. Auden, Arthur Miller, and Graham Greene.

21. For the names of these writers and the text of their letter of protest, see Ginzburg 385–87.

22. Kochetov also accused Patricia Blake of spying while she was fact-finding and shooting pictures for *Life*. As you will see in chapter nine, he attacked Sinyavsky again in 1989.

Chapter Three

Platforms for Satire

Other than "phantasmagoric," there has been no better label for Andrei Sinyavsky's fiction. After all, Sinyavsky himself applied it to his works in a very defining way (*Fantasticheskii mir Abrama Tertsa* 446). But while this label explains important features, especially in regard to his representation and juxtaposition of images, it does divert our attention from the tradition of literature to which Sinyavsky's writing belongs: satire—the tradition that develops in response to the abuses of power in almost every nation. Such development, which was very pronounced in both tsarist and Soviet Russia, may be illustrated by a long list of writers, including Gogol, Nekrasov, Saltykov-Shchedrin, Olesha, Zamyatin, Bulgakov, Ilf and Petrov, Zoshchenko, and Voinovich.[1] It is no coincidence that there are echoes of these authors in Sinyavsky's writing, particularly in the expression of the fantastic, the grotesque, and the absurd. It may be argued, moreover, that Sinyavsky's irreverent approach to authority and his playful projection of lightheartedness into a "dark August night" are, after all, the primary ingredients for this mode of writing. Considering that he viewed his authorship as the treatment of forbidden topics and the violation of taboos, satire in his work was inevitable.[2]

It is possible to argue that satire is the basis for Sinyavsky's clash with Soviet authorities, for without this irreverent mode in the initial works that he published abroad, there would have been an entirely different response both in the West and in Moscow. Sinyavsky did not simply publish literature abroad, but satiric literature, which at his trial he argued was the easiest kind of writing to attack (Ginzburg 305). But this satiric literature is without any pro-Western bias. While his opposition is genuine, it is not coupled with an endorsement of the West. In fact, he is more like Dostoevsky than Turgenev, that is, a Slavophile rather than a Westernizer. Moreover, he is not a lone voice. Like many writers of the era of the Thaw, he was emboldened to take issue with Stalin's Russia.[3] In the following chapter, let us consider several of his targets, but let us consider, above all, how his satire is socially constituted, that is, born of the erosion of the dominant discourse of Marxism-Leninism, a discourse, for an intellectual like Sinyavsky, that is haunted by irony and challenged by the persistence of Russian folktales and anecdotes (jokes).

It must be recalled that Sinyavsky's first "underground" works, *Chto takoe sotsialisticheskii realism* (*What Is Socialist Realism*) and *Sud idet* (*The Trial Begins*), published respectively in 1959 and 1960, were perceived mainly as political statements both in the West and in the Soviet Union. Such perception served both sides of the cold war, culminating on the one hand in the exploitation of dissent and on the other in the indictment of a dissenter. In the urgency of breaking stories and news-making analysis about Sinyavsky's arrest and trial, there was no time to consider that Sinyavsky's writing went beyond politics; moreover, that his representations were not literal but literary; that writing, especially when it unfolds as parody and caricature, is evidence of humor and wit rather than "truth." It became more apparent what kind of discourse shaped Sinyavsky's admirers and detractors rather than what kind of discourse shaped Sinyavsky. In fact, after the politically driven reportage and analysis subsided, no one could really say much about him. In the interviews that journalists and scholars arranged with Sinyavsky after he immigrated to France, the most fundamental questions about him and his writing persisted.[4]

In spite of how Sinyavsky's writing was politicized, it turned out that he was not the kind of writer the cold war made him out to be. He saw political satire as an extension of a political agenda—something completely absent from his writing. On the other hand, it is not possible to say that Sinyavsky's writing was free of ideological irreverence. In fact his writing was filled with irreverence, a good part of which is ideological. It is this irreverence that became Sinyavsky's antidote to what he considered an era of unprecedented misinformation. In the light of his article "*Anekdot v anekdote*" ("An Anecdote within an Anecdote"), it is clear that Sinyavsky champions irreverence, fully savoring its manifestations and widespread currency in funny stories, including those with references to Soviet institutions and the people who ran them ("*Anekdot*" 356).[5] Seeing the anecdote as a vehicle for irreverence, he acknowledges its "transgressional potential." "It simply does not exist without crossing into forbidden territory," he declares ("*Anekdot*" 357). Sinyavsky crosses into this forbidden territory when he speaks about Lenin's promise to make toilets out of pure gold, or Stalin's economic circumlocutions regarding the base producing the superstructure so that it would serve the base (*Chto takoe sotsialisticheskii realizm* 405, 409).

For Sinyavsky the anecdote is a vital genre, a type of discourse related to fundamental patterns of storytelling which, in many respects, express the issues of the day with well-developed paradigms and a large measure of carnivalization, that is, a playful assault on authority.[6] He, in fact, engages in Bakhtinian oratory when he speaks about the capacity of an anecdote "perforating and galvanizing, not only recreating, but actually restoring reality" ("*Anekdot*" 360).[7] Moreover, when he underscores the importance of fantasy, the grotesque and the absurd in the substance of the anecdote, he returns to the very features that he considered vital to literature in the conclusion to *Chto takoe sotsialisticheskii realizm* (446). Speaking about a transgression into forbidden territory and a transformation of reality through humor and wit, Sinyavsky, in fact, touches upon the essential features of satire, features that are endemic to his writing. When we look closer at Sinyavsky's fiction and discover further reverberations of the anecdote, it is an indication of how this ritual of communication, practiced so often in Russian kitchens, secured a place in Russian literature—which is to say Russian culture. In fact Sinyavsky begins his study of Pushkin, claiming that all of the poet's works were nothing more than anecdotes (*Progulki* 8). Further along in his study he pauses to discuss the power of the anecdote in Pushkin's works and in literature in general (*Progulki* 43–45).

In "The Literary Process in Russia" Sinyavsky maintains:

> In recent times only the anecdote has kept that unique, spontaneous vigor which is inherent in art and which stands for something more than freedom of speech. No matter how much the anecdote is suppressed (in my time you could get from five to ten years for telling one—imagine: for words!), it only gets strength from this suppression—not the strength of malice, but of humor and sunshine. Throughout the thirty-year-long night, anecdotes have shone and shine to this day like stars in the darkness. ("*Literaurnyi protsess v Rossii,*" 165–66)[8]

Given that humor and wit characterize much of Sinyavsky's satire, the anecdote is clearly germane, especially in its evocative potential.[9] When Sinyavsky explains the difference between the MVD and the KGB in terms of one organization wearing crimson caps and the other light blue, he is joking, anticipating that he will get a rise out of the reader (*Sobranie sochinenii* 2:395). Very much in the tradition of the anecdote, Sinyavsky resorts to stock characters, that is, to socially recognizable types such as insiders and outsiders with special attention to a gallery of *intriguers* who match wits with security men and the police. To this explosive mix Sinyavsky adds specific references to Lenin, Stalin, Khrushchev, prominent judges (e.g., chairman of the Supreme Court, Smirnov), KGB officials (e.g., Semichastny, Volkov, Pakhomov, Postnikov, Andropov), and watchdogs of the literary canon (e.g., Shcherbina, Kochetov, Sofronov, Khrapchenko, Ovcharenko, and Zelinsky). Savoring the anecdote's concision, he mimics its emblems and codes, baiting his audience with references to bald heads, mustaches, and not-so-subtle echoes of well-worn exhortations such as "encirclement by the enemy," "deviation," "necessary sacrifices," and "glorious aim."

In keeping with the anecdote, Sinyavsky builds his fiction upon yarns, upon humorous vignettes—many with bawdy language, nudity, and sex.[10] With Rabelaisian delight he focuses on lust, sexual performance, and voyeurism. Readers of "*V tsirke*" ("At the Circus") may recall Konstantin's "acrobatics" with Tamara in the bathhouse, the breathless lovemaking in a snowy stairwell in "*Ty i ya*" ("You and I"), or the necrophilia in the basement in "*Gololeditsa*" ("Icy Conditions"). But more in line with satire is the episode with Golbov, the party careerist in "*Sud idet*" (*The Trial Begins*), peeking through the keyhole at his naked wife, or the prison camp official, Lieutenant Kishka in *Spokoinoi nochi* (*Goodnight!*), peeking through the keyhole of a prisoner's room on visitors' day. In *Golos iz khora* (*Voice from the Chorus*), which is interspersed with funny and racy stories, Sinyavsky gives what he calls the complete paradigm of man according to the wording of tattoos:

> On the chest (or shoulders) a stock phrase—"There is no happiness in life." On the belly—"Still hungry." On the legs—"Tired." On the penis—"Crude." (*Golos* 43)

In this paradigm he makes a playful but telling appraisal of the human condition, putting the punch line of a stand-up comic at the end.

While the Marxist-Leninist rhetoric that Sinyavsky had to learn as a student and use as a literary critic seems to be a great distance from anecdotes, it was an unavoidable feature of official language, reaching deep into textbooks and the media. With its fixed phrases, it was a very distinct form of expression; everyone could recognize its modulation of praising and blaming. As jokes and anecdotes spoke through Sinyavsky's writing, so did Marxist-Leninist rhetoric, adding a characteristic measure of bombast and arrogance. Lurking in Sinyavsky's expression of sustained derision, especially in his early literary analysis, is the unmistakable imprint of this rhetoric. Suffice it to say, through constant exposure to this invidious discursive practice, he reached a point where he could mimic and then fully orchestrate its singular tone as he did in reports on dialectical materialism for his uncle, Evgenii Nikolaevich, a professor at a Fish Institute (*Sobranie sochinenii* 2:472). Even after he came to recognize that this purposeful disclosure of economic and ideological determinants was essentially an attack on enemies of socialism, he nevertheless resorted to its ceremonial bellowing of positive and negative attributions. His position as a literary scholar at the Gorky Institute of World Literature depended upon it. In fact, He became a master at addressing Marxist-Leninist anxieties—even in his initial underground publication, *Chto takoe sotsialisticheskii realism* (*What Is Socialist Realism*). While his writing at the Institute and his writing published abroad in the late 1950s and early 1960s are marked by different targets, they nevertheless shared the same kind of imputations, ideological innuendos, and arrogant tone.

Ironically, Marxist-Leninist rhetoric provided a basis not only for ideological inferences, but also for satire, the attacking type of satire that we usually associate with Juvenal (Griffin 11). In keeping with this satire, Sinyavsky's early literary criticism is very direct, acerbic, and filled with ridicule whether he is talking about socialist realism in a foreign publication or the work of Russian writers in a Moscow journal.

"Unmasking" (*razoblachenie*) of enemies, one of the cornerstones of Marxist-Leninist rhetoric, was easily inculcated into literature and literary analysis. Promoted by the Russian Association of Proletarian Writers in the 1920s (RAPP), this disclosure of allegedly masked characteristics was in fact a type of ideological exposé or smear campaign (Fitzpatrick 27). Under the guise of getting below the surface, this class-conscious criticism resulted in the practice of blaming one group, for example, the bourgeois intelligentsia, and praising another, for example, the progressive intelligentsia, a bipolar practice fundamental to elementary satire. Lunacharsky maintained that a satirist should "launch an attack against an enemy while simultaneously declaring him already vanquished and laughable" (*On Literature and Art* 309). In his article "Gor'kii—Satirik," Sinyavsky suggests that "unmasking" and "accusatory laughter" (*oblichitel'nyi smekh*) are central to turning literature into satire (131). He goes on to discuss several facets of Gorky's satire, but not without establishing Gorky's contempt for the bourgeois intelligentsia. After all, in Marxist-Leninist criticism, satire and scorn are in the same semantic field. As Sinyavsky explains, satire for Gorky is not just a genre, but a defining genre, clarifying the relationship of the artist to reality, identifying what is obsolete and therefore standing in the path of progress (172). Quoting Gorky, he conveys the idea that the function of writing is purgative: "A

Soviet writer," in Gorky's words, "must take up the work of satire, making an effort to get rid of all of the infectious dirt and rubbish from life" (172).

In Sinyavsky's hands "unmasking" became not only the primary path of explication in his early academic writing, but also the basis for defending his own positions and opposing the positions of other critics. Essentially a style of indictment and condemnation, "unmasking" made Russian scholarship and journalism a volatile territory, especially when its practitioners turned on each other. Sinyavsky's dissertation, which we will examine in chapter four, is, in fact, a good example of "unmasking"—with a good measure of scorn for enemies of socialism. But his "unmasking," especially in his articles and reviews in *Novyi mir* (*The New World*) during the first half of the 1960s, became centered on artistic rather than ideological issues. Using the Marxist-Leninist style of heavy shelling, Sinyavsky wrote merciless attacks on the poetry and prose of a number of establishment writers, including V. Dolmatovsky, A. Sofronov, and I. Shevtsov.[11] He even chastised Evgenii Evtushenko, the darling of the young generation at the beginning of the 1960s, for his poem, *Bratsk GES* (*The Bratsk Hydroelectric Station*), calling it "highly superficial" (*samoe poverkhnostnoe*), "extremely saccharine" (*do krainosti slashchavo*), "banal"(*shablonoe*), and "cheap" (*deshevoe*).[12]

We should not assume that Sinyavsky's scathing assessments are a reflection of a malicious nature. In the context of Marxist-Leninist criticism, especially in its application to literary assessment, his assault and his tone are proforma. Without this form and tone, he would not have been entrusted to write literary encyclopedia entries on "Acmeism," "M. A. Voloshin," and "N. S. Gumilev" or banner scholarly pieces in the *History of Russian Literature* series published by the Academy of Sciences.[13] But in his contributions to *Novyi mir* (*The New World*), where he insists on innovation and individuality of voice, it is possible to discern not just malignment, but also irony—its indirectness and playfulness providing a departure from canonic calculations and blunt incriminations.

Sinyavsky's irony is rooted in a well-recognized phenomenon, namely the gap between ideals and their realization, as well as the practice of touting these ideals with shameless exaggeration. This kind of gap, with its aura of hypocrisy, breeds not simply anecdotes about empty rhetoric, but irony, which Sinyavsky compares to a loss of faith. Speaking about irony in *Chto takoe sotsialisticheskii realizm* (*What Is Socialist Realism*), Sinyavsky suggests its link with laughter, which, in his opinion, became a disease in Russian culture during the one-hundred-year period from Pushkin to Blok (433). Citing Blok's essay on irony from 1908, Sinyavsky underscores the path of irony, which begins with mockery and a smirk and ends with rebellion and sacrilege (433). It is what the prosecution characterized as Sinyavsky's path at his trial in February of 1966.

A child of irony, Sinyavsky is capable of brandishing the word as a sharp critical instrument or a blunt form of insult. Using, for example, understatement and overstatement, the traditional paths to irony, Sinyavsky manages to ridicule Anatoly Sofronov's collection of poems, *Ot vsekh shirot* (*From All Latitudes*), as well as the critics who praised it. According to Sinyavsky, A. Markov, a critic from *Literaturnaya gazeta*, tries to pass off Sofronov's "elementary knowledge about literature" (*elementarnaya literaturnaya gramotnost'*) as a literary breakthrough ("*O novom sbornike*" 253). At one point he wonders how Makarov could rave about the use of an adjective such as "captivating." Sinyavsky exclaims, "Imagine, the notion of 'captivating' and not just any object, but the sky." "Outside of 'captivating' any other word would have been out of place," he says with tongue in cheek (253). When he enumerates the fundamentally inconsistent tones in Evgenii Dolmatovsky's travel-based poems, he quips:

> Once these poets get away from home for two weeks they do not grow tired of writing about how they yearn to be back and how gloomy and burdensome it is to be on the road. Permit me to ask: would it not be better to give up these depressing trips and spare one's nerves? ("*Est' takie stikhi*" 246)

In a scene from prison in the second chapter of *Spokoinoi nochi* (*Goodnight!*), one of Sinyavsky's cell mates tells him to encourage his son, Yegor, to go into the military, suggesting that he might become an important officer, perhaps, the warden of a prison. Rather than expressing outrage, Sinyavsky feigns a revelation, using some well-worn clichés:

> I am beginning to understand how things work. Do you think by bayonets? Fear? Deception? Nothing of the sort. Through the great, unique class unity of our country, stitched together with steel upon a living filament, an unbroken and untarnished bond between the KGB, the party, industrialists, generals, lieutenants, and the lowest World War II collaborator rotting in a camp. (*Sobranie sochinenii* 2:436)[14]

Namely through irony Sinyavsky mocks the ideological rhetoric of his day, which, in its taut and inflated idiom, was ripe for ridicule. Speaking about a Marxist education, for example, he exclaims: "It has been a long time since men had such exact knowledge of the meaning of the world's destiny—not since the Middle Ages, most likely" (*Chto takoe sotsialisticheskii realizm* 408). The mere echo of this pervasive canonic language, combined with an extra measure of exaggeration, was enough to undermine its integrity, as in: "The ape stood up on its hind legs and began his triumphant march toward Communism" (*Chto takoe sotsialisticheskii realizm* 406). Using irony then, Sinyavsky becomes a ventriloquist, expressing more than one voice and addressing more than one type of reader. One can only imagine Sinyavsky, looking over his shoulder during six years of "underground" writing, hinting, winking, smiling, imagining the reactions of the KGB, the Western press, scholars, enemies, and friends. Through the anticipation of these reactions alone, irony was most tempting.

For Sinyavsky irony is more than a gap between what is said and what is meant. It is the basis for playing an implicit position against an explicit position, for drawing the reader into contingencies rather than into what may be necessarily true or false. Through irony, Sinyavsky carries on a type of disputation, not simply making the reader a witness, but an unwitting partner in a tug-of-war. Using irony, Sinyavsky not only enriches his text with allusions and innuendos, but he carries on a hermeneutical process from which the reader cannot escape. In *Chto takoe sotsialisticheskii realizm*, for example, just when readers from the West are enjoying a witty attack upon Communism, Sinyavsky suddenly shifts his addressivity, as if overhearing their laughter:

> Why do you laugh scum? Why do you claw the spots of blood and dirt on our uniforms with your well-cared-for nails? You say that this is not Communism, that we took the wrong turn and that we are further from it than when we started. Well then, where is *your* Kingdom of God? Show it! Where is the free personality of the superman that you promised? (*Fantasticheskii mir* 411)

In this sharp discursive turn readers may coil or recoil, uncertain about the author's words, but they may not easily turn the page without rethinking what is and what is not being said. When Sinyavsky shifts in *Chto takoe sotsialisticheskii realizm* from "I" to "we," from the playful to the professional, from sarcastic to earnest, from defiant to confessional, no reader should fail to consider what measure of masquerade goes into this kind of tonal artifice. There is, after all, no other course for a satirist who uses irony.

In view of Sinyavsky's anxiety about the arrest of his father in 1951 and the attempts by the KGB in 1948 and 1952 to coerce him into a deceptive relationship with Hélène Peltier, one might have expected him to use his pen in a discourse of pro and contra. But he never set out to write according to a facile dialectic. He became a satirist not a propagandist. His stance as a writer is free of the proselytizing and the prophesy of writers such as Tolstoy or Solzhenitsyn or the "purposeful" Gogol. Rather than simplifying the relationship between victims and victimizers, or fastening upon the struggle between the powerful and the powerless, he planted clues for readers to do their own taxonomy. Sinyavsky's writing is filled with clues—the kind that satirists count on to be discovered.

Sinyavsky's most important clue to the nature of his projects was his double identity. In fact Sinyavsky and Terts represent two-sidedness, the crucial ingredient of satire, which, in this case, has an underside in the underworld. Speaking of these sides, he declares:

> Sinyavsky is a quiet, plain, boring person, who lives most of his life in his study, devoting his energy to his academic career. Terts is lean and wiry, surly and abrasive. He could stick a knife into anybody's ribs. His name is as expressive as a knife. (Brezna 55)

In *Spokoinoi nochi* (*Goodnight!*), where Sinyavsky actually introduces the knife-wielding Terts into the text, he pauses to explain two-sidedness in terms of a telling relationship between a pen and a pocketknife (*Sobranie sochinenii* 2:345). Underscoring how the references to these instruments overlap in prison (knife=pen), Sinyavsky suggests how semantic connections in Soviet society reflect a system of fantastic reciprocities—one that creates Sinyavsky/Terts, that is, one that makes outlaws out of authors and authors out of outlaws.[15] The connection between writing and the underworld is of course restated more poignantly in Sinyavsky's decision to write satire and to smuggle it out of the country. To be sure, smuggling manuscripts abroad and smuggling another layer of meaning into a text are not the same, but, under Soviet law, both could be considered criminal activity. In both cases something is circumvented, for example, customs and censorship, not to mention the literary canon. Of course, the seriousness of the circumvention depends upon the nature of the smuggled contents—which the customs agent and the censor see with the same eyes.

Through a pseudonym like Abram Terts, Sinyavsky was providing one of his many poignant clues, linking his satire with the underground activities of a legendary Jewish outlaw from Odessa who had been celebrated in thieves' songs that were revived in the early 1950s during Stalin's final pogrom.[16] With this pseudonym, Sinyavsky was suggesting a link not simply to another identity, but to a provocative identity. The name Abram Terts was like a shot across the bow, a name adopted to rile the establishment with its highly charged semantic load, clearly echoing Sinyavsky's notion about "transgression" or "crossing into a forbidden territory." Unlike other

Russian authors who had chosen a lofty or a catchy pseudonym, Sinyavsky decided on an outrageous persona that he fleshed out in his fiction and in his life.[17] As Sinyavsky explained later in interviews, there was much that he shared with this criminal (Nepomnyashchy 7; Brezna 55). After all, he had read banned books and had smuggled his satire abroad—activity that was considered criminal under the Soviet legal code. Moreover, the Jewish identity of Terts suggested otherness, someone officially singled out as different and marked solely by this difference. Linking otherness not only with the maginalized, but also with thieves and artists, Sinyavsky suggests likenesses that could only sound an alarm among members of the establishment.

If Terts appears to be an unlikely part of the double discourse of the Russian intelligentsia, what can be said about the abundance of what is unlikely or implausible in Sinyavsky's writing? While it is customary to claim that the unlikely and the implausible link Sinyavsky's fiction with fantasy, the features of this fantasy are more indicative of Russian folklore than science fiction. After all, Sinyavsky has only written one genuine science fiction story, "*Pkhents*" ("Pkhents"), whereas most of his fiction contains folktale elements, for example, magic, becoming, for some readers, a source for old-world rituals. He weaves these elements into his writing to make indirect commentary, treating old traditions like mirrors to another reality, pausing to point out, for example, that not Marxism-Leninism, but Russian fairy tales open our eyes to the world and remind us what lies behind as well as ahead of us (*Sobranie sochinenii* 2:504). We should not overlook that Sinyavsky has contributed to the study of Russian folklore, pausing to introduce it in lectures at the Sorbonne, lectures which were later published as *Ivan-Durak: Ocherk russkoi narodnoi very* (*Ivan the Fool: An Essay about Russian Folk Beliefs*). Moreover, he moved the subject of Russian folklore to a central place in *V teni Gogolya* (*In the Shadow of Gogol*) underscoring its presence and importance even in Gogol's later works.[18]

Most of Sinyavsky's characters—and we must include Terts in this category—are built upon a large measure of unlikeliness, moreover, a particular type of fabled unlikeliness that recalls the archetypal, Russian folktale hero: Ivan the Fool. Such unlikeliness is, in fact, the narrative basis for this particular Ivan whom Sinyavsky considers a most endearing hero (*Ivan-Durak* 34).[19] Ivan the Fool, the one most unlikely to succeed, is the one who, in fact, does succeed. Terts, clearly a variant of this potential ne'er-do-well, is also not likely to succeed, yet he too succeeds in an astonishing way. He would not likely be celebrated in song (outside of thieves' circles) or welcomed into a literary partnership with Sinyavsky.

But it turns out otherwise. In fact, it turns out that both Ivan the Fool and Terts belong to a similar kind of narrative model for a startling deviation. In drawing attention to this kind of model, especially when he is enmeshed in allusions to hushed-up pages from Russian history, Sinyavsky mocks the notion of life as a scientific system, that is, life determined from the start and free from unlikely developments.

Like Ivan the Fool, most of Sinyavsky's unlikely heroes are blessed by "magic" agencies such as clairvoyance ("*Gololeditsa*") ("Icy Conditions") or hypnosis (*Lyubimov*) (*The Makepeace Experiment*), the ability to perform tricks ("*V tsirke*") ("At the Circus"), or the capacity to "see" the transformations of witches, house spirits, and water sprites ("*Kvartiranty*") ("Tenants"), or grant wishes *Kroska Tsores* (*Little Jinx*).[20] In *Lyubimov* (*The Makepeace Experiment*), in fact, which is saturated with folk-tale elements, Sinyavsky gets very close to the Ivan the Fool mold, putting together a composite character who resembles, in his sudden leap from the obscurity of a bicycle repairman to the status of the "supreme ruler" (*verkhovnyi pravitel'*) of the city of Lyubimov, a Soviet variant of this hero.[21] This updated Ivan, Lenya Tikhomirov (Lenny Makepeace), unknown, unschooled, and unlikely to acquire power, is actually elected without any ideological readiness. When the astounding results of the election are announced, Sinyavsky's narrator says that only the chattering of the teeth of the head of security is heard, then the mooing of a cow and finally the crowd, uncertain at first, shouting in unison, "Long live Tikhomirov" (*Sobranie sochinenii* 1:22). In this way Sinyavsky begins the story of what he calls a "scientific revolution" (*nauchnyi perevorot*).

Clearly Sinyavsky's writing is calculated—as calculated as the era in which he lived. Both a product of and a reaction to his era, he uses its canonic language to make arguments as well as to draw attention to its abuses and follies. On the one hand, he praises and blames his way to a position as a literary critic; on the other, he risks this position, turning against second-rate writers and critics who defend them. Taking up fiction, he carnivalizes the building of socialism, going so far as to spotlight a peasant in *Lyubimov* who steps forward among the unfinished monuments to urinate into a half-filled cement foundation (*Sobranie sochinenii* 1: 103). It is one of many times that his humor not only violates a taboo, but also makes a "forbidden" juncture. At such junctures, whether they are the meeting places of anecdotes and historical accounts, irony and official rhetoric, or folklore and ideology, Sinyavsky displays not only his fantastic coat of arms, but also his satirist banner. In the following chapters let us further examine this banner, from its sturdy shaft to the threads that make up its intricate fabric.

NOTES

1. In the nineteenth century, both Dobrolyubov and Rozanov claimed that Russian literature not only began with satire, but also that satire dominated several periods (Draitser xvi). Clearly, modern Russian literature began with the satire of Kantimir, Sumarokov, Fonvizin, Novikov, Krylov, and Griboedov. Moreover, it dominated the early Soviet period in the works of Zoshchenko, I'lf and Petrov, Olesha, Bulgakov, Erenburg, Kataev, Evgeny Shvarts, and Daniil Kharms, coming to the fore once again in the works of Sinyavsky, Voinovich, Iskander, Aleshkovsky, and Zinoviev.

2. In Catharine Nepomnyashchy's interview with Andrei Sinyavsky he claims, "There is a need to violate something, and I often catch myself thinking that I only truly find it interesting to write if there is a prohibition, a taboo" ("An Interview with Andrei Sinyavsky," 9). In his essay "The Literary Process in Russia," Sinyavsky maintains that a Russian writer writes about things that are most vital and most dangerous: things that are forbidden. Otherwise, he says, why write (85). In another interview, he says, "I usually write on forbidden topics, I'm not interested in writing about everyday matters, like what people have for lunch and that sort of thing. That's why my subject matter is often piquant. In the Soviet Union there are many taboo subjects, but I still maintain that such subjects are the very stuff of any real literary work" (Brezna 55). In an interview with John Glad he speaks about his writing as transgression, as entry into forbidden and risky discourse (157).

3. While it is important to consider that Sinyavsky became disillusioned when his father was arrested on trumped-up charges in 1951 and when the KGB tried to coerce him into a deceptive relationship with Hélène Peltier in 1948 and 1952, the period of the Thaw, with Khrushchev's agenda of de-Stalinization, emboldened a number of Russian writers to speak out, such as Pomerantsev, Ehrenburg, Dudintsev, Zorin, Panova, and Pasternak. In spite of the bumpy course of reforms during this period, social, economic, political, and cultural life were changed forever. In fact, the first steps toward glasnost' (openness) were taken not under Gorbachev in the mid-1980s, but between 1953 and 1964.

4. Because so little was known about Sinyavsky, any scrap of information seemed like a major discovery. Questions formed a circle around Sinyavsky's pseudonym, the meaning of phantasmagoria, and the turning points in the life of a man who suddenly became a *succès de scandale* at age 40. As late as the 1980s we were still discovering when Sinyavsky actually wrote a number of his works as well as what he had read and how he managed to survive.

5. Although "anekdote" is roughly equivalent to a joke in English, it also may refer to a funny story or an entertaining short narrative.

6. Sinyavsky claims, "All of Soviet history could be told through anecdotes (*Soviet Civilization* 224). And he speaks very much like a satirist making his case when he says,

> The future of Russian literature, if it is destined to have a future at all, has been nourished on political jokes, just as Pushkin grew up on the fairy tales told by his nanny. In its pure form, the joke demonstrates the miracle of art, deriving as it does nothing but good from the savagery and fury of dictators. ("The Literary Process in Russia," 97)

7. Sinyavsky's *Soviet Civilization* contains a wealth of jokes. He claims: "Given no freedom of speech, no freedom of the press, people took to the joke the way a duck takes to water. Thus it has become the leading folklore genre, the constant companion of Soviet life, with great influence upon contemporary language" (224).

8. While Michael Glenny's translation, *Kontinent* (Garden City, N.Y.: Anchor-Doubleday, 1976), 77–118 is generally accurate, sometimes there are unexplainable gaffs. For some reason or other he includes a statement that is not in the original: "The Soviet leaders are, of course, a natural target for political jokes" (97).

9. Anyone who has interviewed Sinyavsky knows that he had a sense of humor. In fact, he was fond of telling stories with hilarious outcomes. He was filled with stories and he told them with a twinkle in his eye. In the midst of what seemed to be an ordinary story he would suddenly add some shock value such as references to blowing up bridges, spying for the United States, or selling plans for a new class of submarine.

10. In *Mysli vrasplokh* (*Thoughts Unaware*) Sinyavsky leads the reader into the forbidden territory of sex. For comments about Sinyavsky's treatment of sex, see Dalton (129–31); Lourie (106–10), Deming Brown, "The Art of Andrei Sinyavsky" (385–86); Field, "Abram Tertz's Ordeal By Mirror" (12–13), Nepomnyashchy, *Abram Tertz and the Poetics of Crime* (157–58). For a recent discussion of Sinyavsky's treatment of sex, see Sandler (295).

11. We will examine these attacks in the context of all of Sinyavsky's contributions to *Novyi mir* (*The New World*) in chapter five.

12. While many in Russia and in the West viewed Evtushenko as a pawn of the establishment in the 1960s, no one made an issue of his sanctioned critiques or individualist posturing. Sinyavsky's article on Evtushenko, which was rejected for publication in Moscow, appeared abroad in *Grani* (*Facets*) 1967, almost two years after his arrest.

13. "Akmeism" and "M. A. Voloshin," *Kratkaya literaturnaya entsiklopediya*, 1:118–19, 1021. Moscow: Sovetskaya entsiklopedya, 1962. "A. M. Gor'kii," *Istoria russkoi sovetskoi literatury*, 1:99–167. Moscow: Akademiya nauk, 1958; "Eduard Bagritskii," *Istoriya russkoi sovetskoi literatury*, 1:397–420. Moscow: Akademiya nauk, 1958; "*Literatura perioda velikoi otechestvennoi voiny*," *Istoriya russkoi sovetskoi literatury*, 3:5–53. Moscow: Akademiya nauk, 1961; "*O khudozhestvennoi structure romana 'Zhizn' Klima Samgina,'*" *Tvorchestvo M. Gor'kogo i voprosy sotsialistcheskogo realizma*, 132–74. Moscow: Akademiya nauk, 1958.

14. The word "steel" (*stal'naya*) in this quotation could suggest "stitched together with a steel needle" as well as " Stalin's needle."

15. The link between criminality and writing is at the heart of Catharine Nepomnyashchy's *Abram Tertz and the Poetics of Crime*. In her opinion, "If the writer is an outlaw, then the act of writing literature becomes a crime and the text a site of transgression" (2). In *Soviet Civilization: A Cultural History,* Sinyavsky takes criminality further: "In the broadest sense, then, I would say that every Soviet citizen is, by definition, and necessity, a criminal, for the simple reason that survival in a socialist society is somehow always a matter of breaking the law" (138–34).

16. For a reconstruction of one of these songs, see John Updike's "The Lament of Abrashka Tertz," 3.

17. The list of Russian authors who adopted pseudonyms is quite extensive. Here are a few: Boris Pilnyak (Vogau), Vladimir Sirin (Nabokov), Lev Schwartzman (Shestov), Mikhail Saltykov (Shchedrin), Yefim Pridvorov (Demian Bedny), Andrei Bely (Bugaev), Alexei Peshkov (Gorky), Eduard Dzyubin (Bagritsky), Fedor Sologub (Teternikov), Andrei Bely (Bugayev), Anna Gorenko (Akhmatova).

18. It is Russian folklore that drew Sinyavsky and his wife, Mariya Vasilevna, to Pereslavl'-Zalesskii in the lake region of northern Russia where they photographed old architecture and collected artifacts such as icons and distaffs (Dalton 15).

19. For two examples of tales about Ivan the Fool, see Afanasiev's *Narodnye russkie skazki*, 3:3, 195, 315. In Sinyavsky's monograph on Russian folk beliefs, he draws attention to Ivan's "openness" (otkrytost') and "passiveness" (passivnost'). He describes him as an international type, a variant of the ne'er-do-well whose contradictory triumph is not contingent upon wit, diligence, or volition. By implication, Ivan The Fool possesses what for Sinyavsky is most admirable: a lack of purposefulness (*Ivan-Durak* 38–39).

20. In *Ivan-Durak* Sinyavsky draws attention to the agency of magic in Ivan's success (41). As in "V tsirke" ("At the Circus"), he speaks about magic in terms of "conjuring" (fokus) and the capacity of Ivan to play the role of a "magician" (fokusnik) (44).

21. The term "composite" here designates a combination of characteristics, including features of Ivan the Fool, a Soviet version of Ivan the Fool, a caricature of Soviet leadership and, in Lenya's ability to turn himself into a hawk, a borzoi, and a motorcycle, a playful allusion to early Russian princes as they are hyperbolized in *The Tale of Bygone Years* (*Povest' vremennykh let*), a chronicle of events and narratives from approximately 1040 to 1118.

During his trial Sinyavsky argues that *Lyubimov* is complex, that it is filled with a deliberate farrago of nonsense, with contradictions and gibberish (Ginzburg 230–31). It appears first in his two-volume collection (1992) because it was his favorite.

Chapter Four

Constant Polarities, Scholarship, Ventriloquism

Andrei Sinyavsky's dissertation contains layers of praise and blame—the official discourse of Soviet scholarship. It also contains a measure of voicing, which palliates the satiric flow of booing and cheering. Completed in 1952, during Stalin's final years, "Maksim Gorky's Novel *Klim Samgin* and the History of Russian Social Thought at the End of the Nineteenth and the Beginning of the Twentieth Century" ("*Roman M. Gor'kogo 'Klim Samgina' i istoriya russkoi obshchestvennoi mysli kontsa XIX— nachala XX veka*"), is, in many respects, an archeologist's find, extracted not long ago from the depths of the main library (*fundamental'naya biblioteka*) of Moscow University.[1] There is much to sift through in this 404-page dissertation, including Sinyavsky's mastery of the Marxist-Leninist idiom, his scholarly rigor, as well as his erudition in idealist philosophy and decadent literature. Moreover, because of Sinyavsky's disillusionment with Soviet society in 1948, it is the earliest record of a Sinyavskian masquerade, in this case, the seemingly contemptuous treatment of the bourgeois intelligentsia accompanied by a steady stream of Marxist-Leninist assaults.[2] In fact, by means of a veil of denunciations, Sinyavsky creates a suitable rhetorical atmosphere for introducing and examining literature that had been banned. Both attacking and at the same time amplifying the place of this literature, Sinyavsky displays his skills at orchestrating more than one voice (*The Dialogical Imagination* 324). In the following pages I would like to discuss the context and the dynamics of this orchestration, factoring in important connections with Sinyavsky's life as well as his other writing.

Sinyavsky completed his dissertation in the year prior to Stalin's death, a year that culminated in the so-called "doctors' plot," stemming from accusations that nine physicians, through intentional medical malpractice, murdered a number of Soviet leaders, including Zhdanov (Riasanovsky 538). The events of Sinyavsky's "underground" novella, *The Trial Begins* (*Sud idet*), published abroad in 1959, are set precisely in this period. Given the atmosphere of suspicion and increasing arrests, signaling another round of purges, Sinyavsky did not submit a dissertation that could have been ideologically misleading. Even Aesopian language was out of the question. Yet, as we shall see, his research was not entirely subsumed by ideological expediency. His canonical utterances, extracanonical revelations, and critical calibrations give his study an intricate quality, the kind of quality that is absent from his M.A. thesis (*diplomnaya rabota*) in 1949 on Mayakovsky, "On Mayakovsky's Esthetics" ("Ob estetike Mayakovskogo").

Most dissertations are written under stress, resulting quite often in a candidate's anxiety and soul-searching. In Sinyavsky's case, there was cause for much inner turmoil. It is no secret that he had a profound change of heart regarding the merits of the Soviet system in the late 1940s. In his novel *Goodnight!* (*Spokoinoi nochi*), he points to 1948, a year before he received his first degree from Moscow University, as his final break with Communism (*Spokoinoi nochi* 181). Up until that time, he had been a staunch defender of the ideals of the Revolution, joining the *Komsomol* not because of others' expectations, but out of his own convictions. To make matters worse, in 1951, while Sinyavsky was in the final stages of his dissertation research, his father, Donat Evgenevich, was arrested for espionage in connection with his role in the distribution of U.S. famine relief to Russian schools and kindergartens in 1922 (*Spokoinoi nochi* 167). While his father presented documentary proof that he was carrying out his official duties rather than spying, he was nevertheless sentenced to five years of exile for agitation and propaganda—thirty years after his alleged crime. In 1952, the year that Sinyavsky completed his dissertation, his father was sent to a transfer prison and then on to Rameno, his place of exile.

The KGB had a file on both father and son. During that very summer they turned to the younger Sinyavsky about his relationship with Hélène Peltier, the daughter of a French naval attaché.[3] In fact, they took him under escort to Vienna in order to meet and deceive her, and eventually to use her to obtain information. Sinyavsky made every effort to ensure that the Peltier operation failed. This harrowing experience completely alienated Sinyavsky from the Soviet system. It was in Vienna that he asked Hélène to consider smuggling out one of his manuscripts on her next trip to Moscow. Indeed, he soon began writing "for the drawer." In the course of the following two years, he finished the first part of a biting satire that he entitled "Point of Departure," which is also known as "An Essay in Self-Analysis" ("*Tochka otscheta*," "*Opyt samoanaliza*") (Ginzburg 238), and the core of a monograph on art called "Between Heaven and Earth." By the mid-fifties he had several manuscripts ready for Hélène.

Before looking into the body of Sinyavsky's dissertation, I should say a few words about the novel to which it is devoted, *Klim Samgin*. After Gorky's canonization, this four-volume epic became a classic model for socialist realism, a suitable topic for suitable scholarship. It tells the story of forty years of Russian intellectual and political life from the 1870s to the Revolution, shifting its focus from the Volga region to St. Petersburg, to Moscow, and other Russian cities, as well as abroad. The novel's center is Samgin, who at first shows promise, but who falters, not finding his niche in life, failing to commit himself to anyone or anything. In one revealing episode from book one, fear for his own safety prevents him from saving his companions, Boris and Varya, from drowning, a drowning that he will later deny more than once (*Samgin* 79–82). For Gorky, Samgin represents the typical bourgeois intellectual, an unquestionable antihero, surrounded by others like himself, juxtaposed, in no uncertain terms, to the novel's exemplary Marxist, Kutuzov. Filled with historical events and historical personages, the novel reaches its denouement during the events of January 1905 with Samgin, not unlike Pierre Bezukov at Borodino, stumbling in and out of harm's way. In the end, Gorky shows how Samgin, along with the class to which he belongs, is swept away by the October Revolution.

Gorky's *Klim Samgin* is overly ambitious in scope and in psychological analysis and complicated by so many characters, events, and narrative leaps that the unifying thread of Samgin's life does not hold together. *Klim Samgin*, of course, is an unfinished piece, the latter parts of which Gorky had planned to revise. Boris Pasternak supposedly enjoyed the first part because of its complexity, saying that it forced the reader to make an effort to follow Samgin's growth and development (305).[4] Gleb Struve thought that all parts of the novel suffered from compositional problems (62). B. Shcherbina praised it for its epic qualities (168). In the opening pages of his dissertation, Sinyavsky calls it the realization of Gorky's efforts to portray the bourgeois intelligentsia, efforts that begin as early as the 1890s (2). Speaking about *Klim Samgin* in 1933, Gorky declared:

> I wrote it in the most heavy-handed way, tediously and altogether badly. And it seems that I do not have the time to make it right, to make it better,

old age is against me and I am aging fast. Believe me, I am not exaggerating.[5]

While Sinyavsky's dissertation is a reflection of the times, it does not belong to the 550 dissertations written about Soviet literature during the first decade after the war that resemble "padded newspaper articles" (Slonim 309). It has a lofty foreword, a carefully chosen bibliography, and, by in large, ideologically appropriate chapter headings such as: "The Affirmation of Socialist Ideology and the Unmasking of Bourgeois Ideology in the Novel *Klim Samgin*"; "Politics and Sociology;" "Philosophy and Esthetics"; "The Artistic Structure of This Novel and the Problem of Reflecting the History of Social Thought"; "The System of Imagery in This Novel: Some Questions Regarding Its Composition and Syuzhet"; "*Klim Samgin* as a Philosophic and Political Novel." In keeping with the requirements for the acceptability of a dissertation during this period, it is filled with quotes from Lenin, Stalin, and Zhdanov, not to mention Fadeev, as well as Belinsky, Chernyshevsky, and Dobrolyubov. There are no surprises in the short bibliography of seven pages, which consists of two alphabetical lists, one political, the other literary. In spite of the fact that "idealist" philosophers such as Berdyaev, Rozanov, Shestov, and Merezhkovsky or "decadent" writers such as Bryusov, Bal'mont, and Bely, are cited in the body of the dissertation, they do not appear in the bibliography.

Authority, against which Sinyavsky posits antithetical images in his fiction written under the pseudonym of "Terts," is central to his dissertation. It is authority, which speaks through Sinyavsky and through which Sinyavsky speaks. Sinyavsky does not simply cite or refer to authority; he appropriates it. Not only does he include forty-nine entries in his bibliography on Lenin and twelve on Stalin, but he also takes the additional step of establishing the centrality of his investigation to the canon (the unmasking of the bourgeoisie) in the precise language and tone of Marxist-Leninist criticism. Through such ideological centrality and authenticity of pronouncement, he puts forward arguments whose inferences are an end in themselves. In other words, he engineers a discourse not of revelation, but of replication, which, in a dissertation written within a closed system, is not unexpected. Sinyavsky had an opportunity to demonstrate his skill at this kind of discourse earlier, when he wrote reports on dialectical materialism for his uncle, Evgenii Nikolaevich, a professor at a Fish Institute (*Spokoinoi nochi* 183). He points out that his "crib notes" (*spargalki)* were instrumental in establishing his uncle as a prominent Marxist at the institute. Analogously, Sinyavsky's dissertation research helped to establish his own authority on Gorky, an author, ironically, whom he attacked in no uncertain terms several years later in *Chto takoe sotsialisticheskii realizm* (*What Is Socialist Realism*).[6]

Sinyavsky proclaims *Klim Samgin* to be the culmination of the "unmasking" (*razoblachenie*) of the bourgeois intelligentsia, a proclamation that echoes the Juvenalian side of Marxist-Leninist criticism, that is, the satire of praise and blame. Underscoring Gorky's corroboration of official ideology and history, Sinyavsky develops a level of discourse that combines authoritative generalization ("*chto revolyutsiya obogoshchaet trudyashchikhsya mass, opredleyaet rastsvet lichnost, obnaruzhivaya skrytye sily, sposobnosti i talant*") (54) and accusation ("*revizionizm, soglashatel'stvo, opportunizm*") (40) with praise ("*Gor'kii reshal problemy imevshie, printsipial'no-vazhnoe znachenie dlya stanovleniya i razvitiya sovetskoi literatury*") (17). It is this type of discourse that gives Sinyavsky's dissertation an institutional quality. Given this quality, there is something parodic about its marked presence in the writing of a dissenter, a recent dissenter—and something ironic when this writing is a dissertation. Sinyavsky's "own" voice lies in the orchestration of the excess of such canonical simulation.

The institutional traits of Sinyavsky's discourse are often expressed in watchwords, fixed epithets, and clichés. Adhering to well-known pronouncements and labels, Sinyavsky reduces, for example, the essence of six characters (Turoboev, Kozlov, Nekhaeva, Zotova, Tomilin, Nikonova) to "skepticism," "monarchism," "decadence," "occultism," "subjective idealism," and "provocation" (244), or one character (Berdnikov) to "greed," "undisguised egoism," "misanthropy," "extreme unscrupulousness," and "cynicism" (116). Listing "emigrants," "saboteurs," "capitulators," and "factionalists" as extensions of the bourgeoisie intelligentsia (14), he echoes the type of classification that has enabled critics to lump together "Trotskiites," "Zinovevites," and "Buxarinites" (28) or explain "falseness," "duplicity," "secrecy," and "pretentiousness" as the sociopolitical features of bourgeois liberalism (90). Marked by expressions such as "relentless struggle" (*besposhchadnaya bor'ba)*, "class contradiction" (*klassovoe protivorechie)*, "departure from day-to-day reality" (*ukhod ot zlobodnevnoi deistvitel'nosti*), "enemy of the working class and the revolution" (*vrag rabochego klassa i revolyutsii*), the language that Sinyavsky adopts is the official language of denunciation.

It goes without saying that Marxist criticism dismisses what is known as "bourgeois phrase mongering." Sinyavsky, therefore, does not engage in lengthy deductions and vacillations. Moreover, given the aim of this novel, Sinyavsky's analysis does not unfold apart from Gorky's indictment of a class enemy. In view of this indictment, what Sinyavsky is examining is not simply a text, but evidence in a case against Samgin. Hence, Sinyavsky's language carries the arrogant accent of a prosecutor rather than a literary critic. When Sinyavsky calls Samgin a "subjectivist" (*sub'ektivist)*, a "skeptic" (*skeptik)*, a "renegade" (*renegat*), and a "liar" (*lzhets*), his language bristles with imputations (231).

While Sinyavsky's analysis is never free from the language of the canon, it is not completely vitiated by this language. In fact, his official-sounding utterances are unevenly distributed, condensing now and then for maximum effect, but mostly framing beginnings, endings, and transitions from textual example to ideology. His critical positions, upon close examination, do not always lead to ready-made appraisals, but to thoughtful formulations and deductions. While he attacks the critics of the late 1920s (E'lsberg, Shklovsky, Polyakova, and Mikhailov) and unnamed "vulgarizers" (*vul'garizatory*) from RAPP, or praises established Gorky scholars (Saburov, Bushmin, Belkin, Novich, Kanaev), including his dissertation advisor, L. M. Timofeev, he does not hesitate to consider troublesome omissions and assumptions, or to explore ideologically underdeveloped territories.

When Sinyavsky suggests that (1) the study of the novel's artistic form, (2) its place in the literature of the Soviet period, (3) its impact upon the meaning and development of socialist realism, (4) its relationship to Russian literature of the nineteenth century, and (5) its historical concordance is sorely lacking, he does not simply justify the need for his study, but he makes a statement about the modest state of *Samgin* scholarship (31). There is, of course, nothing extraordinary about this admission, except for what it suggests about Gorky's novel: official endorsement of this work had not been fully substantiated by literary criticism. Its reputation was based largely on the sponsorship of the literary establishment. On the other hand, given this state of scholarship in the early 1950s, Gorky's novel offered significant opportunities for further research, which, for Sinyavsky, meant access to the literature of the bourgeois intelligentsia, that is, banned books.[7]

Sinyavsky's assault upon unnamed critics regarding their treatment of Marina Zotova, a member of Samgin's circle who was known as the high priestess of decadence, is also telling. It is, in fact, another layer of his discourse, a layer with challenges to "opinion." He claims, "for a long time there has been a widespread opinion that was publicly promulgated or quietly acknowledged" (*dolgoe vremya bylo rasprostraneno sformylirovannoe ili molchalivo priznannoe mnenie* 99) regarding Zotova's "incongruous" (*neumestnyi*) place in the given historical period. Taking issue with this opinion, he argues that Zotova's historical place lies unquestionably in her connection with religious sects (*khlystovstvo*) and their connection with the bourgeois intelligentsia at the turn of the century. Rejecting how critics defined her relationship to Samgin, Sinyavsky insists on her tutorial attitude toward Samgin and her cultivation of his interest in sects. Essentially, Sinyavsky challenges an accepted interpretation of Zotova's place in the novel, putting forward a new perspective on her, legitimizing, above all, a discussion of the influence of sects on Samgin and his circle.

Sinyavsky is at his best when he discusses the interconnecting properties of Gorky's novel. At his best, Sinyavsky meets the irreconcilable expectations of two audiences: literary critics and literary censors. The result is a layered discussion with uneven paths of extrapolation from one layer to another. It is this kind of layered discussion that is most poignant in Sinyavsky's chapter on the structure and composition of *Samgin*, a chapter that was later published as "The Artistic Structure of *Klim Samgin*" in a collection of essays on Gorky.[8] Here Sinyavsky advances one of his substantive premises, saying that what is original about *Samgin* is its "mirror construction" (*zerkal'noe postroenie*). Drawing upon Lunacharsky's notion (149) of the "concentric" (*kontsentricheskii*) features of this novel, Sinyavsky underscores the function of Samgin as a locus of both projection and reflection. He argues that Samgin exemplifies all of the features of the bourgeois intelligentsia which, in turn, exemplify all of Samgin's features. Not anticipating any questions about the primacy of the chicken or the egg, Sinyavsky discusses Gorky's methods of mirroring the one in many and the many in one, that is, his representation of doubles, likenesses, parallels, analogies, as well as mutually reflecting scenes, images, and ideas (242). To add conclusive ideological perspective to his analysis, Sinyavsky reaffirms the unified social essence of the bourgeois intelligentsia, and therefore of Samgin's circle. Three successive quotes from Lenin emphasize this kind of unity through corollaries regarding the oneness of "legal Marxism," "economism" and "menshevism," and the lack of real differences among the idealists.

Often there is an obvious seam in the way that Sinyavsky splices together Gorky's compositional devices with canonical expectations. For example, his insights into the novel's "multi-linearity of plot" (*mnogolineinost' syuzheta)*, the "multi-layered nature of its narrative" (*mnogoplannost' povestvovaniya)*, and the "polyphony" (*mnogogolosie*) of its verbal exchanges are hardly in accord with the purposefulness of the novel. Moreover, they suggest that Gorky is one of the great stylists of his era—which is hardly the case. But in order to move his focus to the formal elements of the novel, Sinyavsky must defend Gorky's style. Through attacks on the claims of the critics of the late 1920s regarding the shortcomings of Gorky's style, Sinyavsky dispels any doubts about the relevance of his focus. On the other hand, by enumerating the claims of these critics about the "formlessness," "strategic paucity," and "compositional weakness" of Gorky's novel (297), he spells out more than one counteropinion to the canon.

After Sinyavsky discusses the prominent features of *Samgin*—what he calls juxtapositional exposition in nature, recurring images and motifs, and dramatic and satiric circumstances—he boils them down to a true-to-life, historically specific, and well-motivated context. It is this well-prepared context that Sinyavsky uses to compare the bourgeois intelligentsia with Stepan Kutuzov, the ideological opposite to Klim Samgin. Praising Gorky's art of contextualization, Sinyavsky prepares a path for weighty canonical considerations. Fully aware of the implications of Kutuzov's impeccable image, Sinyavsky argues that Gorky solved "one of the fundamental problems of Soviet literature: the representation of the positive Bolshevik-hero" (261). Thus, Sinyavsky links his discussion of literary strategies to one of the central issues of Soviet literature then to a recognition of Gorky's model hero. In praising the singular appearance of an effective Bolshevik-hero, however, Sinyavsky acknowledges an embarrassing shortfall in the development of what should be a leading and pervasive character.

Buried in Sinyavsky's final chapter, where *Samgin* is largely illuminated by the insights of the "progressive" critics and writers of the nineteenth century, is a brief discussion about the novel in terms that we associate with Bakhtin.[9] Sinyavsky begins this discussion with regard to the speech characteristics of Gorky's characters. While he formulates the features of an unflattering class jargon, consisting of fragments, contradictions, empty phrases, weak emotional coloration, and clichés (357), he also acknowledges the shared territory of speech and the interrelationship of characters within a mode of speech. To this discussion he adds his notion of Samgin's "elastic biography" (*elastichnaya biografiya*), from which and to which is transmitted a wealth of sociohistorical material, including the accent of others' speech. In the manner of Bakhtin, Sinyavsky points to Samgin's use of "others' words" (*chuzhie slova)*, to interlocution where there is no interlocutor, to passages where speech is the only attribute of a character. In a footnote he adds, "Klim Samgin reads his own thoughts in books, finds them in the words of his friends and finally hears them in the streets" (325). Returning to his argument about the unprepossessing speech of the bourgeois intelligentsia, Sinyavsky does not go deeper into the dialogical realities that he posits.

There are, of course, ideological differences between the reflection of characters (the mirror principle) and the refraction of characters (the dialogical principle). Sinyavsky bases his analysis on the former; it could not be otherwise. Clarifying his position, he argues that while the events of the novel unfold only through Samgin's eyes, Gorky exercises control over Samgin. Wanting to distance himself from the "vulgar-mechanistic approach" (*vul'garno-mekhanicheskii podkhod)* to literature, Sinyavsky dismisses any notion of Gorky as an author who depicted reality through the eyes of a negative character. According to Sinyavsky, notions such as "Samgin's eyes" or "Samgin's perception" are conventions. Pointing out the difference between figurative and literal meaning, he pauses to make a fundamental distinction: "Let's not forget that we are talking about a literary work, that Samgin is not a living, perceiving person, but a literary character" (268). Little did Sinyavsky then suspect that he would make the same distinction about characters in his own literary work at his trial on February 12, 1966 (Ginzburg 302).

It is Sinyavsky's examination of the philosophical and literary influences on the bourgeois intelligentsia that lends his dissertation an extraordinary quality, for most of the sources that he cites were then banned. Only with special permission was it possible to have access to authors such as Berdyaev, Rozanov, Merezhkovsky, Shestov, Bryusov, F. Sologub, Bal'mont, and Gippius, permission which Sinyavsky was granted. In 1951, when Sinyavsky's father was arrested, a twenty-one-hour search was conducted in the family's small Moscow apartment on Khlebnyi Street. Upon discovering a large collection of books written by "idealist" philosophers and "decadent" poets, the KGB operatives raised a lot of questions. Even though Sinyavsky explained that the books were needed for his research on Gorky, one of the operatives said, "The son is worse than the father" (*Spokoinoi nochi* 237).

Following Gorky's lead regarding the reading tastes and recurring issues in Samgin's circle, Sinyavsky reconstructs the bourgeois intelligentsia's "passions of the mind." He traces these passions to this group's search for answers, for the meaning of life, for an antidote to what Marx posited as materialist philosophy and objective truth. Samgin, according to Sinyavsky, finds his antidote in Nietzsche, Shestov, and Merezhkovsky. Thirty-two years later, Sinyavsky will claim that this kind of writing, which he collected for years before his dissertation research, was a "substitute for an antidote" (*vmesto protivoyadiya)* (*Spokoinoi nochi* 236). Tracing Tomilin's skepticism to Berdyaev, Shestov, and Rozanov, Krasnov's meditation to the teachings of Buddha, Samgin's inspiration to F. Sologub, and Lidiya Varvarka's poetic aspirations to Gippius, Sinyavsky suggests their path from epistemological inquiry to some form of religion through empiricism, skepticism, relativism, solipsism, and mysticism. Along this path Sinyavsky displays one of his best gifts: what Igor' Golomshtok has called his "great philosophical range" (*bol'shogo filosofskogo mashtaba*) (Ginzburg 162).[10] Only with such range, which could not be easily acquired in Soviet schools, was it possible for Sinyavsky to move easily, for example, from Schopenhauer to Nietzsche to Rozanov. In fact without it, he would not have had any basis for his argument against teleology in *What Is Socialist Realism* (*Chto takoe sotsialisticheskii realizm*), his first and foremost underground essay written only four years after his dissertation.

Arguing that Zotova's participation in sects that practiced rituals of flagellation is an indication of the level of degradation to which the bourgeois intelligentsia had succumbed at the turn of the century, he underscores this class's deviations from mainstream religion. According to Sinyavsky, with the loss of credibility of the Orthodox church, "God-seeking" (*bogoiskatel'stvo)* and "God-constructing" (*bogostroitel'stvo*) took a dissolute path: a path that he finds elucidated in Merezhkovsky's "Not Peace but the Sword" ("*Ne mir, no mech*"). For proof of the spread of "wild fanaticism" (*izuverstvo)* he turns to "decadent" literature, citing Bal'mont's "Green Petrograd" ("*Zelenyi Petrograd*"), Belyi's *Silver Dove* ("*Serebryanyi golub*"), Gippius's "Bright Lake" ("*Svetloe ozero*"), *The Devil's Doll* ("*Chertova kukla*") and *Roman, Son of the Tsar* ("*Roman-tsarevich*"), as well as P. Karpov's *The Flame* ("*Plamen'*"). To further illuminate his argument, Sinyavsky quotes a long passage from one of Blok's letters to E. P. Ivanov, providing an account of a ritual that culminated in dancing, writhing, and symbolic contortions of the body (209).

Throughout this dissertation, it is as if Sinyavsky the scholar and Sinyavsky the pragmatist were coauthors, agreeing only about the audience for which it was written. The former chooses the topic and explores the territory beyond the canonical walls; the latter denounces this territory, aligning the canon to check the progress of exploration. Thus, one of Sinyavsky's voices makes important distinctions regarding the preoccupations of the bourgeois intelligentsia; the other levels these distinctions, underscoring their homogeneity and typicality, as well as baseness. Such is the double-voiced quality of this dissertation, with one voice guided by givens (the canon) and the other by research (discoveries). The presence of these voices makes the flow of discourse uneven, jumping, for example, from Berdyaev's *Reason and Common Sense* ("*Razum i zdravyi smysl*'") to Lenin's *Materialism and Empirical Criticism* ("*Materializm i empiriokrititsizm*"), resulting in feeble connections, such as the placement of religious protest and religious fervor in the same category, or fundamentalists and obscurantists in the same camp. Most feeble is the attribution of the reading habits of the bourgeois intelligentsia to an "omnivorous appetite" (*vseyadnost'*) for any book (197). Claims about eclecticism and undisciplined behavior sound ideologically correct, but hardly convincing.

There is no doubt that these voices are in opposition to each other; however, they do not collide. Such a collision, with its ensuing contradictions, would not have been tolerated by Sinyavsky's dissertation committee—especially in 1952. These voices, it goes without saying, are never on the same rhetorical level. The authoritative voice, as I have indicated, sounds like an old script, repeating the canon with such excess that parody was within reach. With its fixed intonations, and recognizable baggage, it is easy to stage. In fact, Sinyavsky stages it well as his subsequent works attest. He stages it here in order to draw attention away from a scholarly discussion about the "other," that is, the bourgeois intelligentsia. Using more than one voice, Sinyavsky does not champion what the establishment condemns, at least not in his dissertation. He does, however, orchestrate a succession of denunciations, ideological clichés, and arrogant imputations followed by intermittent analyses of forbidden writing and extra-canonical arguments. What is ironic about this orchestration is that Sinyavsky used a model socialist realist novel to obtain forbidden literature and discuss it with impunity.

This dissertation is clearly a starting point for what we sense as Sinyavsky's remarkable insight into literature, his potential for parodic practices, and his philosophical disputation. It is this disputation especially that takes him beyond Marxist theories, in this case, to the hypotheses of thinkers such as Berdyaev, Merezhkovsky, Rozanov, and Shestov. While it is not possible to document what Sinyavsky gleans from these thinkers, there should be no doubt about later traces of Rozanov in Sinyavsky's exploration of the self, his rambling utterances, and his highly polemical positions. The stamp of Rozanov's style, for example, is undeniable in *Thoughts Unaware* (*"Mysly vrasplokh"*), and *Voice from the Chorus* (*"Golos iz khora"*). Also undeniable is Sinyavsky's serious regard for this eccentric writer in *"Fallen Leaves" of V. V. Rozanov* (*"'Opavshie list'ya' V. V. Rozanova")*, which he put together from his lectures at the Sorbonne. Such linkage, however, should not suggest that Sinyavsky is a direct product of the bourgeois intelligentsia. Sinyavsky's dissertation points to his erudition rather than his espousal of a particular ideology. It is namely through this erudition that Sinyavsky is able to consider positions both inside and outside Marxism. The first steps in the evolution of Sinyavsky/Terts are here in the way that he makes his way through a minefield of explosive issues, making certain that the bluster of ideological authority will muffle other sounds.

NOTES

1. Sinyavsky's dissertation has not been examined to date. Unavailable to the reading public until recently, it has been a noncirculating item at the University of Moscow library.

2. In Marxist-Leninist parlance, the "bourgeois intelligentsia" is of course distinct from the "progressive intelligentsia." In *Soviet Civilization*, Sinyavsky pauses to provide a list of traits that were usually attributed to the former, the group that had allegedly betrayed the working-class cause: individualism, abstract humanism, flabbiness, spinelessness, a lack of principles, half-heartedness, no collective spirit, introspection, free thinking, decadence, skepticism, cynicism, and opportunism (135). A later reflection of Sinyavsky's focus on the bourgeois intelligentsia and Gorky is his discussion of "god-building" *(bogostroitel'stvo)* in "Roman M. Gor'kogo *Mat'* kak rannii obrazets sotsialisticheskogo realizma," *Cahiers du monde russe et sovietique* 24 (January–March 1988): 38–40.

3. Sinyavsky befriended Hélène Peltier at Moscow University in 1947.

4. The page numbers in parenthesis correspond to Sinyavsky's dissertation, "Roman M. Gor'kogo."

5. In a letter to Romain Rolland on January 30, 1933 (*Pis'ma o Literature* 442).

6. In addition to his dissertation, Sinyavsky published two articles on Gorky: "O khudozhestvennoi strukture romana *Zhizn' Klima Samgina*," *Tvorchestvo M. Gor'kogo i voprosy sotsialisticheskogo realizma*. ANSSR, Inst. mirovoi literatury, 1958, 132–74, and "Gor'kii-Satirik," *O khudozhestvennom masterstve M. Gor'kogo*. ANSSR, Inst. mirovoi literatury, 1960, 131–73. In an article on Issac Babel, *Oeuvres et opinions*, no. 8 (1964): 160–61, Sinyavsky underscores Gorky's role in encouraging and defending promising young authors before and after the Revolution. In *Chto takoe sotsialisticheskii realizm* he suggests that socialist realism may be Gorky's "senile fancy" (*starcheskaya prichuda)*. He also

argues that Gorky's romantic notions were in conflict with socialist realism, stressing that many of his formulations were treated with an embarrassed silence or an awkward explanation (435). In *Soviet Civilization* he claims that Gorky led a smear campaign against the intelligentsia, spending his last decade indicting intellectuals with charges of treason and sabotage (139). In an interview, Sinyavsky said that he was not at all close to Gorky ("Exile and Writer," 17). In 1988 he published an article on Gorky's novel *Mat'* (*Mother*), reminding everyone that this model of socialist realism also included links between the Revolution and the Christian faith, not to mention "God-building" (*bogostroitel'stvo*) which, to the embarrassment of the establishment, was associated with the bourgeois intelligentsia.

7. In an interview with Catharine Nepomnyashchy, Sinyavsky specifically addresses the question of decadent literature. He said, "I remembered reading banned books. I loved these books, and they were condemned" (*Formations* 7). In my own interview with Sinyavsky (June 29, 1993), he said that the topic of his dissertation gave him further access to what was considered "decadent" literature.

8. For a complete reference, see note 6.

9. Sinyavsky was a student at Moscow University when Bakhtin defended his dissertation. Although he did not know him at the time, he later became acquainted with his work on Dostoevsky and Rabelais.

10. Igor' Golomshtok is an art historian who is now living in Great Britain. In the late 1950s he and Sinyavsky wrote a monograph on Pablo Picasso. At first their manuscript was held up by the censors. In fact, they thought that it had been rejected. After a long delay (almost two years), the censors allowed it to be published. *Pikasso*, "Znanie," Moskva, 1960, was the first study of Picasso to be made available to the Russian public.

Chapter Five

Early Polemics

What Is Socialist Realism (*Chto takoe sotsialisticheskii realism*), is as much a continuation of Sinyavsky's work as a literary critic as it is the first step in his semipublic life as a satirist.[1] It is, of course, rooted in the verbal assaults that characterize Marxist-Leninist rhetoric—the Soviet version of Juvenalian satire. While the substance of *What Is Socialist Realism* is dissent, its expression is marked by contempt and irritation, not to mention mockery. Only wit and intermittent humor mitigate its frontal attacks. Such attacks remind us that while Sinyavsky raises objections to the establishment, he does it in the language of the day, a language inherited from the Russian radicals of the late nineteenth century. In other words, his imputations do not come from enemy camps outside of the country. They come from within, from the dominant discourse, a discourse truly cultivated, promulgated, inculcated, and adapted to unmasking a succession of enemies.[2] If we see in *What Is Socialist Realism* a genuine measure of onslaught, then we cannot help but see the same in the articles and reviews that Sinyavsky published in Moscow between 1959 and 1965. The barbed accent is unmistakable.

There is no need to make another case for the audacious nature of *What Is Socialist Realism* or to bewail the efficacies of a *succès de scandale*.[3] Yet the very scandal that drew attention to *What Is Socialist Realism* is the very scandal that isolated it from Sinyavsky's other essays in literary criticism. By examining the articles and reviews that Sinyavsky published between 1959 and 1965, we will not only discover how they are in the same maligning mode as *What Is Socialist Realism*, but also how they share the same risks in attacking the establishment. Arguably, the risks that Sinyavsky took when he published *What Is Socialist Realism* abroad under the identity of Abram Terts are similar to the risks that he took in Moscow under his own identity as a literary critic. It turns out that while Sinyavsky was under scrutiny for possible links with Terts, he was also under scrutiny for his outspoken literary criticism in Moscow. His sharp polemics whether under the name of Terts or Sinyavsky provoke the same ideological backlash, drawing increasing attention right up to 1965, just before Sinyavsky's arrest. In the following study let us look at Sinyavsky's other essays from the same period as *What Is Socialist Realism* and in the process lay out a broader context for scathing assessments and witty rejoinders, as well as polemics with and direct salvos at the establishment.

What Is Socialist Realism is, of course, a turning point in Sinyavsky's life. The very ideals that he incorporated into his early scholarship on Gorky and Mayakovsky he repudiates here in this essay, adding a layer of irony for good measure. His reaction to literary authority this time is without any ruse. In this essay he reaches into his arsenal of Marxist-Leninist attacking strategies, unmasking the unmaskers, questioning the very legitimacy of realism that is qualified by any ideology, including socialism. Moreover, he rejects the very notion of institutionalizing a single representation of reality. Enumerating the fixed features of socialist realism, for example, determinism, a narrow range of ideals, a simplification of issues, and a search for enemies, he points to what he considers its preromantic features. Making a case for socialist realism's eighteenth-century qualities, its rigid, hierarchical pronouncements, haughtiness, and intolerance to any further exploration of ideology, Sinyavsky cannot help but incense the literary establishment. Such qualities, in his opinion, take the development of literature backward rather than forward. He is so concerned about this ruinous agenda of literary valuation that he speaks out not only in *What Is Socialist Realism* under the cover of Terts, but also in Moscow journals under his own name.

The same year that *What Is Socialist Realism* appeared in Paris, Sinyavsky submitted an article on science fiction, "No Discount" ("*Bez skidok*"), to *Questions on Literature* (*Voprosy literatury*). It appeared in January of 1960. Almost simultaneously, an excerpted version was published in *The Literary Gazette* (*Literaturnaya gazeta*). The following year, the whole article was republished in *The Paths of Development of the Contemporary Soviet Novel* (*Puti razvitiya sovremennogo sovetskogo romana*). As in *What Is Socialist Realism*, in "No Discount" Sinyavsky focuses on the big picture, that is, on literary developmental issues, on prevailing critical contingencies in the Soviet period with specific reference to science fiction. Given the presence of the fantastic in his fiction and the hope that he expressed for it in the conclusion of *What Is Socialist Realism*, his discussion of science fiction is telling in more than one sense. Once again he argues that fantasy is indispensable to art.

According to Sinyavsky, the lack of good Russian science fiction may be traced not to the ineptness of writers, but to the trends in literary criticism, especially since the end of the 1940s.[4] These trends, he says, seem to be based upon the "perverse opinion" (*prevratnoe mnenie*) that Soviet science fiction need not be "completely fantastic" (*chereschur fantasticheskii*), that "cosmic distances and supernatural inventions are alien to our writers," that "it is only necessary to depict the perspectives of the immediate future" ("*Bez skidok*" 45). While Sinyavsky is hopeful that some of the impediments to the development of science fiction have been pushed aside by the advent of space travel, he nevertheless sees a persistence of mistaken ideas: attempts to limit the imagination, forcing it into a framework of "moderation and propriety" ("*Bez skidok*" 45). As a result of such attempts, in much of the recent Russian science fiction Sinyavsky sees restraint, geocentrism, slavish dependence on ready-made themes, standardization of devices, lack of credible plots, bad taste, and, quite often, a utilitarian understanding of the genre.

In addition to attacking the conceptual barriers to genuine science fiction, Sinyavsky boldly defends I. Efremov's *The Nebula of Andromeda* (*Tumannost' Andromedy*), taking sides in a major polemic regarding this author. While he does not praise every aspect of Efremov's work, he does underscore its new ideas, and, above all, its absence of limits—not unlike, Sinyavsky adds, our dreams or our accumulation of knowledge, which, by nature, know no limits. Only once does he question Efremov's representation of a future time and place wherein the author's protagonists pause to deliver a lecture on dialectic materialism to demonstrate their high mindedness ("*Bez skidok*" 52). In this kind of demonstration Sinyavsky sees the reduction of characters to resonators of the present. Taking issue with what he calls "realistic fantasy" (*realisticheskaya fantastika*), which he finds especially pronounced in science fiction writers such as V. Nemtsov, V. Okhotnikov, V. Saparin, and G. Martynov, Sinyavsky addresses the relationship between realism and fantasy as he did in *What Is Socialist Realism*. In Sinyavsky's opinion, which will be repeated again and again, fantasy takes its material from reality: the most astonishing fantasy is constructed from down-to-earth elements ("*Bez skidok*" 54).[5] Accordingly, he maintains that realism cannot be free of what constitutes fantasy ("*Bez skidok*" 53). Together, these formulations spell out Sinyavsky's further assault on socialist realism, an assault which, in the context of his indictment of the state of Russian science fiction, is no less poignant than what is found in *What Is Socialist Realism*.

During this period (1959–1965), Sinyavsky's derision of artistic and ideological shortcomings is especially apparent in his reviews. In two of them, in fact, he attacks establishment writers who have always enjoyed broad privileges, including easy access to publishing. One of these writers is Anatolii Sofronov; the other is Evgenii Dolmatovsky.[6] In Sofronov's *From All Latitudes* (*Ot vsekh shirot*), for example, Sinyavsky finds "poetic monotony" (*poeticheskoe odnoobrazie*), a repetition of "the same words, formulas and situations" (*te zhe slova, formuly, polozheniya*) ("*O novom sbornike*" 249). Casting aspersions about the privileges of certain writers, Sinyavsky draws attention to Sofronov's numerous trips to India, China, England, Egypt, Indonesia, Australia, and Japan. He then declares that Sofronov's collection is not unique; that in contemporary Russian poetry there are many works that are written on a rather low artistic level ("*O novom sbornike*" 253).

Throughout this review Sinyavsky embarrasses Sofronov, underscoring his lack of style and taste, his limited lexicon, feeble articulation of ideas, cliché-ridden generalizations, lifeless images and, finally, his attempt to imitate Mayakovsky. Such assessment would be devastating to any writer. But Sinyavsky does not stop here. He takes Sofronov to task for "simplification of ideological straight-forwardness" (*uproshchenie pryamolineinosti)* as well as for passing off incongruous ideas "under the single rubric of uprightness" (*pod edinym imeniem pryamoty*). Before concluding his review, he attacks critics such as A. Markov and V. Litvinov for their "exaggerated evaluations" (*zavyshennye otsenki*) of Sofronov's poetry, saying, "Strange things do happen. One has only to put together a few recognizable images and immediately this is considered a tremendous achievement" ("*O novom sbornike*" 253). It is not simply inappropriate, according to Sinyavsky, but harmful to praise this level of poetry, for it lowers standards, bewilders readers, and misguides aspiring writers.

While Sinyavsky does not relegate Evgenii Dolmatovsky's collection of poetry, *Poems about Us* (*Stokhi o nas*), to the same rung as Sofronov's, he does call it "mediocre" (*srednego kachestva).* In fact, he states that the purpose of his review is to "settle accounts" (*pred'yavit' schet*) with mediocre poetry. He does not hesitate to praise Dolmatovsky's occasional concreteness: the routing of personal experience and biographical details into the projection of his lyrical "I." On the other hand, he does not hesitate to scoff at his "doctrinaire pose" (*doktrinerskaya poza*), especially when the poet puts on an air of importance, as if speaking for society, bearing witness to lofty events. At one point in a discussion of a poem called *The Old Drummer* (*Staryi barabanshchik*), Sinyavsky recalls Heinrich Heine's and Ilja Selvinsky's treatment of the same theme, reminding Dolmatovsky and his readers about derivational implications. He does not raise the issue of deliberate imitation, but of the "unconscious submission to another's rhythm" (*bessoznatel'noe podchinenie chuzhomu ritmu*). According to Sinyavsky, such submission is the result of the insufficient clarity of Dolmatovsky's poetic persona. Dolmatovsky does not find his own register, failing therefore to rise above the "common rung" (*oshchego ryada*) of poets.

During this period, which may be called Sinyavsky's *New World* (*Novyi mir*) years, he does not hesitate to start or sustain a polemic, openly taking sides, expressing his objections to what he perceives as ideological or artistic failings. He, for example, joins reviewers in *Literaturnaja gazeta*, *Komsomolskaja pravda*, and *Ogonek* in condemning a novel by Ivan Shevtsov called *The Blight* (*Tlya*). Responding to Shevtsov's crude representation of a struggle between formalists and realists, Sinyavsky recommends not further attacks, but pity and compassion for the author. Underscoring Shevtsov's method of attributing vices as well as criminal behavior to the villains, Sinyavsky argues that the novel recalls the suspicions, allegations, and threats associated with the era of "the cult of personality" ("*Pamflet*" 230). According to Sinyavsky, Shevtsov puts the struggle for the development of Russian literature on a level with a military or intelligence operation. Outraged by Shevtsov's dark insinuations about diversity in socialist realism, Sinyavsky makes a case for the author's pedestrian understanding of art, drawing attention, for example, to the unwarranted denigration of French paintings in the novel. Before concluding his review, he poses the following questions: (1) How is it possible that the publishing house, "*Sovetskaya Rossiya*," printed 100,000 copies of Shevtsov's novel? (2) Is it only Shevtsov who "preaches ignorance under the guise of realism and slings mud at the artistic intelligentsia?" (*propoveduet nevezhestvo pod vidom realizma i smeshivaet graz'yu khudozhestvennuyu intelligentsiyu*).

Needless to say, such literary assessments provoked many authors and literary critics, especially in the atmosphere of posturing that followed Khrushchev's call for literary tolerance and professionalism at the third congress of the Union of Soviet Writers. Two extended reviews, "A Day of Russian Poetry" ("*Den' russkoi poezii*") and "For Poetic Vigor" (*Za poeticheskuyu aktivnost'*), in the February 1959 and the January 1961 issue of *The New World*, which Sinyavsky coauthored with A. Menshutin, led to a major polemic, involving critics from *Literature and Life* (*Literatura i zhizn'*), *The Little Fire* (*Ogonek*), *Siberian Lights* (*Sibirskie ogni*), *The Young Guard* (*Molodaya gvardiya*), *October* (*Oktyabr'*), and *Questions about Philosophy* (*Voprosy filosofii*).[7] In the August 1961 issue of *The New World* following Sinyavsky and Menshutin's detailed rebuttal, "Let's Speak Professionally" ("*Davaite govorit' professional'no*"), the editorial board of *The New World* printed its own response, defending Menshutin and Sinyavsky as well as B. Runin whose rejoinder, "The Logic of Argument and the Logic of Art" ("*Logika spora I logika iskusstva)*, was also included. Given the tone of this editorial, with its lengthy quotations of Khrushchev ("*Ot redaktsii*" 256–57), and the critical space afforded to Menshutin, Sinyavsky, and Runin to air their views, the stakes in this polemic were high.[8]

Sinyavsky and Menshutin provided the primary spark. In their first review, "A Day of Russian Poetry," they not only express disappointment with the "low level of artistry" (*nizkii uroven' masterstva*), but also take issue with A. Kovalenov and V. Soloukhin whose comments about this collection had already appeared. Kovalenov, in their opinion, did not discriminate between poems that contain pretentious positions and stylistic ornamentation, and poems that contain spontaneity and originality. In Soloukhin's evaluation they found something worse: a readiness to attribute the exploration of rhythmic possibilities, as well as every irregularity of style, to formalism. They argue, moreover, that the use of themes recalling the most representative and consequential moments of the Russian past does not insure artistic merit, that the "artistic materialization" (*khudozhestvennaya konkretizatsiya*) of the basic idea of a poem is far more important than historical references. What Sinyavsky and Menshutin recommend for the development of Russian poetry is what they find lacking: intense work, bold pursuit, discovery, and above all, a projection of "the self" (*avtorskoe "ya"*), which they also call "individuality" (*individual'noe litso*).

Two months after B. Runin's defense of the lyrical "I" in Russian poetry, which drew *The New World* deeper into this polemic, Sinyavsky and Menshutin take sides with Runin, adding ballast to their own argument for poetic "self-definition" (*samoopredilenie*) and "self-assertion" (*samo-utverzhdenie*). In a follow-up review they praise the young Russian poets of the 1959 "Day of Russian Poetry," especially Voznesensky and Okudzhava, whose images of the world are closely bound with the self. While they caution readers about the excesses of an author's "I" (*yakan'e*), they are convinced that the realization of an author's "I" in a poem is indispensable. Not willing to overlook an "unrealistic" assessment (*daleko ot real'nogo polozheniya*), Sinyavsky and Menshutin discuss P. Vyxodtsev's approach to the young poets, "The Poetic Generation of the Epoch of Earth Satellites" ("*Poeticheskoe pokolenie epokhi sputnikov*"). What they criticize is Vyxodtsev's "polemical one sidedness" (*polemicheskaya odnostoronost'*), his interest not in the presence or absence of talent, but in the direction of talent. According to Sinyavsky and Menshutin, the development of Russian poetry is not advanced by Vyxodtsev's insistence upon the poets' close ties with life and the activities of the masses. In fact, in their August 1961 rebuttal, "Let's Speak Professionally" ("*Davaite govorit' professional'no*"), they point out that any claims about the relationship between life and poetry are beside the point, for this relationship is a generally accepted fact in Russian literature (249).

With the publication of "Let's Speak Professionally," Sinyavsky and Menshutin advance the issues of this polemic beyond the discourse of the "Thaw." It could be argued that this rejoinder not only restated the probing questions of the "Thaw," but also foreshadowed the dissenting opinions of the second half of the 1960s, making it a precursor to the emergence of widespread opposition movements and emerging public opinion. Speaking very openly, Sinyavsky and Menshutin compare the personal attacks, labeling, and misinformation of this polemic to those of the 1920s, a time when after an author "slipped up" (*proshtrafilsya*), endless condemnation followed. Questioning whether it is possible to defend themselves against the "poison arrows" (*yadovitye strely)* of V. Bushin, D. Starikov, S. Smirnov, K. Lisovsky, V. Fedorov, B. Solov'ev, as well as P. Vyxodtsev, they attempt, at least, to set the record straight. Accordingly, they argue that "purely professional" (*sugubo professional'nye)* or "intraliterary" (*vnutreliteraturnye*) concerns do not define their approach to poetry, that questions about talent, skill, poetic vision, and artistic unity are germane to literary criticism. Moreover, they hasten to point out that nothing can be inferred from their use of the foreign word "tendency" (*tendentsiya*).[9] Furthermore, they deny that they are predisposed to Voznesensky's poetic "onslaught" (*natisk*) or that they underrate B. Kuznetsov's work because of his proleterian background.

Not shying away from addressing fundamental ideological givens, Sinyavsky and Menshutin suggest that achievements are not the same for poets, workers, and revolutionaries, that the criteria for excellence in each area are quite different. Recalling an innocuous example of the practice of transferring achievement from one area to another, they turn to an anecdote from the 1920s about Jakubovsky's defense of I. Filipchenko's poetry. Clearly addressing the questionable link between Kuznetsov's verse and his "worker's biography," Sinyavsky and Menshutin cite Jakubovsky's artistically naive but ideologically correct question: "Could a poet with such a biography write bad poetry?" (*Razve mozhet poet s takoi biografiei pisat' plokhie stikhi*?) In doing so, they brazenly challenge socialist assumptions about art's connection to "life" as well as its roots in class consciousness.

More than once, Sinyavsky and Menshutin deride critics for distorting the issues. In exasperation, they ask: "Where does this unwillingness to consider the facts come from?" (*Otkuda eto nezhelanie schitat'sya s faktami*? "*Davaite*" 249). Outraged by allegations of Voznesensky's expression of misanthropy and pornography, and his portrayal of an evil caricature of Soviet reality, they accuse namely K. Lisovsky of attempting to play the part not of a literary critic, but a public prosecutor. Rather than going into detail about what they consider Lisovsky's libelous and threatening behavior, Sinyavsky and Menshutin point to the central problem among Russian critics: a lack of competence, which they find in Lisovsky's inability to recognize hyperbole or metaphoric substitution ("*Davaite*" 251). To Sinyavsky and Menshutin this lack of competence is a result of fostering old arguments, general assumptions, intimidation, and monochromatic assessments. In their concluding remarks, they turn to this problem. In fact, they call for what amounts to be a sweeping reform in the criteria and the methods of Russian literary criticism:

> It is understandable that we can't get by without disagreements and polemics. It is important, however, that our differences of opinion move away from this dead end, that we get out of this enchanted circle where everything whirls around a shuffle of names and excessively abstract categories, threatening one and all with the same old evaluations and assessments. ("*Davaite*" 252)

Sinyavsky and Menshutin's unmasking here is unprecedented. They in fact expose the established practice of literary criticism, spelling out what other critics would dare not mention. Needless to say, those whom they implicate as hacks join a growing number of writers and critics waiting for an opportunity to get even.

Given Sinyavsky and Menshutin's spate of critical ambushes, such an opportunity was easy to seize. During the same year, they are reproached by a number of critics for their separate contributions to the third volume of *The History of Soviet Russian Literature* (*Istoriya russkoi sovetskoi literatury*).[10] In the September issue of *October* (*Oktyabr'*), which includes the proceedings of a conference devoted to reviewing the aforementioned volume, G. Brovman attacks Menshutin for defending Sinyavsky's focus on the poets and their poetry rather than the heroism of the participants of The Great Patriotic War ("*Pisat' pravdivo*" 181). Meanwhile, A. Vlasenko attacks Menshutin for focusing not on the main features of the poetry of the post-war period, but on the self-expression of a small number of poets, the kind of focus that he calls "formalism, pure and simple" (*chisteishii formalizm*) ("*Opisatel'nym metodom*" 186). But it is Sinyavsky who is castigated at length by almost all of the reviewers for what they consider significant omissions. Among their objections, moreover, there are serious charges. G. Brovman, for example, suggests that Sinyavsky equates praise for the heroes of The Great Patriotic War with embellishment (180). Similarly, A. Dymshits holds Sinyavsky responsible for slighting the heroic character of the literature of this period (204). A. Vlasenko, who calls Sinyavsky's essay the poorest in the collection, maintains that Sinyavsky did not know how to show the greatness of the period or its literature (184). Sinyavsky, who also participated in this conference, admits to a number of shortcomings in the third volume of *The History of Soviet Russian Literature*. He points out, however, that his colleagues exhibit more gloating over the volume's weakness than genuine concern for the period and its literature (195).

Adopting the Marxist-Leninist language of acrimony and accusation to his own ends, Sinyavsky changes the distribution of official praise and blame. In his defiance, his fierce attacks on literary apparatchiks, he resembles his literary persona, Terts, the knife-wielding bully who does not hesitate to pounce on anyone who challenges his views.[11] In fact Sinyavsky describes Terts as someone "honed down by years of polemics" (*Sobranie sochinenii* 2:345). These polemics turn out to be an ideological battleground from which emerges not a quiet academic, but someone combative, picking up a pen the same way that one would pick up a weapon. In his initial period as a critic Sinyavsky truly carries on the agitation that was expected in literary assessment. But this agitation, recalibrated to different satirical settings, targeted the very institutions that legitimized it. Meanwhile, Sinyavsky's praise for the contributions of Akhmatova, Babel', Bagritsky, Berggol'ts, Voznesensky, Pasternak, and Picasso left no doubt what kind of ideals he championed.[12]

At his trial, Sinyavsky explained that his life as a literary critic had not been easy (Ginzburg 247). He often faced "editorial" rejections and delays, especially in connection with his writing on Babel', Pasternak, and Picasso. *The New World*, the most liberal journal of the period, turned down, or was forced to turn down, his essay on Evtushenko.[13] He was attacked in the press and at meetings, receiving official reprimands at the Institute of World Literature (Ginzburg 304). As the newspaper *Literature and Life* (*Literatura i zhizn'*, 29 July 1962, 3) found "serious shortcomings" (*ser'eznye nedostatki*) and "a concession to bourgeois decadence" (*kompromiss s burzhuaznym dekadentstvom*) in his entry on "Acmeism" in *The Concise Literary Encyclopedia* (*Kratkaya literaturnaya entsiklopediya*), so the Institute of World Literature found ideological vagueness and a partiality for un-Soviet writers such as Tsvetaeva, Mandelshtam, and Pasternak in his work, demoting him, subsequently, from a senior to a junior staff member (Ginzburg 303).

Between 1959 and 1965, Sinyavsky exhibits a number of skills, especially in the Soviet style of Juvenalian satire that provides an ideal platform for praise and blame. It is clear that *What Is Socialist Realism* belongs to this kind of literary criticism, its intermittent humor and irony notwithstanding. Actually *What Is Socialist Realism* provided themes not only for Sinyavsky's criticism in Moscow journals, but also for his lifelong work. It is in the Moscow journals, however, that he contests the inadequacies of socialist realism without the cover of Terts. Needless to say, such contestation led Sinyavsky down a dangerous path. Unwittingly, he became one of the prominent voices for reforming literary policy during this period. For his positions, whether attacking unoriginal novelists, defending bold new poets, or advocating a break with critics who use abstractions, clichés, and labels, he made enemies in the literary establishment. While he was arrested for what he had published abroad, it was what he had published in Moscow that set the stage for this arrest.[14] Given his enemies, Sinyavsky's work as a literary critic came under close scrutiny. Long before his arrest, his career as a literary critic in Moscow was at risk. In fact, it was coming to an end.

NOTES

1. *What Is Socialist Realism* appeared in the journal *Esprit.* Anon. "*Le realism socialiste*," *Esprit*, no. 2 (February 1959): 335–67. It was translated into Russian by E. Neledinskii in *Mosty*, no. 2 (1959): 269–302. It was then translated into Polish by Jozef Lobodowski in the *Kultura* library series, "*Anonim, Co to jest realizm socjalistyczny*" (Paris: Institut Literaci, 1959).

2. Ilya Ehrenburg's article in *Kul'tura i zhizn'* (*Culture and Life*, February 21, 1948) about the American film *The Iron Curtain* is a good example of Marxist-Leninist criticism. Heller and Nekrich claim that Ehrenburg uses "the full range of unflattering epithets so typical of the style of the Stalin era" (*Utopia in Power,* 489). During the Zhdanov period, which coincides with Sinyavsky's years as an undergraduate, the language of the press was exceptional in its use of smear campaigns. Incriminations in the press were commonplace. Attacks upon "cosmopolitans" and "anti-patriotic" groups in *Pravda* (January 28, 1949), for example, included not only indictable charges, but also vulgar references and anti-Semitic language.

3. For previous discussions of *What Is Socialist Realism* see: Lourie, *Letters to the Future,* 51–74; Dalton, *Andrei Siniavskii and Julii Daniel',* 22–32; Leatherbarrow, "The Sense of Purpose and Socialist Realism in Tertz's *The Trial Begins,*" 268–79; McLean, "Abram Tertz and His Translators," 434–40; Pevear, "Sinyavsky in Two Worlds," 385–91; Clardy, "Andrei Sinyavsky's 'On Socialist Realism': An Analysis," 29–32; Nepomnyashchy, *Abram Tertz and the Poetics of Crime,* 40–50.

4. Sinyavsky certainly has in mind the repressive period called "*Zhdanovshchina*."

5. This statement, repeated again and again by Sinyavsky whenever he is questioned about "departures from reality," is his own understanding of fantasy.

6. The writing establishment is one of Sinyavsky's major targets. Not only does he attack writers such as Dolmatovsky, Sofronov, and Shevtsov in Moscow literary journals, he also ridicules, for example, Kochetov and Sofronov in *The Trial Begins* and *The Makepeace Experiment*. In "Graphomaniacs" he satirizes the Moscow literary scene, focusing on the machinations of authors and would-be authors. Later, in an essay called "*Literaturnyi protsess v Rossii*" ("The Literary Process in Russia"), he returns to the subject of writing policies in Russia, proceeding with an extended verbal shelling from his Paris suburb. In *Spokoinoi nochi* (*Goodnight!*) Sinyavsky recalls the corruption and hypocrisy at the Institute of World Literature, naming scurrilous scholars such as Shchebrina, Khrapchenko, and Ovcharenko (*Spokoinoi nochi* 138).

7. The first "Day of Russian Poetry" was held in 1955 when over one hundred poets gathered to read their works in a large auditorium in Moscow. Since then, Poetry Day has been celebrated annually in Moscow as well as in other cities. Beginning with 1956, a collection of poems called *Den' russkoi poezii* has been published to mark this event. This polemic directly involved the following critics: Bushin, "*Fialki pakhnut ne tem,*" 1–3; Starikov, "*Sporit po sushchestvu!*" 1–3; Lisovsky, "*Kuda–to ne tuda,*" 6–9; Fedorov, "*Vechernyaya vstrecha,*" 14–18; Solov'ev, "*Legkii nesesser i tyazhelaya klad',*" 197–93; Smirnov, "*Metnulo! Replika dvum kritikam,*" 29; Runin, "*Spor neobkhodimo prodolzhit,*" 195–220. Sinyavsky and Menshutin coauthored three articles in *The New World* and a book, *The Poetry of the First Years of the Revolution*. Like Sinyavsky, Menshutin submitted his dissertation ("The

Satire of Mayakovsky from 1921 to 1930") to the Department of Philology at Moscow State University in 1952. After receiving a *kandidat nauk* degree, both Sinyavsky and Menshutin received positions at the Gorky Institute of World Literature. In their collaborative work they seem to have a common interest in poetry, an appreciation for originality, and an indefatigable admiration for Mayakovsky.

8. Sinyavsky was constantly worried that Tvardovsky, the editor of *The New World*, would be replaced. After his trial, Tvardovsky was crossed off the list of candidates from the Moscow party organization to be elected as delegates to the Twenty-third Party Congress (Heller and Nekrich 615).

9. The term "*tendentsiya*" was actually used by Mayakovsky.

10. "*Literatura pirioda velikoi otechestvennoi voiny,*" 5–53.

11. Sinyavsky characterizes Terts in an interview (Brezna 55) and in *Spokoinoi nochi* (*Sobranie sochinenii* 2:345).

12. "*Raskovannyi golos,*" 174–76; "Isaak Babel," 157–63; "Eduard Bagritsky," 397–402; "*Poeziya I proza Ol'gi Berggol'ts*," 225–36; with A. Menshutin. "*Davaite govorit' professional'no,*" 248–57; "*Poeticheskii sbornik B. Pasternaka,*" 261–63; "*Poeziya Pasternaka,*" 9–62; with I. Golomshtok, *Picasso*.

13. "*V zashchitu piramidy*" was finally published abroad in *Grani* in 1967.

14. According to Donald Jameson, who worked for the CIA in the Russian section, the literary intelligentsia in Moscow knew the identity of Terts in 1965. He adds that in 1964 either the novelist, Ivan Shevtsov, or the poet, Evgeny Dolmatovsky, had gone to the Central Commitee of the Communist Party, seeking action against Sinyavsky for his savage literary assessments in Moscow journals ("What Yevgeny Knew" 40).

Chapter Six

Sword and Shield: Mayakovsky

During his initial period as a literary critic Sinyavsky balances his attacks against bad writing with applause for good writing. After all, satire is built upon this kind of modulation. In fact without any relief from ridicule and condemnation, satire seems to cut a very narrow path. Moreover, only through a consideration of Sinyavsky's praise is it possible to piece together his complete satiric discourse. Given that Sinyavsky is not inclined to moralizing or to subordinating everything to "truth," there is no other way to get a good grasp of his ideals. Unlike his attacks, which carried the same rhetoric and rancor as other Moscow critics, his unpolarized applause is a departure from that of his ideologically minded colleagues. Instead of vaunting the officially prescribed purpose of art, Sinyavsky makes a case for the capacity of art, an uncommon case in view of the focused agenda of socialist realism. Given that he praises a wide range of authors—Anna Akhmatova, Eduard Bagritsky, Isaac Babel, Vladimir Mayakovsky, Ol'ga Berggolts, Robert Frost, Aleksandr Pushkin, Nikolai Gogol, Boris Pasternak, and Vasily Rozanov—it cannot be said that he prefers a particular artistic movement or style. But clearly he lauds works that are distinguished by innovation and an author's personal stamp, rather than works that are vehicles for moralizing, prophesy, or loftiness of purpose. While the list of authors whom Sinyavsky admired is large, there are, of course, recurring favorites, such as Mayakovsky.[1] In fact Sinyavsky seems to venerate this poet's personal and artistic prowess in a tireless way. Mayakovsky, it turns out, was the subject of one of his very last projects. Before his project is entirely forgotten or pieced together without its original focus, let us examine not only Sinyavsky's unusual record of praise, but also the way he turns this controversial author into both sword and shield against bogus art and vengeful critics.[2]

Mayakovsky is, after all, the only twentieth-century Russian author whom Sinyavsky includes among his models for phantasmagoria, the only twentieth-century Russian author whom he considers to be a singular example of socialist realism. In what may be considered his literary credo, he distinctly says, "May the exaggerated images of Hoffmann, Dostoevsky, Goya, Chagall and Mayakovsky, the most socialist realist of all, and many other realists and non-realists, teach us to be truthful with the aid of preposterous fantasy" (*Chto takoe sotsialisticheskii realizm* 446). Sinyavsky's placement of him in the company of Hoffmann, Dostoevsky, Goya, and Chagall is, of course, a telling tribute—in this context the highest tribute. In fact, in his first essay published abroad, *Chto takoe sotsialisticheskii realizm* (*What Is Socialist Realism*), he makes Mayakovsky the thematic bridge between the last paragraphs and the famous concluding page, which was sent abroad later.[3] Casting aspersions at establishment writers, he expresses astonishment at Mayakovsky's uniqueness in the territory of socialist realism, calling him a genius and an exception, the writer who interpreted the ideals of socialist realism with boldness, inventiveness, and passion. Besides conveying unqualified admiration, Sinyavsky reminds readers of the discrepancy between Mayakovsky's official reputation as a celebrated poet of the Revolution and his embattled position in the literary politics of the day, underscoring that for all of Mayakovsky's poetic timeliness, he remained a solitary figure "to the point of horror" (*do zhuti*) (*Chto takoe sotsialisticheskii realizm* 441).

Throughout Sinyavsky's fiction and literary criticism, he does not lose sight of Mayakovsky. From his M.A. thesis, "Esteticheskii pozitsii Mayakovskogo" ("Mayakovsky's Aesthetic Positions"), to his autobiographical novel, *Spokoinoi nochi* (*Goodnight!*), Mayakovsky is not only critically acclaimed, but also savored like a rare phenomenon. Tikos and Peppard argue that for a time Mayakovsky was a symbol for the "courage to experiment" (*For Freedom of Imagination* xvii). For Sinyavsky he was the embodiment of courage and artistic experiment. Had Mayakovsky been merely a convenient symbol for originality in Sinyavsky's criticism in Moscow, he surely would have been replaced in his writing later on in Paris, when he no longer had to look over his shoulder. But Sinyavsky does not replace him; Mayakovsky remains his model for originality until his very last days. The same high regard that Sinyavsky expressed for Mayakovsky at the beginning of his career, he expresses in an article in 1994, "*Refleksy simvolizma v poeme 'Chelovek',*" lionizing him once again.

Sinyavsky's first major research project was his master's thesis (*diplomnaya rabota*) from which he published two articles: "*Ob estetike Mayakovskogo*" ("Mayakovsky's Aesthetics") and "*Osnovnye printsipy estetiki V. V. Mayakovskogo*" ("The Fundamental Principles of Mayakovsky's Aesthetics"). While both articles are very similar, the former, which appeared in *Vestnik moskovskogo universiteta* (*The Herald of Moscow University*) in 1950, is actually a part of his thesis. In it Sinyavsky argues that Mayakovsky's aesthetics are rooted in the primacy of life over art, and after the Bolshevik Revolution, in the socialist foundation for this primacy under the leadership of the party. Like many critics of the day Sinyavsky discusses Mayakovsky's poetry as a merger of art and politics with emphasis on the differences between his prerevolutionary and postrevolutionary projects. While his discussion takes a narrow ideological route, he does allude to a wide range of elements in Mayakovsky's poetry: Communism, the October Revolution, the theme of labor, one's homeland, life, love, and poetry (*Vestnik* 138). These allusions, however, are not developed and therefore do not become a part of his principal discourse which, although acknowledging Mayakovsky's "fullness" (*polnota*) and "richness" (*bogatstvo*), clearly departs from any notion of a multifaceted or an avant-garde poet.

Sinyavsky's formulation of Mayakovsky's subordination of art to life, although at variance with his own views at that time, follows the official literary discourse of the day.[4] His review of I. V. Gutorov's textbook, however, *Poeticheskoe masterstvo V. V. Mayakovskogo* (*The Poetic Mastery of Mayakovsky*), which was published a year later, reveals a testy tone, if not a different set of sensibilities. In fact, it marks the beginning of Sinyavsky's querulous defense of Mayakovsky as well as his conflict with other literary critics regarding Mayakovsky's artistic status. In this review he insists on a full, scholarly measure of Mayakovsky, a measure that he says should include a holistic view, a historical perspective, and a discussion of principal strategies and images. But Sinyavsky goes further. Using a bit of demagoguery, he calls the book irresponsible in regard to its pedagogical goals (a textbook, after all), especially in its treatment of a poet like Mayakovsky whose role, he reminds the reader, is of primary importance to the development of Russian poetry.

In the early 1950s Sinyavsky was one of the evaluators for the defense of a dissertation on Mayakovsky. It turned out that the student, a Vietnamese who had received part of his education in the West, relied on Hegel for his hermeneutics; moreover, his enthusiasm for Russian futurism was without qualification. Because he was at variance with Soviet ideology on two counts, other evaluators raised objections. Sinyavsky, on the other hand, defended the soundness of the dissertation. Aware that his colleagues could not ignore Stalin's blessings upon Mayakovsky or the propaganda value of the success of a Vietnamese student at Moscow State University, he turned to them and said:

> Comrades! This is the first dissertation written by a Vietnamese and not just on anyone, but the premier poet of the Russian revolution, on Vladimir Mayakovsky. Wouldn't it be a political mistake for the academic council not to approve it? (*Soviet Civilization* 204)

Even at this early stage in Sinyavsky's career it is possible to sense that he does not shy away from a number of awkward disclaimers regarding Mayakovsky's avant-garde art. He takes the assessment of Mayakovsky beyond a well-known circle of timely references, acknowledging, by degrees, the poet's very personal and modernistic expression. It is originality that Sinyavsky ultimately defends, especially against pretenders to the Mayakovskian brand of lyric-civic poetry. In fact, during his *Novyi mir* (*New World*) period (1959–1965), this defense becomes a recurring feature of his literary criticism. One cannot help but notice how many poets he accuses of imitating Mayakovsky, or what, in his exposure of their counterfeit representations, comprises his criteria for good poetry, as well as his insistence upon Mayakovsky's inimitability.

In a review of Anatolii Sofronov's collection of poems about far-off places, *Ot vsex shirot* (*From All Latitudes*), for example, Sinyavsky recalls Mayakovsky, pointing to his image as "cultural ambassador" for a new society and a new poetry, for like Sofronov, Mayakovsky traveled widely and wrote about the places that he visited. But Sinyavsky maintains that Mayakovsky made real discoveries abroad, as in his *Moe otkrytie Ameriki* (*My Discovery of America*), discoveries no less important than those of Columbus. Turning to Sofronov's imitation of Mayakovsky, Sinyavsky identifies a number of problems. Not only does he consider Sofronov's mimicry clumsy, but also devoid of essential Mayakovskian features. In Sinyavsky's opinion, Mayakovsky looked at the West in a sophisticated way, taking into account both its social contradictions and its technological vitality. Citing Mayakovsky's poem about the Brooklyn Bridge, Sinyavsky underscores the poet's enthusiasm regarding this great span, as well as his anger and pain regarding the unemployed Americans who jumped from it.

Addressing the weakness of Sofronov's mannered poetics, Sinyavsky reminds A. Makarov, a defender of Sofronov's collection, that the essence of Mayakovsky is more than bold figures of speech, staircase stanzas, and clever rhymes. Summarizing his objections to Sofronov's simulations, Sinyavsky claims that the weakest poems in the collection are those that rely upon Mayakovskian elements. Rather than ending his review with a recapitulation of his main points or further deductions, Sinyavsky cites Mayakovsky's verse, letting the poet's words echo his own:

> Let there be powerful verse
> so that for a hundred years,
> It may not dissipate
> like a puff of smoke,
> So that with this verse
> we may resound
> and boast
> To our era,
> our republic,
> and the one whom we love.
> ("*O novom sbornike*" 252)

Insisting on the inimitability of Mayakovsky's poetry, Sinyavsky does not hesitate to assail popular poets, even if he risks the displeasure of a journal's editorial board. Moreover, in holding poets who imitate Mayakovsky accountable to specific Mayakovskian standards, he advances several challenging positions—some that sound like a shot across the bow of the literary establishment. In a review of Evtushenko's *Bratskaya GES* (*Bratsk Hydroelectric Station*), for example, Sinyavsky calls Evtushenko's role as the inheritor of the Mayakovskian tradition circumstantial, his use of the lyrical biography and the civic poem strategic ("*V zashchitu piramidy*" 119). He argues that the topicality of Evtushenko's poems as well as his civic posture are bogus claims to Mayakovsky's inheritance. Compared to Mayakovsky, Evtushenko, in the opinion of Sinyavsky, is a weak variant of commitment. He argues that Evtushenko does not have the forcefulness of Mayakovsky, who always went straight to the point, allowing no circumlocutions or camouflage ("*V zashchitu piramidy*" 120). Explaining that Evtushenko's verse, unlike that of Mayakovsky, betokens fluff and bluster, Sinyavsky warns, once again, that the writing of many poets who imitate Mayakovsky is at best publicizing his work.

It is not only Mayakovsky's art, but also Mayakovsky's positions on art that Sinyavsky advocates. In fact, Mayakovsky often becomes the sole ideological authority that he uses in his attacks on other writers. In a review of Evgenii Dolmatovsky's collection of verse, *Stikhi o nas* (*Verse about Us*), he cites, for example, one of Mayakovsky's well-known positions: "*Poeziya nachinaetsya tam, gde est' tendentsiya*" ("Poetry begins where a definite tendency exists," "*Est' takie stikhi*" 246).[5] What brings Sinyavsky to Mayakovsky's maxim is the "bland quality" (bloodlessness) that he finds not only in Dolmatovsky's poems, but also in much of Soviet poetry ("*Est' takie stikhi*" 247). Comparing Mayakovsky's understanding of "tendency" to a biblical formulation, "*O, esli by ty byl kholoden ili goryach! No . . . ty tepl*" (O that thou wert cold or hot! But . . . thou art lukewarm), Sinyavsky inveighs against the low state of Russian poetry in 1964.[6] Emboldened by Mayakovsky's notion of "tendency," he expands its definition in very confrontational terms: "*zhivoe formoobrazuyushchee, tvoryashchee nachalo* v *stikhe, dvizhenie, lomayushchee dogmy i shtampy, ne terpyashchee kompromissov, zhelayushchee zhit' po-novomu, po svoemu*" (a living, formative, and creative principle in verse, a principle that breaks down dogmas and clichés, avoiding compromises, manifesting itself in what is new and distinctive ("*Est' takie stikhi*" 247–48). Using Mayakovsky's authority then about what constitutes good poetry, Sinyavsky makes a wholesale attack on dogma and standardized writing, advancing, in the process, what, in his opinion, is central to Mayakovsky and to art: innovation and an author's individual voice.

Sinyavsky coauthors several pro-Mayakovsky projects with A. N. Menshutin, a colleague at the Gorky Institute of World Literature. Together they write three provocative articles for *Novyi mir* (*The New World*) with numerous references to Mayakovsky. In 1964 they complete a pioneering book called *Poeziya pervykh let revolyutsii* (*The Poetry of the First Years of the Revolution*) in which Mayakovsky figures prominently. Whether they focus directly on Mayakovsky, as in their book, or illustrate their positions with his poetry, as in their articles, they do not conceal their complete admiration for this poet. Coauthorship notwithstanding, it is clear that Sinyavsky and Menshutin are united in a recurring discourse about Mayakovsky's unblemished record of ideological clarity and poetic originality. It is this record with which they buttress their arguments and challenge their opponents.

In their review of the 1958 *Den' russkoi poezii* (*Day of Russian Poetry*), which sets the stage for a very heated polemic, they criticize almost all of the contributors, including Lev Oshanin, who wrote the lyrics to "*Pust' vsegda budet solntse*" (*Let There Always Be Sunshine*). After spending an entire page discussing Oshanin's ill-conceived treatment of good and bad fortune, they cite several lines of Mayakovsky ("*Den' russkoi poezii*" 215). But in this case poetics are not at issue; they turn to Mayakovsky for his interpretation, for his ideological authority. Demonstrating that Mayakovsky views a freshly washed shirt not in terms of comfort, but in terms of his only necessity, Sinyavsky and Menshutin take sharp aim at Oshanin's catalogue of needs. Forgoing their briefly mentioned objections to Oshanin's lack of diachronic and synchronic orchestration, they simply explain that Mayakovsky did not put on airs regarding creature comforts.

Actually Sinyavsky and Menshutin brandish Mayakovsky in a major polemic with other critics during the same years that witnessed a tug of war between students and authorities over poetry readings in front of the monument to Mayakovsky in Moscow. In 1958, the very year of the Day of Russian Poetry that Sinyavsky and Menshutin reviewed, a monument was erected to Mayakovsky in Mayakovsky Square (Heller and Nekrich 584). Hoping to mollify and at the same time spy upon students, the *Komsomol* organized readings in front of this monument. But as it turned out, the readings lead to shouting and heated arguments just as in the days of the futurist poets. Those who gathered at the monument were soon subjected to provocation and beatings, together with searches of their homes and confiscation of books and manuscripts (Heller and Nekrich 585).[7] Some students were expelled from their universities. In the press the students in Mayakovsky Square were called "sluggards" and "idlers." In May of 1961, during the reading of a poem dedicated to the thirtieth anniversary of Mayakovsky's suicide, the KGB provoked a fight in which they beat up a number of students (Heller and Nekrich 585). That year Aleksander Tvardovsky, the editor of *The New World*, while publicly defending the positions of Sinyavsky and Menshutin, commented on the savage shift in the discourse about poetry.[8]

In *Poeziya pervykh let revolyutsii* (*The Poetry of the First Years of the Revolution*) Sinyavsky and Menshutin refer to Mayakovsky more than two hundred times. Although the subject of this book is not Mayakovsky, they manage to sandwich him into every possible discussion that gravitates toward praise. Tracing the development of artistic renewal through the competing groups of poets of the era (e.g., the Proletcult, the Futurists, Octobrists, Smithies, Cosmists, Acmeists, and Sythians), they examine a wealth of poetry. But when they need to make an analogy, demonstrate an artistic phenomenon, or provide further illustration, they characteristically turn to Mayakovsky's poems. In works as diverse as those of Gastev, Eisenstein, Shershenevich, Gumilov, Klyuev, Dmitriev, Burlyuk, and Bednyi, for example, they cite numerous connections and disconnections with Mayakovsky, or make asides in which he is artistically or ideologically relevant.[9] When Sinyavsky and Menshutin are talking about bold images, neologisms, transformations, satire, history, or fantasy, they, in fact, never leave Mayakovskian territory, circling around it again and again. While they acknowledge the contributions of the groups of this period, they stress that a few geniuses (Bedny, Blok, and Mayakovsky) had the greatest effect on the development of poetry. Needless to say who among these geniuses transformed Russian life into "an extraordinary spectacle of art" (*Poeziya pervykh let* 144).

It should be clear that, with and without Menshutin, Sinyavsky establishes himself as a strong advocate of Mayakovsky. Moreover, as we have seen, he stands behind Mayakovsky as behind a shield, brandishing him, when necessary, as a weapon. Having grown up in the shadow of Stalin, Sinyavsky cannot escape such strategies. He understands that positions in art are positions on a battlefield where casualties are not imaginary. But not all of Sinyavsky's references to Mayakovsky are used for defensive or offensive purposes. In a number of articles, where the context is not a call to arms, Sinyavsky turns to Mayakovsky for refinement and reinforcement of his analysis, as in his celebrated introduction to Pasternak's poetry in *B. Pasternak: Sikhotvoreniya i poemy* (*The Poetry of Boris Pasternak*). In this essay, Sinyavsky makes several important comparisons between Mayakovsky and Pasternak, illuminating the work of both poets.

In Pasternak's dislocation of reality through emotion, Sinyavsky sees Mayakovsky's metaphorical modes. He explains, however, that Mayakovsky's emotional extensions are highly charged. Waxing hyperbolic, Mayakovsky says, "*Ya ne mogu byt' spokoinei*" (I cannot be calmer). Pasternak, according to Sinyavsky, is less anxious, quieter, more restrained (*Stkhotvoreniya i poemy* 18). While Sinyavsky underscores that the projection of the lyrical "I" is different for each poet, he suggests that their renewal of poetry, that is, their liberation of "things" from fixed categories of perception, is remarkably similar. Speaking specifically about the disengagement of literature from old forms, about the democratization of language, Sinyavsky maintains that Mayakovsky proceeded far ahead of his contemporaries, mixing conversational speech, vulgarisms, and political positions, whereas Pasternak, through similar linguistic orchestrations, revitalized a circle of traditional themes. Comparing the brilliance of Mayakovsky's and Pasternak's tonal organization, Sinyavsky concludes, along with Bryusov, that Pasternak's correspondence of sound and meaning make *him* rather than Mayakovsky the leading innovator of rhymes.

Mayakovsky once said that he and Pasternak lived in different rooms of the same house. Sinyavsky gives us a tour of this house, taking us well beyond the common meeting places for poets from the Futurist or Centrifuge groups. He takes us namely to rooms with mirrors where Mayakovsky and Pasternak are reflected in a relative way. Above all, Sinyavsky takes us to a house that has two compelling centers of art, the proximity of which is telling.

Decades after his ordeal as a writer in Moscow, after arrest, imprisonment, and emigration to France, Sinyavsky writes about Mayakovsky with renewed enthusiasm. Not only does he cite him in his literary criticism, but also in his fiction, reiterating what he said earlier and advancing his admiration to a higher register. In his *Soviet Civilization*, for example, Mayakovsky becomes one of the chief coordinates of this reconstruction of the past, the primary source for authenticating the ideals of the Revolution and revolutionary art. In spite of Sinyavsky's retelling of Russian literary history from an entirely different vantage point in the 1990s, he does not revise his opinions about Mayakovsky. In fact, writing without the restraints of censorship, he puts forward a compassionate image of Mayakovsky. For the first time, he spells out Mayakovsky's fundamental dilemma, making bold to say: "Mayakovsky was a deeply moral person with a pure and tender soul, but as a real revolutionary, he understood that the road to a radiant future was paved with blood and filth" (*Soviet Civilization* 130). Putting this dilemma in terms of a dark Dostoevskian paradox, he adds that through the Bolshevik Revolution Mayakovsky sensed that violence to oneself and to others was inevitable.

Fleshing out a Christlike image of Mayakovsky, Sinyavsky cites the poem *Pro eto* (*About It*):

> On the bridge of time
> abused and despised,
> redeemer of earthly love,
> I'll keep
> my vigil here
> and for all be chastised,
> I'll pay for all
> and for all I'll weep.
> (*Soviet Civilization* 12)

Here Sinyavsky underscores what, in his opinion, became the enduring symbol of Mayakovsky's life and art: a poet who had crucified himself, bearing the pain and love of all men (*Soviet Civilization* 12). According to

Sinyavsky, in difficult times, while hunger and cold bred hostility, mutual suspicion, fear, and alienation, Mayakovsky did not repeat the message of Zamyatin's "Cave," for in this story the protagonist, Martin, gives his beloved a vial of poison. In Mayakovsky's *Khorosho* (*Good*), the poet in similar circumstances gives his beloved the best and last that he has: two carrots and a birch log. Qualifying both authors' choices, Sinyavsky adds that although Zamyatin's path of mercy and Mayakovsky's path of hope were different, they were not clearly in opposition.

In the final chapter of *Soviet Civilization*, Sinyavsky pauses to remind readers about the two sides to Mayakovsky's legacy: standard-bearer of the Revolution and the Soviet state and symbol of opposition (232). Thus Sinyavsky provides an update to his lifelong, intermittent analysis of Mayakovsky, pointing to two entirely different constructions of the poet. For dissident youth, he says, the importance of Mayakovsky lay in rebelliousness, nonconformism, a refusal to compromise, an utter lack of anything "bourgeois" or "establishment."[10] Recalling his graduate school days in *Spokoinoi nochi* (*Good Night!*), Sinyavsky makes it clear that he himself belonged to this dissident youth which, under Stalin, discovered that Mayakovsky was "the only lawful representative of the avant-garde, the sole delegate on the scorched earth of Russian poetry" (*Spokoinoi nochi* 325). He underscores that Mayakovsky's poetry was a lightning rod, charging the atmosphere in Viktor Dmitrievich Duvakin's celebrated seminar at Moscow University (*Spokoinoi nochi* 396). Only through Mayakovsky, he maintains, was there access to a world that was officially denied.

In "*Refleksy simvolizma v poeme* 'Chelovek'" ("Reactions to Symbolism in the Poem *Man*"), Sinyavsky continues Viktor Shklovsky's discussion of Mayakovsky's links with the symbolists ("*O Mayakovskom*" 38–41).[11] He not only revives this discussion, but also suggests a portrait of Mayakovsky in line with Lawrence L. Stahlberger's view of this poet's bondage, Nietzschean eternal recurrence, and cosmic alienation (*The Symbolic System of Majakovskij* 14, 62). Underscoring Mayakovsky's parodic use of well-worn symbolist references (e.g., abyss, glassy surface, distance, heaven), he quickly moves to the poet's earnest adaptation of images from Bely and Blok. Pointing to evidence of such adaptations in a number of Mayakovsky's poems, librettos, scenarios, and drawings, Sinyavsky then claims that *Chelovek* (*Man*) is Mayakovsky's central link with symbolist poetry. It is, moreover, Sinyavsky adds, a quintessential work, proclaiming the duty of a writer as well as the redemptive and destructive power of love.

Sinyavsky argues that Mayakovsky incorporates features of Blok's *Neznakomka* (*The Stranger*) and Bely's *Petersburg* into his poem, clearly drawing attention to associations with the other world, with alienation, suicide, and the fantastic side of a fantastic city—the coveted territories of the symbolists. Sinyavsky sees a further extension of these territories in Mayakovsky's attention to clouds, fog, mist, the sea and, above all, the disk of the sun, which he interprets as a regulator of time, and therefore Mayakovsky's enemy. Although *Man* is a parody of the life of a saint, Mayakovsky's reference to "*Povelitel' Vsego*" (Sovereign of the World), in the opinion of Sinyavsky, refers not to God, but to the supreme power of money through which Mayakovsky is shackled to mundane matters.

What emerges from Sinyavsky's consideration of the symbolist discourse in this poem is a portrait of a doomed poet, doomed to be, in the words of Sinyavsky, "*vechnyi zhid revolyutsii*" (the wandering Jew of the Revolution), that is, kept by Soviets in an intractable relationship with the Revolution. Linking this relationship to the notion of the eternal return, Sinyavsky concludes:

> Mayakovsky is eternally born, eternally in bondage to the Sovereign of the World, eternally ascending into heaven and returning to earth, eternally standing and doomed to stand on a bridge in the flameless fire of senseless love. ("*Refleksy smvolisma*" 322)

In the light of this endless birth, death, and rebirth, this disappointing servitude to the world, to faith and love, he reemphasizes the tragic figure of Mayakovsky for whom the other world of the symbolists, with all of its paradoxes, seemed plausible—as plausible as his suicide in 1930.

In a 1989 essay in the journal *Iskusstvo kino* (*The Art of the Cinema*), Sinyavsky once again takes up his defense of Mayakovsky, who was vilified in *Voskresenie Mayakovskogo* (*The Resurrection of Mayakovsky*), a monograph that was published in Munich in 1985. Still reeling from attacks on his book about Pushkin, *Progulki s Pushkinym* (*Strolls with Pushkin*), this time from both inside and outside of Russia, Sinyavsky puts his defense of Mayakovsky and his defense of himself into the same context. Without mincing words, Sinyavsky accuses the author, Iu. Karabchievsky, of having written an unflattering portrait of Mayakovsky. He especially takes issue with Karabchievsky's representation of Mayakovsky as a "vortex" (*zasasy-vayushchaya voronka*) that draws in and destroys whatever and whomever is nearby ("*Stilisticheskoe raznoglasie*" 35). Explaining that Karabchievsky's discussion about "bad influence" (*durnoe vozdeistvie*) is not limited to Mayakovsky, Sinyavsky argues that the positions behind this discussion lie not only in a rejection of the avant-garde, but also in a nationalism that targets "Russophobia" and "pluralism."

Putting himself in the same defensive context with Mayakovsky, Sinyavsky suggests a personal identification with this poet, especially in terms of facing constant mean-spirited assessments. Certainly Sinyavsky could not overlook that both he and Mayakovsky shared a similar paraliterary profile, consisting not only of attacks in the press, but also scandals and rumors. Moreover, he could not fail to acknowledge that his disdain for realism and worn literary conventions, as well as his penchant for fantasy and provocation was in no way different from that of Mayakovsky. Sinyavsky was not a literary bohemian like Mayakovsky, creating himself, or what passed for himself, in his art. But in creating Terts, Sinyavsky came up with a similar version of this persona, a persona at once defiant to what was commonplace or doctrinaire.

Every satirist needs a model, but not every satirist needs a moral model. Besides, socialist realism co-opted all models for its own ends. Sinyavsky looked to Mayakovsky for art that anticipated its era in an original way. He praised his full and clear expression that resulted not from realism, but from Homeric proportions, poster-style exaggerations and less-than-lofty expressions (*Fantasticheskii mir* 443).[12] It is namely Mayakovsky's artistic anticipation that Sinyavsky restates in his own literary manifesto, proposing to capture, through means most Mayakovskian, the times—the consciousness of the era. It is this kind of anticipation that Sinyavsky spelled out in his arguments with other critics, undermining, with irony, their claims to orthodox interpretation with the lines of a poet whose art was by no means orthodox.

Mayakovsky, of course, fits into Sinyavsky's bold revisions of writers such as Pushkin, Gogol, and Rozanov, about whom I will speak later. In Mayakovsky's case, as in the case of Pushkin, Gogol, and Rozanov, he carries on a polemic with literary taxonomists, questioning the most fundamental assessments. In each case Sinyavsky takes issue, not simply as a literary critic, but as a social critic, challenging the record not only in regard to taste, but also in regard to the values of the day, pointing out, in no uncertain terms, the disposition of some cultural monuments and their utilitarian foundations.

NOTES

1. Tikos and Peppard point to Sinyavsky's many references to Mayakovsky in their introductory essay to *For Freedom of Imagination* (xviii).

2. Mayakovsky (1893–1930) is a controversial poet not only because of the life that he led, but also because of claims and counterclaims about his work. Eschewing the avant-garde, Stalin nevertheless considered him the most talented poet of the Soviet period. Although he came to occupy a hallowed place in Russian literary history, it was not his artistic innovation that Russian ideological opportunists celebrated. Owing namely to misgivings regarding artistic innovation, the development of a Mayakovskian "school" of poetry never got off the ground. On the other hand, many Western critics saw his postrevolutionary work as that of a court poet. What can be said about a remarkable avant-garde writer who also made his mark as a cartoonist and propagandist? It was clear that he was a revolutionary poet as well as a poet of the Revolution. According to Sinyavsky, he inspired two entirely different reactions:

> Paradoxically, many young Soviet people arrived at dissidence via Mayakovsky, via the revolution's officially recognized poet. In the early sixties in Moscow, young people began gathering by Mayakovsky's statue to read poems and argue about everything under the sun. For some, the statue on Mayakovsky Square became a baptism of fire, even the execution place of unofficial poetry. Others waited for the plainclothes agents they knew were coming. Thus Mayakovsky was transformed from standard-bearer of the revolution and the Soviet state into—for certain people at least—a symbol of opposition. (*Soviet Civilization* 232)

3. It should be pointed out that Sinyavsky first published *What Is Socialist Realism* anonymously. Only later was it attributed to Terts. At his trial Sinyavsky indicated that he sent out one additional page to this essay through Remezov. He called it an "addendum" (*dopolnenie*) rather than a conclusion (Ginzburg 204).

4. Hélène Peltier says that Sinyavsky was not in agreement with Marxist aesthetics at that time. In fact, during the year that his master's thesis was accepted, he claimed what was in opposition to his thesis: that literature was more important than life (Ginzburg 281).

5. Sinyavsky and Menshutin point to V. Bushin's objections to their use of the "the foreign word" (*zagrannichnoe slovo*) "tendency" in "*Davaite govorit' professional'no,*" 248.

6. Sinyavsky quotes from the Bible, Revelation 3:15. He quotes the same passage in his discussion of Rozanov who was, according to Sinyavsky, always "hot" (*goryach*) and never "warm" (*tepl*) ("*Opavshie list'ya" V. V. Rozanova* 278).

7. See Sinyavsky's comments about these poetry readings in front of the Mayakovsky monument (*Soviet Civilization* 232).

8. "*Ot redaksii,*" *Novyi mir* 37, no. 8 (1961): 253–57. B. Runin's rejoinder, "*Logika spora I logika iskusstva,*" is also included in this issue (236–48), an issue containing twenty-eight pages of rebuttal very reminiscent of the heated claims and counterclaims of the literary groups of the 1920s.

9. For a discussion of these poets with regard to Mayakovsky see *Poeziya pervykh let* 72, 82, 99, 101, 110, 132, 163, 166, and 184.

10. Sinyavsky goes so far as to say that Pushkin, Lermontov, Dostoevsky, and Mayakovsky were all dissidents and that dissidence is simply a synonym for art ("*Iskusstvo i deistvitel'nost*'" 112).

11. Sinyavsky sent me a copy of "Reactions" in manuscript form in 1996. All page references in the body of this chapter correspond to it.

12. Only Rozanov, according to Sinyavsky, came close to Mayakovsky's exaggerated materialization of lifeless images and abstractions ("*Opavshie list'ya" V. V. Rozanova* 216).

Chapter Seven

Forbidden Themes, Disputation, Autobiography

Unlike the satire in Sinyavsky's early literary criticism, the satire in his early fiction, that is, *Sud idet* (*The Trial Begins*), *Lyubimov* (*The Makepeace Experiment*), "*Ty i ya*" ("You and I"), "*V tsirke*" ("At the Circus"), "*Kvartiranty*" ("The Tenants"), "*Grafomany*" ("Graphomaniacs"), and "*Gololeditsa*" ("Icy Conditions"), is essentially indirect.[1] Although it discloses the abuses and follies of the era, it does so in a vast intertext of public and private moments, stories within stories, fantastic images, literary allusions, and philosophic positions. In other words, there is a complexity about Sinyavsky's fiction, abetted by an overriding playfulness that leads to taboo breaking and a great measure of humor.[2] Rather than officiate in the pronouncement of a particular doctrine, Sinyavsky provides the reader with metaphors, with pieces to a puzzle of the human condition. In the Menippean tradition, he even displays a contest of ideas to enhance this puzzle not unlike Dostoevsky, entangling the reader in a web of hypotheses.[3] Mischievously rather than maliciously, he mixes nonsense with volatile issues, twisting and turning the perspective of events as well as the emotions of the reader who tries to make sense of them. In the following chapter let us examine this playfulness, paying particular attention to an intertext of forbidden themes, emplotments of personal history, and recurring philosophical disputation.

Before proceeding, a few words about fantasy and philosophy are in order. They are, after all, the chief ingredients of Menippean satire, which finds much expression in Sinyavsky's writing. While the fantastic elements of Sinyavsky's fiction are rather obvious, the philosophical considerations that inform his stories may not strike us immediately. Such considerations are part and parcel of Sinyavsky's scholarly preparation, his teaching and research—his erudition. With this erudition he joins Menippean satirists such as Swift who create fantastic albeit philosophical paradigms. Thus Gulliver as well as the creature in "Pkhents" are put into what they perceive as startling and unexpected circumstances, circumstances that hypothesize the plight of man. Dostoevsky, to whom Bakhtin attributes Menippean satire, is, of course, a master of these circumstances. In the opinion of Bakhtin, "The Menippean satirist uses fantasy to create extraordinary situations for provoking and testing of a philosophical idea" (*Problems* 41). Clearly Sinyavsky's writing moves in this direction, posing and illustrating questions namely about teleology, as in *Sud idet* (*The Trial Begins*), identity, as in "*Gololeditsa*" ("Icy Conditions"), and ontology, as in "*Ty i ya*" ("You and I"). Thus Sinyavsky explores thorny theoretical issues against a backdrop that is quite often outrageous.

Sinyavsky's fantastic constructs, whether built upon folklore or science fiction, should be regarded as means rather than ends. For Sinyavsky fantasy opens up the text, permitting leaps into almost every area of discourse, including philosophy. It is a platform, above all, for a circuitous deployment of earnest argument and humorous disclosure. In *The Trial Begins*, however, Sinyavsky's first work of fiction to be published in the West, this platform is barely in place. Is it possible that Sinyavsky's misgivings about this novella are in part due to its dearth of fantasy. Given, for example, Sinyavsky's literary manifesto at the end of *Chto takoe sotsialisticheski realizm* (*What Is Socialist Realism*), it was reasonable to assume that its companion piece, *Sud idet* (*The Trial Begins*), was an example of phantasmagoria.[4] Yet, there is very little of the fantastic in *The Trial Begins*—a soap opera about Globov, a public prosecutor, whose wife, Marina, has an affair with Karlinsky, and whose teenage son is arrested for counterrevolutionary activity. Widening the Globov circle are Skromnykh, an interrogator, and Rabinovich, an obstetrician, who help to thicken the plot as well as the supply of stock characters. This novella is certainly not in the fantastic register of "*Ty i ya*" ("You and I"), "*Gololeditsa*" ("Icy Conditions") or *Lyubimov* (*The Makepeace Experiment*).

The Trial Begins, on the other hand, has a rich philosophical vein. It clearly continues the disputation of *What Is Socialist Realism*, providing not only illustrations for the philosophy of Purpose, but pretexts for comedy. As Swift recontextualizes assumptions about spirit and matter in *The Tale of a Tub*, Sinyavsky recontextualizes assumptions about ends and means in *The Trial Begins*. Certainly every reader will immediately recognize that in this novella Marina's vanity, Globov's careerism, Karlinsky's solipsism, Serezha's idealism, or Globov's mother-in-law's old-fashioned Bolshevism are all emanations of Purpose, placed in the context of the "doctors' plot," Stalin's final scheme in the name of Purpose.[5]

With playful images of Lenin and Stalin, security men, arrests, prisons, courtrooms, spies, and outcasts, it would seem that *The Trial Begins* is front-loaded for satire. But such images, which appear again and again in Sinyavsky's works, are not simply introduced for jeering. In this novella they are part of a larger discourse about the folly of Purpose, which is dramatized not by one, but by all of the principal characters, leaving no heroes to follow.[6] It is insufficient to point to individual outcomes such as Globov's madness or Marina's spiteful abortion. Everything leads to a dead end, like the blind movement of the masses at Stalin's funeral, or to prison, the destiny of the narrator, Rabinovich, and Serezha.[7] Moreover, the loftiest goals are framed with uncertainty. Questioning freedom in a very Dostoevskian way, Rabinovich maintains that it not only replaced Christ and established the bourgeois way of life, but also that in the name of freedom one person suffocates another (*Sobranie sochinenii* 1:286). Even Serezha's revolutionary idealism is disputed when the narrator alludes to the young man's plan to camouflage the barbed wire in the zoo so that animals would think that they were free (*Sobranie sochinenii* 1:282). Again and again, Sinyavsky poses variations on the folly of Purpose, suggesting that even a worthy goal consumes itself, for, according to Rabinovich, when someone finally gets to this goal, it has been turned inside out (*Sobranie sochinenii* 1:286).

Actually, what may pass for fantastic are the narrator's candid remarks about his own impending arrest and imprisonment, as well as playful references to Stalin, not to mention the parodic use of epithets and slogans.[8] Outside of jokes, references to the dark side of sovietization and out-and-out mimicking of "newspaper lyrics" (*gazetnaya lirika*) did not come to the surface in Russian society—especially the printed surface. More fantastic, however, is Sinyavsky's way of spoofing archetypes such as party careerists, Jewish doctors, security men, lechers, and young idealists. With tongue in cheek, Sinyavsky leads readers into territories where alarms that usually signal the violation of a taboo are muffled by laughter. Feigning a sincere and authoritative tone, for example, his chatty narrator gives the impression of overturning a misconception about members of the KGB:

> How deluded was the mercenary Western press whose scribblers portrayed these men as somber villains. In reality, they could not be nicer; they were

> witty, home-loving; according to Skromnykh, many of them liked fishing in their spare time, or cooking, or making toys for children. One senior interrogator, employed on cases of utmost gravity, used his leisure time knitting gloves and embroidering doilies and cushion covers. (*Sobranie sochinenii* 1:294)[9]

The reader can only imagine Sinyavsky, trying to keep a straight face, as he whitewashes the members of a dreaded invisible army, turning them into model husbands and fathers.

In the epilogue of *The Trial Begins* Sinyavsky recapitulates his philosophical inquiry, introducing the most Dostoevskian image into his discourse on Purpose: a dagger with a handle in the form of a crucifix. The setting is a prison camp in Siberia where a writer (the narrator), Rabinovich, and Serezha are thrown together by fate. Although no details are given, the writer was probably sentenced for his manuscript, that is, *The Trial Begins*; Rabinovich for his "involvement" in the "doctors' plot," and Serezha for his junior high conspiracy to overthrow the government. It is Rabinovich who shows his fellow inmates the rusty dagger that he had found earlier while on ditch-digging detail. Addressing the central issue of the story, he exclaims:

> A nice place they found for God—the handle of a deadly weapon. Are you going to deny it? God was the end and they turned him into the means—a handle. And the dagger was the means and became the end. (*Sobranie sochinenii* 1:311)

His growing madness puts him in a position to raise this issue with poignancy, to take center stage, alluding to teleological and existential matters in the most dramatic way. Seizing the cross in both hands and raising it to the sky, Rabinovich exclaims:

> In the name of God! With the help of God! In place of God! Against God! And now there is no God, only dialectics. Forge a new dagger for the new Purpose at once! (*Sobranie sochinenii* 1:311)

These exclamations could have ended the story: a summation of the stages of Russian history from a man on the brink of madness in a deep ditch in a Siberian prison. But they are denied a place as a coda. They, in fact, are followed by the silence and oneness of prison camp labor. It is the prison camp guard, awakened by Rabinovich's exclamations, who has the last word, ordering an end to blabbering (*chesat' yazykom*) and a return to digging. What the guard mistakes for blabbering, however, is a hypothesis, one of many in this story, which, as Sinyavsky declares in *Chto takoe sotsialisticheskii realizm*, constitutes the basis of art (*Fantasticheskii mir* 446).

Sinyavsky criticizes *The Trial Begins* for being excessively intellectualized, lifeless, and too much of a given. He faults himself for yielding to the need to write something important about the times, that is, for directing his art toward a larger Purpose (Nepomnyashchy "Interview," 7–8). It is this very fault that he sees in Gogol's and Solzhenitsyn's lofty, artistic Purpose. If by "intellectualized, lifeless, and too much of a given" Sinyavsky means meticulously organized and referentially unclouded, he has a point. In this respect *The Trial Begins* is, arguably, an anomaly among his works of fiction. But it does not suffer from any sort of philosophic or artistic compression. Whatever feelings originally launched this novella, they seem to be checked by Sinyavsky's cat-and-mouse argumentation, his comic side, his exploratory rather than declarative manner. In spite of Sinyavsky's misgivings, *The Trial Begins* remains a marvelously de-centered work. For all of its "intellectualization" of the issue of Purpose, this novel ultimately shows the quandary that is inherent in the subordination of means to ends. Above all, it places this quandary at the same table with laughter and serious debate.

Sinyavsky's personal side should not be overlooked in *The Trial Begins*, or in his other works, for he not only emplots events from Russian history, but also events from his own life into his fiction. In his efforts to unmask abuses, he circles around the horror of his generation, referring to or hinting at what he himself had experienced, such as his father's arrest, the possibility of his own arrest, the KGB's coercion in regard to his friendship with Hélène Peltier, and his growing conflicts with the literary establishment. More often than not, he enhances the personal side of his writing by providing a story line for a writer or a privileged place for a first-person narrator. Besides, with a first-person narrator Sinyavsky establishes an "I" with which to make asides about castaways and letters to the future. In the tradition of *skaz* (a highly marked narration), he gives the narrator a dramatic role, allowing him to move in and out of the story and, above all, to play the buffoon or make remarks that seem confidential. It is this kind of narrator in *The Trial Begins* who declares that everyone is on trial at the end of chapter three (*Sobranie sochinenii* 1:278). Pointing to the moment when the police come to make an arrest as the point when one becomes a writer, he alludes to the motivation for starting to write as well as for sharing the very story the reader is reading.

From reading *What Is Socialist Realism* and *The Trial Begins*, it is easy to guess that the issue of Purpose is a very personal issue—one that haunts Sinyavsky's writing. His critique of social order stems from considerations of this issue rather than from formulations about capitalism and socialism. Rejecting Machiavellianism, that is, a philosophy in which the ends justify the means, Sinyavsky makes the same objections as Dostoevsky's underground man, as well as Ivan Karamazov in *Brat'ya Karamozovy* (*The Brothers Karamazov*).[10] Moreover, he questions the whole notion of a goal (purpose). In *Lyubimov* (*The Makepeace Experiment*), a comic chronicle about a Russian provincial town, Sinyavsky continues his discourse on Purpose, adding a broader perspective by illustrating a parodic path to an ideal through science, hypnotism, Christian miracle, the magic of folklore, and even vodka. Creating the illusion of a historical account, he allows two chroniclers from two different centuries, Savely Kuzmich and Samson Samsonovich, to "record" a major turning point: Lenya Tikhomirov's "revolution," that is, his assumption of power through winning the hearts and minds of the inhabitants of Lyubimov. It is precisely his means to winning hearts and minds, that is, his use of hypnosis (a spoof on the Marxist notion of altering consciousness) that is targeted in this mock epic.

Lyubimov is of course a satire about Russian history with substantial emphasis on historiography, in this case on mythmaking and record keeping, complete with parodies of utopian plans and propaganda practices, as well as veiled references to Lenin and Khrushchev. But this satire has many components. Its comic dimension adds ballast to weighty issues of a Dostoevskian caste, such as free will, the persistence of the irrational, and the politics of progress. For Sinyavsky there is no better way to consider the contradictions of a utopia than to show the fortunes and misfortunes of a bicycle repairman who, having gained absolute power, attempts to "improve" the human condition. To this philosophical disquisition Sinyavsky adds several other layers of discourse—what he calls gibberish (*tarabarshchina*) and cock-and-bull stories (*nebylitsy*) (Ginzburg 230–31), giving *Lyubimov* a true measure of farrago (originally, a platter full of mixed fruits).

Lyubimov, like *Gulliver's Travels*, is an allegory of ideas about the development of man, about his institutions and the passions that make these institutions inevitable. Samson Samsonovich, the principal source of wisdom and inspiration in *Lyubimov*, relates these ideas to Russian history, which, he insists, can only be told in layers (*Sobranie sochinenii* 1:37). One of the principal layers is, of course, Russian folklore with fantastic creatures, some of which Sinyavsky introduced earlier with metaphoric uncertainty in "The Tenants" ("*Kvartiranty*") and later discussed with scholarly and anecdotal flair in *Ivan the Fool* (*Ivan-Durak*). Such layers are indispensable to demonstrating the existence of more than one Russian discursive practice, more than one voice, indispensable, of course, to satire, namely, to bringing the reader face to face with the leaps, gaps, and unexplained phenomena that contribute to man's folly. If Lenya's rise to power is rooted in (1) his desire to impress Serafima Petrovna, (2) his association with Savelii Kuzmich, (3) his belief in the benefits of reading, and (4) his discovery of a magic book, there can be no claims about the workings of dialectical materialism or any other philosophy of totalization.

Several binary oppositions in *Lyubimov* lead us to that Sinyavskian mixture of philosophy and comedy that lends both depth and levity to his satire. One such opposition is the logic of a utopia versus the irrationality of man. Using "scientific" methods, Lenya does what he can to improve society. In spite of innumerable problems, he is filled with hope for altering human nature. But when he paints a picture of a future society at a high stage of development, where, at the push of a button, all wishes are granted, the narrator counters:

> So that's it? We got to the highest level? We started out with the steam engine and what happened? Why I would be better off crawling in lice, better in my primitive state, upside down hanging by my tail, swinging on a eucalyptus branch! Give me darkness! A shadow! A place where I can hide my face in shame. (*Sobranie sochinenii* 1:28–29)

Echoing Dostoevsky's underground man in *Zapiski iz podpol'ya* (*Notes from the Underground*), the narrator restates a major attack on the rational utopia of the radical intelligentsia. Pointing to the illogical side of man, he suggests the folly of Lenya's dream. But this folly is further suggested by the implications of another opposition: scientific deductions versus simple intuitions. Throughout *Lyubimov* the sequence of unusual events is punctuated with opinions from both sides of this opposition. Lenya, of course, hastens to show that science explains everything. Yet, the nature of these unusual events seems to mock science. To many inhabitants, for example, it appeared that the city of Lyubimov had simply vanished at one point. On the other hand, "experts" maintained that the city was still there, that a geological subsidence had taken place (*Sobranie sochinenii* 1:61). While many inhabitants of Lyubimov claimed that there was something "miraculous" (*chudesnyi*) or "supernatural" (*sverkh'estestvennyi*) about Lenya, the narrator, allegedly Savely Kuzmich, insisted that everything could be explained in "scientific terms," beginning with their leader's proletarian roots (*Sobranie sochinenii* 1:26). Even simple technological devices are rejected. When Lenya offers people from the villages a lightning rod, they grumble, seeing it as nonsense. What they want him to do is cast a spell on the weather to regulate the rainfall (*Sobranie sochinenii* 1:90).

We, of course, should not overlook the opposition between Lenya and Father Ignatius—as well as the false likeness. It would seem that both, in their own way, are interested in saving humanity, that both follow their faith in a higher cause. In fact Lenya's mother brings cottage cheese (*tvorozhok*) to both her son and to Father Ignatius (*Sobranie sochinenii* 1:70, 107).[11] But on the chain around his neck, Lenya wears a key instead of a cross (*Sobranie sochinenii* 1:100). It is a key to the metal container in his study in which he keeps the book on hypnotism. It is through the power of hypnotism that Lenya competes with miracles, that he attempts to imitate them, changing, for example, mineral water into alcohol and river water into champagne. When his hypnotic power begins to fail him, however, it becomes clear that it was all he had. The makepeace experiment fails. Lenya did not raise the consciousness of the people; he merely "transmitted" his own wishes, which, in the end, come from his irrational side.

In *The Makepeace Experiment* Sinyavsky experiments further with the narrative point of view. In fact he works out an entire drama between two narrators, Savely Kuzmich, a local chronicler of events, and Samson Samsonovich, a distinguished professor from the past. In their struggle for the text, Sinyavsky suggests, among other things, the struggle between himself and Terts, that is, between author and invented author. It is the kind of struggle that Sinyavsky mythifies in his "relationship" with Terts and which he pauses to discuss in *Spokoinoi nochi!* (*Goodnight!*) (*Sobranie sochinenii* 2:345–46). Mirroring this struggle, the narrators in *The Makepeace Experiment* clash over how history is to be written, especially Russian history; moreover, they spar about who is the real source for the text. A further development of this relationship is put forward in "*Ty i ya*" ("You and I") and "*Kvartiranty*" ("The Tenants") where Sinyavsky continues to straddle the fence between one and another source for a point of view.

The personal side of Sinyavsky reverberates both in the title of "Graphomaniacs" ("*Grafomany*"), one of six of his "fantastic stories," and in its subheading, "From Stories of My Life."[12] Although this kind of subheading is a convention, in this case a narrative hook, it is also filled with irony, for it turns out that Sinyavsky's fingerprints as a writer and literary scholar are clearly present in the story. Only someone quite familiar with Russian literature and the literary process in Russia could have written "Graphomaniacs." Built on four comic scenes, it is a story about two writers, Galkin and Straustin; it is also a discussion of the question of talent, as well as the conditions for authorship in tsarist and Soviet society.

The narrator, Straustin, is contemptuous of Galkin, taking every opportunity to show him as a mediocre writer with a fondness for hackneyed phrases. At a literary evening, for example, he describes how Galkin reads a passage from his own work where the protagonist rhapsodizes on spring, "when everyone wants to join nature in weeping with joy and cry, 'O Russia! Wither art thou rushing'" (*Sobranie sochinenii* 1:171).[13] Galkin's protaganist begins this effusion of feelings after a description of a kiss, when a certain General Ptitsyn senses in his soul "one of those pieces of curd tarts and mushroom pies, and half a dozen strong pickles, cold as icicles and smelling of fresh dill" (*Sobranie sochinenii* 1:171). This Gogolian reference to spring and food, which immediately follows the kiss, cannot but draw a knowing smile from the reader. The same kind of smile is also possible when the reader recognizes that the wretched existence of Straustin resembles that of Akaky Akakievich in Gogol's "*Shinel'*" (*The Overcoat*), complete with a humiliation scene in an editorial office (*Sobranie sochinenii* 1:161).[14] Lourie also comments on this parody, claiming that Sinyavsky was hinting at his debt to Gogol (*Letters to the Future* 145).[15]

With few events, "Graphomaniacs" contains an intermittent discussion of writing, which, of course, haunts Sinyavsky's fiction. From this discussion, it is apparent that Galkin and Straustin are different, but that they share the same mania. Metaphorically speaking, Galkin (jackdaw) and Straustin (ostrich) are birds of a feather not unlike Gogol (duck) whose famous troika comparison is restated not coincidentally by Ptitsyn (bird).[16] It is possible to say that Galkin's "obsession with becoming a historical figure" (*odno na ume—voiti v istoriyu*) not only links him with Gogol, but also links Gogol with graphomania (*Sobranie sochinenii* 1:165). In this discussion about writing, with its many allusions to authors such as Pushkin, Lermontov, Gogol, Dostoevsky, Turgenev, Nekrasov, Tolstoi, Chekhov, Mayakovsky, Esenin, Fedin, Leonov, Paustovsky, Fadeev, Sholokhov, Shakespeare, Alexander Dumas fils, Dickens, Stendhal, and Swift, the voice of Sinyavsky, the literary critic, is clearly heard, a voice that mediates between the playfulness of the story and the dictates and motivations of authorship in Russia and the West.

"Graphomaniacs" is a good measure of Sinyavsky's satire, for it demonstrates an absence of polarities and an absence of malice. In the hands of another Russian satirist, it would not have been surprising to find undisguised hostility for the Soviet writing establishment and a genuine showdown between a hack and a genuine writer. But Sinyavsky's satire playfully explores rather than cheaply exploits this kind of tension. For Sinyavsky, more important than privileging one writer over another is exploring the nature of authorship and the hurdles that surround it. Graphomania, according to this story, is at the heart of writing, including that of Galkin and Straustin. The former deceives himself about what he has written; the latter does too—until he gives up writing as a means of recognition.

It is Straustin, a late-blooming Sinyavskian protagonist, who comes to understand the scramble for literary greatness, the forging of literary celebrities, the lies, the authors who have turned literature into "an impregnable fortress" (*Sobranie sochinenii* 1:173). Feeling hurt and angry after his manuscript is rejected, he even thinks about writing a book about the editor, his secretary, and B., the famous writer, "in satirical colors" (*v satiricheskikh kraskakh*) (*Sobranie sochinenii* 1:160). But his plans for revenge are displaced by anxieties about writers stealing phrases from his manuscript. Not only does he suspect Galkin, but also Fedin, Leonov, Paustovsky, Fadeyev, and Sholokhov of plagiarism. Beside himself almost to the point of a complete breakdown, he finally vents his anger at Russian "classics" such as Tolstoy and Chekhov for what he sees as their easy success and unwarranted monumentalization.

When Straustin tells his wife that he is giving up the idea of becoming a writer, it is a painful decision. After she leaves for work, he approaches his son, Pavel, about writing, encouraging him, this time, to continue. He also takes out a sheet of paper for himself, explaining to Pavel that although he was finished with writing, he had to write his very last work, his "swan song" (*lebedinaya pesn'*). It would be for his son, if he wished to read it. It would not be for publication. Echoing a belief in fantastic literature as it was expressed in *What Is Socialist Realism*, Straustin tells his son, "Paul, write your fairy tales about your funny dwarfs. And I'll write about mine" (*Sobranie sochinenii* 1:179).[17] In fact, he thinks that he or his son, or someone else, will "make it" (*doidet*), will "get a message through" (*doneset*).[18] Unlike Galkin, who aspires to greatness and a place among the giants of literature, Straustin puts his hope in dwarfs, in Lilliputians, as he further characterized them (*Sobranie sochinenii* 1:163).[19] He is finally ready to give up his novels about Russia's revolution and its civil war.

In "*V tsirke*" ("At the Circus"), which is also informed by autobiographical innuendos, Sinyavsky focuses not just on a daring act, but a daring act that ends in death as in "*Pkhents*," and "You and I," making suicide a motivated outcome in half of his "fantastic stories." In this double discourse about links between art and crime, Konstantin, a thief with Promethean potential, commits murder, that is, he transgresses, in the Russian meaning of "*prestuplenie*," as posited in Dostoevsky's *Prestuplenie i nakazanie* (*Crime and Punishment*). Inspired by a magician at a circus, he demonstrates that the hand is quicker than the eye when he picks the pocket of a stranger. Breaking into an apartment later, he inadvertently shoots the very magician who inspires him. Sentenced to a prison camp, Konstantin decides to lunge for freedom, performing a graceful somersault like a circus performer, during which he is shot by a guard. Behind Konstantin's criminal activity (art) as well as his artistic lunge to freedom is "inspiration" (*vdokhnovenie*), "a strange and magnanimous supernatural power" (*postoronnaya i velikodushnaya sverkh'estestvennaya sila*). Thus crime and art are rooted in magic, that is, "tricks" and "miracles" (*fokusy*, *chudesa*) and carried out with daring.

In regard to the actual application of article 70 of the criminal code, the relationship between art and crime is clearly at issue in "The Circus."[20] Also at issue is the magician who, although a master of his art, is vain, vulgar, and possibly evil. For Konstantin, he is the source for temptation, for kindling a desire for something extraordinary. To Konstantin, a simple thief with a taste for carousing in bathhouses and restaurants and breaking into apartments, he is, in fact, the muse of daring. Drunk in a tavern with Solomon Moiseevich, his philosophic interlocutor, Konstantin spells out what daring means when he imagines that he is performing on a tightwire rope high above a crowd that is begging for a *salto mortale* (a somersault: literally, a mortal leap), or, as a writer would have it, for the expression of "an extraordinary word" that would change the world (*Sobranie sochinenii* 1:117). In *Spokoinoi nochi* (*Goodnight!*) Sinyavsky echoes this analogy in regard to his own writing, speaking about doing a few somersaults (*salto mortale*) and landing on his feet on an equal footing with thieves (*Sobranie sochinenii* 2:401). This kind of daring, of exercising one's will, is further suggested in several allusions to Dostoevsky's *Crime and Punishment*.

Allusions to *Crime and Punishment* begin in earnest, moreover, with the "new life" (*u Konstantina Petrovicha nachalas' novaya zhizn'*) that Konstantin experiences after the theft of a wallet and the possible murder of its owner (*Sobranie sochinenii* 1:116). This theft, which is thoroughly de-familiarized, is marked by "magic" (*focus*), "otherworldly presence" (*potustoronnee prisutstvie*), a "miracle" (*chudo*), and a "fairy-tale transformation" (*skazochnoe prevrashchenie*). It is really not clear what happened.[21] In keeping with Raskol'nikov's overtures to the beneficence of his deed, Konstantin's farewell words to the owner of the wallet also underscore how his actions will serve some good:

> What's more, you will be grateful to me for this. I make bold to assure you. You'll think that I am some writer, performer, or sports celebrity. (*Sobranie sochinenii* 1:116)[22]

The owner of the wallet, of course, never utters a word. Later in the tavern, right before his vision of himself high above on a tightwire rope, Konstantin feels something shift inside him. Here, in this very Dostoevskian setting, Konstantin and Solomon Moiseevich carry on a Dostoevskian conversation about the existence of God and the nature of the Russian soul, which exhibits the propensity for stealing and drinking. It is in the tavern that Konstantin, in the melodramatic manner of Marmeladov, carries on about ruining his starving mother, drinking away the money that was needed for her medications (*Sobranie sochinenii* 1:119).[23]

The serious Dostoevskian implications in this story come together in Solomon Moiseevich's exhortations:

> Sin! Thou shalt not sin! There are no barriers in the game! Thou shalt not kill! Thou shalt not kill! God! Devil! (*Sobranie sochinenii* 1:121)

They, in fact, overshadow the physical peril that is underscored in the disabled soldier's adage: "Someone who works with mines only makes one mistake" (*Sobranie sochinenii* 1:121). It is Solomon Moiseevich who speaks about sin, the absence of barriers, and shattered love, extending the loop of art and crime into the moral realm. He draws attention to the connection between the circus and homiletic images namely in the acrobatic postures of the saints depicted on the ceilings and walls of a church. Later this acrobatic motif is recontextualized in a prison camp at night: "a space filled with electric light and kilometers of wire stretching beneath the cupola of a worldwide circus" (*Sobranie sochinenii* 1:125). It is here that Konstantin performs his "somersault" (*salto mortale*), which was foreshadowed earlier. Here, it has the weight of a parable, drawing our attention to the consequences of the daring act of an artist in Russia, which, in this satirical context, is illuminated namely by the lights of a prison camp.

As a satirist, Sinyavsky hints at fault lines, pointing to tremors rather than laying out a seismological report. In fact, he uses the short story not to argue for faults, but to draw attention to their manifestations in circumstances that are clearly serious, but released from a constant force of gravity by lighthearted incidents. In a short story everything should be mobilized for a single effect, at least according to Edgar Allan Poe, but Sinyavsky avoids this prescription, preferring, in "At the Circus," not to spell out a story of artistry, risks, and penalties. Instead he focuses on relationships, on the links between magic and religion, between crime and art, hinting finally about the promise and the peril that an artist faces. It is for the reader to distill out any truth, to separate the issues from the humorous incidents, to debate about what is emplotted and entangled. And a debate is inevitable, for through it Sinyavsky extends his Menippean reach, causing us to pause at the spiraling implications of "At the Circus," especially the possible link between Konstantin and another remarkable thief called Terts.

More than any other short story, "You and I" captures an atmosphere of suspicion and anxiety, of dread in the face of surveillance.[24] Here, under the watchfulness of KGB agents, tension only yields to comic relief when undercover work takes the form of ungainly operatives wearing women's apparel and makeup. Such slapstick, however, is short-lived, for suspicion and anxiety are reiterated in a metafictional relationship between the narrator and a character in the text called Nikolai Vasilevich. What makes this relationship important and, in fact, extraordinary is that the narrator is an embodiment of Terts, who takes issue with Nikolai Vasilevich, an embodiment of Sinyavsky, who bears the first name and patronymic of Gogol. This relationship is a contest very much like the one between Dostoevsky and his characters (*Problemy* 42). In fact Sinyavsky claims that he chose the legendary Jewish brigand Terts because his character symbolized an endless process of contestation (Beausang 17). Through this relationship, a rather large intertextual path opens up, leading form inside to outside the story and especially to Sinyavsky's "hidden" side before his arrest.

Emplotted in this story is a well-known episode from Sinyavsky's life. It is a window to the Hélène Peltier operation in 1948 and 1952 when Sinyavsky was pressured by the KGB to win the heart of the daughter of a French naval attaché in order to pave the way for obtaining secret information from her father.[25] In this story, Lida (Lidochka) is analogous to Lena (Lenochka), that is, to Hélène Peltier, whom Sinyavsky befriended at the University of Moscow and through whom he sent his manuscripts to the West. Hence in this fictional parallel, Nikolai Vasilevich mirrors Sinyavsky, feeling pressure to win over Lida so that the KGB can proceed with its plan (*Sobranie sochinenii* 1:140, 142). Addressing Nikolai

Nikolaevich, that is, Sinyavsky, the narrator, that is, Terts, scolds him, pointing out his clumsy deception:

> And so began your love affair, in the midst of your game with death, in full view of your persecutors, who were quite annoyed by your sudden display of temperament. (*Sobranie sochinenii* 1:133)

Continuing this scolding, he underscores the suspicion of the KGB in spite of Nikolai Nikolaevich's dramatic performance:

> He was shrewd enough not to take your lightning romance at face value and so, as you walked down the street with Lida, you carried on as before, stumbling along as a drunk and making her various proposals, even including a marriage proposal, so that all and sundry could hear. (*Sobranie sochinenii* 1:134)

When Graube, the head of this KGB operation, utters the double entendre "*Cherchez la femme*" (*Shershe lya fam*), his words, of course, reverberate in another context: the woman in question, Hélène Peltier, is not only the target in this operation, but the one who smuggled out Sinyavsky's literary manuscripts.

In good satire a puzzle must be pieced together. New pieces seem to leap out at us when we learn that Nikolai Vasilevich, like Sinyavsky, is a writer who deals in absurd fantasies, has red hair, a red beard, and fingers covered with freckles (*Sobranie sochinenii* 1:140–41). Above all, he is treated by the narrator as someone close to him. In fact, the narrator hints at personal information as if he were living on the borders of Nikolai Vasilevich's consciousness, which is to say, the "authorial" borders of Sinyavsky's consciousness.[26] In the following explanation to the reader, the narrator describes this author/persona relationship, a relationship in keeping with rather blatant Terts/Sinyavsky interpolations:

> His ideas about me are utter nonsense, but, even if one takes his absurd fantasies as a starting point, I am not sure which one of us has the whip hand. We are both prisoners; we are unable to take our glazed eyes off each other. And although he can't see me, the beam of fear and hatred trained on me from under those reddish eyelashes is so strong that I want to shout, "Stop it, or I will swallow you! I only have to shut my eyes and you will vanish like a fly. This contest is beginning to weary me. (*So-branie sochinenii* 1:135)

Speaking confessionally, the narrator bemoans his bondage, his torment of joint existence:

> I was not jealous, but I was upset by this constant reminder of you, by this awkward proximity to you at a moment when I was hoping to hide well away from you. I was getting dangerously close to you, and I could already see your eyes somewhere next to me. They were dilated with fury. Stop! Stop! It was too late. I entered into your brain, into your fevered mind; and your last secrets, which I had no desire to know, were laid before me. (*Sobranie sochinenii* 1:143)

Satire, especially underground satire, could not have been embedded in a more forbidden topic than the mockery of KGB agents and a veiled version of an actual KGB operation into which Sinyavsky was coerced. Moreover, Sinyavsky allows the narrator to speak about him personally and to focus on what appears to be the shared consciousness of Sinyavsky/Terts. Addressing this shared consciousness and the Hélène Peltier operation, this story has the elements of high drama, giving the title "You and I" great poignancy. In the final moments, Nikolai Vasilevich commits suicide like the protagonist in "At the Circus" and "*Pkhents*." The narrator says: "You are gone and I am still here. I do not feel sorry about your death. I am sorry that I am unable to forget you" (*Sobranie sochinenii* 1:144). Nikolai Vasilevich's suicide is a way out of his dangerous involvement with the KGB. Now the narrator, that is, Terts, faces a genuine Pirandello-like dilemma: that of a literary persona without the author who invented him.

In "*Kvartiranty*" ("The Tenants"), Terts and Sinyavsky are embodied in the same way, that is, Terts is the narrator and Sinyavsky is the central character, Sergei Sergeevich. In this brief satire, consisting of no more than ten pages, there is the same anxiety, the same fear of arrest as in many of Sinyavsky's works. Intermittently there are remarks about squalid living conditions, industrial pollution, dreadful sanitation and a corrupt housing committee, but they are marginal to a sustained urgency to get out of a communal apartment building, to escape before the police arrive. What occupies the center of this story is the narrator's account of dangers not only from the police, but also from the strange inhabitants of this apartment building who are in fact witches, water nymphs, wood spirits, devils, and rats.

In this very sinister world there are only embodiments, the most important of which is Sinyavsky/Terts. As an embodiment of Terts, the narrator establishes the tone of a mentor whose past experience gives him insight into police matters and apartment politics. The more advice that he gives to Sergei Sergeevich, the more that the reader can sense about the Sinyavsky/Terts relationship. Although Sergei Sergeevich does not utter one word, there is no doubt about his all-consuming existence as a writer. In fact, outside of this existence, which is accompanied by heavy drinking, Sergei Sergeevich has no marked characteristics. Advising Sergei Sergeevich to move out of the apartment, the narrator speaks about taking care of books and notes, of creating the proper environment for the writer elsewhere (*Sobranie sochinenii* 1:144–45). Asking Sofiia Frantsevna Vinter to maintain a measure of modesty in the presence of Sergei Sergeevich, the narrator says, "He is, after all, a writer" (*Sobranie sochinenii* 1:147). Again and again he attempts to engage Sergei Sergeevich in conversations about literature, asking him for books, making suggestions about writing. Falling into his arrogant Tertsian tone, he says, "Although you are a writer, you have no powers of observation" (*Sobranie sochinenii* 1:147). In part three he declares:

> But what do our conversations add up to? Just a miserable fragment. I have enough of these fairy tales to fill a whole *Decameron*. All based on personal experience. You can publish them in five volumes. With illustrations. (*Sobranie sochinenii* 1:151–52)

What could be more of a self-parody than Terts, embodied as the narrator, supplying fantastic stories about devils and witches to a very Sinyavskian Sergei Sergeevich, a writer who does not directly speak for himself? Few satirists can refrain from such exhibitionism, from such glimpses at layers close to the self. In one of those glimpses, the narrator cautions Sergei Sergeevich, making sure that his words resonate in more than one context:

> Watch your back, be careful. In both word and deed. Please avoid biting descriptions with allusions. Otherwise, you know what can happen. (*Sobranie sochinenii* 1:152)

In a report, Shestopalov, an official in the City Housing Department, denounces the narrator and Sergei Sergeevich in revealing, if not prophetic, terms:

> And his new friend is a writer—copies down all his words on paper. There may be unpleasant consequences. We must punish this rumor monger as a warning to others. But we will deal with the writer separately. (*Sobranie sochinenii* 1:150)

While there are many glimpses into the risky relationship between the narrator and Sergei Sergeevich, there is a sustained look at their coexistence—

their codependency. More than once the narrator argues how important it is for them to stick together. He first admits that he has no existence without Sergei Sergeevich.[27] He then declares:

> And you too (I speak without false modesty) will be lost without me. Whereas with me, God willing, you will become world-famous. A Charles Dickens, a Mayne Reid. You see, I know all, you cunning fellow, you. When I come through the door, you take up your pen. Even when you are not quite yourself and have poor control over language. (*Sobranie sochinenii* 1:151)

At the end of the story the police are at the door to Sergei Sergeevich's room. The reader, of course, has been in this situation before in Sinyavsky's stories. The narrator is with Sergei Sergeevich. His final words are: "They have come for me. And for you too, Sergei Sergeevich. You too. You too" (*Sobranie sochinenii* 1:154).

In "The Tenants" Sinyavsky makes inferences about authors and their self-reliant characters. But such inferences are sandwiched between the layers of the most playful discourse, between conspiracies and cognac, spiteful creatures and harmless imps, between a silent writer and his "mouthpiece." Only satire is served by such innuendos; none of which is an end in itself; all of which, however, constitute a certain addressivity, serving more than one audience, laying out clues instead of teachings. Such clues give "The Tenants," as well as "You and I," the strangest measure of dramatic irony, for what is said in the text about the Sinyavsky/Terts relationship could not have been fully understood before Sinyavsky's arrest. This dramatic irony, suspended in time, is underscored in the conclusion to "*Gololeditsa*" ("Icy Conditions") when the narrator says: "I am convinced that most books are letters to the future" (*Sobranie sochinenii* 1:230).[28] Speaking about putting a "message in a bottle" (*butylka s pis'mom*) in the forward to "Icy Conditions," the narrator clearly gives his writing a time signature, introducing, of course, an intriguing story about time and the many places and forms humans occupy in its wake.

Few Russian satirists explore philosophical issues such as ontology, especially unstable ontology—a contradiction under the umbrella of dialectical materialism and economic determinism. For Sinyavsky, who is more comfortable with philosophy than the details of daily life, the parameters of being become as central as they were to Dostoevsky, so central, in fact, that in works such as *Mysli vrasplokh* (*Thoughts Unaware*) and *Golos iz khora* (*Voice from the Chorus*) he drops almost all conventions of fiction to ruminate about them. Sinyavsky's ontological concerns, moreover, are signaled by his understanding of his persona in an inside/outside sense, whom he represents as author, narrator, and character. Terts is the first step in Sinyavsky's experimentation with more than one self, with the representation of self-consciousness that is theoretically different from his own. By degrees, Sinyavsky represents voices that belong to characters and narrators who do not fit into the usual conventions of fiction. This idea of limitless essence is Sinyavsky's model for being, a model that he illustrates in detail in "Icy Conditions."

Addressing the ontological implications of Marxism, Sinyavsky returns to the high platform of *Chto takoe sotsialisticheskii realizm* (*On Socialist Realism*). In doing so, he raises his satire to a Menippean level, playing point against counterpoint with great erudition as well as parody. Clearly, he takes Marxism to task. Rejecting Marx's formulation that consciousness determines being, Sinyavsky suggests the opposite—that being determines consciousness (*Essential Writings of Karl Marx* 49). In view of what the narrator says about the "transmigration of souls" (*pereselenie dush*), being is constituted by numerous incarnations of the self from the past, present, and future. Given such incarnations, the notion of man as an exponent of economic forces is turned upside down. It is especially shaken from its foundations by the narrator's facetious references to a "higher state of development" (*vysshii etap istoricheskogo razvitiya*) and a "beautiful future" (*prekrasnoe budushchee*). With tongue in cheek the narrator explains:

> I hasten to say that I am not trying to make a theory of this or take sly digs at anybody. I am perfectly well aware that every man, even a Leonardo da Vinci, is the product of economic forces which are responsible for everything in the world. To this I would only add that the individual, the character, the personality—or even, if you like, the soul—also have no part in life and are only reflexes of our vision, like the spots we see when we press our eyeballs or look at the bright sun for a long time without blinking. (*Sobranie sochinenii* 1:192–93)

For emphasis, he restates his mock argument for determinism, sounding, once again, like a Russian intellectual from the nineteenth century leery of the utopian promise of socialism:

> But I have been saying for a long time and I can only emphasize once more that the personality plays no particular part at all. And how can a man have any kind of independence when everything is preordained? I have to stand

> up and I stand up. I have to lie down and I lie down. I don't want to, but I do. Because that is the law, that is historical inevitability. (*Sobranie sochinenii* 1:219)

In this mock argument he continues the intonation and the irony of Dostoevsky's underground man in *Zapiski iz podpol'ya* (*Notes from the Underground*), who satirizes Chernyshevsky's socialist utopia.

The plot of "Icy Conditions," Sinyavsky's longest short story, is straight-forward, but broken up by the exhortations, illustrations, and meditations of the narrator. The reader is invited into the consciousness of the narrator through which everything is projected and explained, starting with his discovery that his self or soul is not solitary, but consists of many souls from other periods of time, including the future.[29] Because he is constituted by many souls, the narrator is not limited to one time period. In fact, incorporated into a body with other souls, he shares insights into many periods of time. He sees, therefore, into the past and into the future. At a New Year's Eve party the narrator goes public with his clairvoyance, telling several of the guests details about their personal lives in the future. Inadvertently he foresees that Natasha, his beloved, will be killed in Moscow by a falling icicle on January 19th on Gnezdnikovsky Street near a ten-story building.[30] To avoid this event he takes Natasha out of town on a train. On route, however, he is arrested by members of the KGB who were alerted to his powers by Boris Belchikov, Natasha's former husband. While he is held captive by the KGB and pressured to put his clairvoyance at the service of his country, Natasha returns to Moscow where on January 19th she meets her fate as foreseen by the narrator.

As in Sinyavsky's other short stories and novellas, there is more of a tangled web rather than a continuous thread. In "Icy Conditions" the reader must wade through parodies of Marxist theory, embodiments of beings who embody other beings, staggering temporal shifts, allusions to great leaders and artists, the arms race, the year of Stalin's death and the usual Sinyavskian portrayal of arrest, interrogation, and imprisonment. In some respects "Icy Conditions" can be read as a weather report regarding the cold war with the metaphor of the "polypus of ice" (*ledyanyi polip*) as an index to a threatening (Marxist-Leninist) development, "bearing down on neighboring structures with stubbornness of Purpose" (*Sobranie sochinenii* 1:226).[31] But this kind of reading should not overlook the melting of ice (a thaw), or its fall from high places in the form of an icicle. No reading should overlook the comic sides—the guest at the New Year's Eve party, described as a Georgian Apollo with a moustache, who manages to bait the narrator with a Trotskian position about world revolution or the party careerist, Colonel Tarasov, who has no real understanding of dialectical materialism. It is with Colonel Tarasov's naive perception of Marxism in mind that the narrator explains: "I repeated, quoting the dialectic, that we can neither improve on history nor detract from it, otherwise we would have chaos and subjective idealism" (*Sobranie sochinenii* 1:219).

Adding to the tangled web of "Icy Conditions" is the narrator's eulogy to the train, a modern version of Gogol's troika, into which he incorporates Gogol's prophetic hyperbole about "outstripping other nations" (*Sobranie sochinenii* 1:206).[32] Feigning the earnestness of a Russian nineteenth-century narrative, the narrator adds the following aside, a Gogolian aside, executed in theatrical fashion, pointing to authorial intent, truthfulness, and the suspicious reader:

> Please don't misunderstand me by taking these words as some sort of innuendo, or as a trick intended, as you might say, to falsify the historical process with the ulterior motive of casting a shadow over our bright future. "But look here," some suspicious reader will exclaim, "who ever heard of such a thing! a healthy man—and a state official, at that—turning into an icicle at the highest stage of development! What is one to make of it? Isn't this defamation and character-blackening?" (*Sobranie sochinenii* 1: 226)

Thus, the narrator does not simply recall Gogol, but he raises a central question about writing, a question of thorny proportions in a totalitarian state. This playful plea notwithstanding, he draws attention to the kind of charges that are leveled at authors who do not write according to the accepted conventions of realism, namely, socialist realism. In fact, in an uncanny way, he foreshadows the thrust of the argumentation that was put forward by the prosecution at the trial, five years after this short story was published.[33]

Had Sinyavsky lived in the West at the time of the publication of these stories, he would have been welcomed into the camp of modernist writers. In Soviet Russia, however, being a modernist meant being in a suspicious territory of art. Besides, publishing modernist stories abroad that were clearly satirical was a serious matter—a criminal matter. It must be said that in these stories Sinyavsky pushed modernism along its normal course toward fantasy, but he made certain that there were junctures as well as collisions with the "forbidden territories" of reality—territories he knew well. These junctures and collisions mark his writing; they characterize his satire. In spite of all of his illusive metaphors, it was possible to figure out that many of them were clearly aligned with events in Russian history and events in Sinyavsky's life. What with the many images of leaders, security men, writers, friends, and foes, he came close to writing an intermittent roman à clef, as well as a cartoon strip for ideologues. In the final analysis, we must ascribe to these richly speculative stories what Northrop Frye ascribes to Menippean satire, that is, a "play of ideas," "a free play of intellectual fancy and the kind of humorous observation that produces caricature" (*Anatomy* 308–9).

NOTES

1. Two other works belong to Sinyavsky's underground writing. "*Pkhents*" ("Pkhents") is discussed in the following chapter. "*Mysli vrasplokh*" ("*Thoughts Unaware*") is discussed in connection with Rozanov in chapter ten.

2. Focusing on rhetorical performance, Dustin Griffin makes a convincing case for the playfulness of satire (*Satire: A Critical Reintroduction* 83–94). "To claim that satire is in part playful," he says, "is thus to claim little more than satire's artfulness, a point worth making, since we often think of satire as primarily concerned with honesty, morality, truth-telling, or 'real life'" (84).

3. Menippean satire has been largely ignored. Lucian, Apuleius, Petronius, More, Erasmus, Rabelais, Burton, and Fontenelle, for example, have been appreciated for their overall achievement rather than their Menippean ways. In *Satire: A Critical Reintroduction*, Griffin speaks of the motley nature and the variety of examples of Menippean satire, preventing critics like Kernan, Kirk, Frye, Seidel, Palmeri, and Bakhtin from describing it in terms of a single coherent system (32–33). In *Anatomy of Criticism*, Frye claims that the Menippean satirist "is not primarily concerned with the exploits of heroes, but relies on the free play of intellectual fancy" (309–10). He goes on to say that this kind of satirist shows his exuberance in intellectual ways, "by piling up an enormous mass of erudition about his theme or in overwhelming his pedantic targets with an avalanche of their own jargon" (311). In *The Problems of Dostoevsky's Poetics*, Bakhtin claims that fantastic adventure, inserted genres and styles, laughter, irreverence, and philosophical disputation are the principal features of the Menippean (106–37).

4. For further discussion of *The Trial Begins* see Chapple, "The Bible and the Zoo," 349–58; Leatherbarrow, "The Sense and Purpose and Socialist Realism in Tertz's 'The Trial Begins,'" 268–79; Lourie, *Letters to the Future,* 75–79; Dalton, *Andrei Siniavskii and Julii Daniel',* 38–49; and Nepomnyashchy, *Abram Tertz and the Poetics of Crime,* 50–63.

5. Nepomnyashchy underscores the importance of the goals of the characters in *The Trial Begins*, drawing attention to their "relativity" and "counterpoint." *Abram Tertz and the Poetics of Crime,* 52–53.

6. In the epilogue to *The Trial Begins* Sinyavsky allows his narrator to, once again, play the buffoon, pretending to assess the story in Marxist-Leninist terms, going so far as to divide the characters into positive and negative types (*Sobranie sochinenii* 1:310).

7. There is an autobiographical echo in this threesome, for in *Spokoinoi nochi* (*Goodnight!*) Sinyavsky refers to Serezha (Sergei Khmel'nitsky), Yura Krasnyi, and himself telling subversive jokes one night in 1949 or 1950, saying that the three of them will wind up in a prison camp (*Sobranie sochinenii* 2:570–71).

8. For a discussion of slogans and epithets see Sinyavsky's chapter on "Soviet Language" in his *Soviet Civilization: A Cultural History,* 190–225.

9. In *Dead Souls* Gogol's narrator claims that the governor of the town of N. knitted purses in his spare time.

10. Like Sinyavsky, Dostoevsky rails against the subordination of everything to Purpose. From *Notes from the Underground* to *The Brothers Karamazov* Dostoevsky makes his case, allowing, for example, the underground man to speak out against Chernyshevsky's utopia and Ivan Karamazov to speak out against the devil's proposal to end all suffering. Dalton, who considers *Lyubimov* a "book of ideas in a Dostoevskian sense," underscores its links to *Notes from the Underground* (*Andrei Siniavskii and Julii Daniel'* 128, 110). Nepomnyashchy sees philosophic analogs between *Lyubimov* and *Notes from the Underground* as well as Zamyatin's *We* (*Abram Tertz and the Poetics of Crime* 137). On one of my visits to Sinyavsky he told me that on rereading Dostoevsky there was much that he found in common with his own work.

11. Lenya's mother, like Sinyavsky's mother, is presented with tenderness and respect. In *Spokoinoi nochi!* (*Goodnight!*), where Sinyavsky talks about his mother, he attributes the very same words to her as he does to Lenya's mother. As Sinyavsky's father always asked about the delay in publishing a study on Picasso, his mother, even on her death-bed, asked: "you did not forget to eat your cottage cheese, did you?" (*Sobranie sochinenii* 2:474)

12. "*Grafomany*" ("Graphomaniacs"), "*V tsirke*" ("At the Circus"), "*Ty i ya*" ("You and I"), "*Kvartiranty*" ("The Tenants"), and "*Gololeditsa*" ("Icy Conditions") were dubbed Sinyavsky's "fantastic stories" and published in Paris as *Fantasticheskie povesti* by the Institut literacki in 1961. "*Pkhents*" ("Pkhents") was added to these "fantastic stories" and published in a larger collection called *Fantasticheskii mir Abrama Tertsa*. For earlier discussions of these stories see Field, "Abram Tertz's Oreal by Mirror," "Prisoner in Fantasy"; Dalton, *Andrei Siniavskii and Julii Daniel',* 49–98; Lourie, *Letters to the Future,* 124–54; Nepomnyashchy, *Abram Tertz and the Poetics of Crime,* 64–130; Aucouturier, "Writer and Text in the Works of Abram Terc"; Deming Brown, "The Art of Andrei Sinyavsky"; Edward J. Brown, "Exodus into *Samizdat* and *Tamizdat*: Sinyavsky," in *Russian Literature since the Revolution,* 238–50; Filippov, "Priroda i tyur'ma"; Mikhailov, *Abram Terts ili begstvo iz retorty*; Woronzoff, "Writer as Artist and Critic"; Durkin, "Narrator, Metaphor, and Theme."

13. This allusion to Gogol is continued in chapter four of "Icy Conditions" beginning with the narrator's eulogy to the "bird-train" (*ptitsa-poezd*) (*Sobranie sochinenii* 1:206).

14. For further discussion of allusions to Gogol, see chapter thirteen, "The Wit of a Literary Scholar."

15. Nepomnyashchy argues that Straustin has a transforming experience through which he adopts Galkin's literary credo of "self-elimination" (*Abram Tertz and the Poetics of Crime and Punishment* 107). But is difficult to understand how a second-rate writer like Galkin, so filled with himself as well as phrases from other writers, possessed such a credo.

16. In "*Gololeditsa*" ("Icy Conditions") the allusion to a train is "bird-train" (*ptitsa-poezd*) which is parallel to Gogol's "bird-troika" (*ptitsa-troika*) (1:206). Both Durkin and Lourie share my insights regarding birds and ducks (*Letters to the Future* 144; "Narrator, Metaphor, and Theme" 138).

17. It is possible that Straustin and his son echo Sinyavsky and his father. After all, Sinyavsky's father was always giving him advice about what to read and what not to read. While Sinyavsky's father made no claims about being a writer, he did write "for the drawer." In *Spokoinoi nochi* Sinyavsky's mother complained about him being out of work, adding that he spent so much time at his desk, "writing a novel without any hope of getting it published" (*Sobranie sochinenii* 2:483). In *Kroshka Tsores*, which is spawned by *Spokoinoi nochi*, the narrator takes up the issue of the shared territory between father and son, that is, between Sinyavsky and his father. Once again, it is suggested that Sinyavsky's father was also a compulsive writer and that it resulted in unhappiness, the very "unhappiness" ("*tsores*") that is at the autobiographical heart of this parody of E. T. A. Hoffmann's tale. Speaking to Little Jinx, whose name is, of course, Sinyavsky, Dora Aleksanrovna says: "You are just like your father. He also traded in his life for paper—for naught. Drove your mother crazy. To the point of giving birth to you" (*Sobranie sochinenii* 2:649).

18. The notion of "getting a message through" at the end of "Graphomaniacs" is echoed at the very beginning of "Icy Conditions." Here the narrator, shipwrecked on an island, throws a letter in a bottle into the sea "in the hope that the waves and the wind will carry it to people who will read it and learn the truth long after its poor author is dead" (1:179).

19. Sinyavsky mentions Swift a number of times in his fiction. In *Goodnight* he speaks about being carried away with *Gulliver's Travels* (*Sobranie sochinenii* 2:466).

20. In is under this article that Sinyavsky and Daniel were criminally charged. Although addressing the dissemination of anti-Soviet propaganda, this article was applied to works of art, thereby establishing evidence for crime on the basis of the content of fiction.

21. Focusing on the shift of pronouns from the third person to the first person, Nepomnyashchy explains the close encounter between Konstantin and the owner

of the wallet as an exchange of identities (*Abram Tertz and the Poetics of Crime* 77).

22. According to Raskol'nikov's theory, the ends justify the means. To murder a miserable, old pawnbroker and use her ill-gotten money to help the needy is justifiable.

23. Here Sinyavsky makes a playful reference to Marmeladov whom Raskol'nikov meets in chapter two of *Crime and Punishment*. What Marmeladov says about his wife, Konstantin says about his mother, including the close proximity of the tavern to her apartment (*v trekh shagakh otsyuda*). Later, Solomon Moiseevich explains that Konstantin, in fact, did not have a mother and that the whole story was made up to intensify his grief (1:119).

24. Like many of Sinyavsky's works, the story "You and I" lends itself to more than one interpretation. Lourie, Dalton, and Deming Brown claim that it resists interpretation (*Letters to the Future,* 132; "The Art of Andrei Sinyavsky," 334; *Andrei Siniavskii and Julii Daniel',* 71).

25. Sinyavsky, of course, discusses this operation and his relationship with Hélène Peltier in the fourth chapter of *Spokoinoi nochi* (*Goodnight!*), "In the Belly of the Whale."

26. Somewhat parallel is the brief contestation of the narrator, allegedly Sinyavsky, and Terts, identified as "Terts" in *Goodnight* (*Sobranie sochinenii* 2: 344–46). Mikhailov (*Begstvo iz retorty* 18) and Nepomhyashchy (*Abram Tertz and the Poetics of Crime* 83) identify the author-narrator of "You and I" as God. Edith Clowes sees "You and I" as the relationship between the author-narrator and his protagonist, Nikolai Vasilevich ("Kafka and Russian Experimental Fiction" 153).

27. In Larry Gelbart's Broadway musical, *City of Angels*, there are wonderful metafictional episodes. In fact the question of the existence of a character without an author and conversely an author without a character is captured in one of the hit songs, "You Are Nothing without Me."

28. These words of course echo the opening of "*Gololeditsa*," where the narrator speaks about throwing a letter sealed in a bottle into the sea with the hope that someone in the future will find it (*Sobranie sochinenii* 1:179). This same idea is echoed in *Spokoinoi nochi* (*Goodnight!*): "Perhaps history continues to develop because we without a twinge of conscience send dispatches from the gallows, salutatory sacrifices, deep, deep into the future" (*Sobranie sochinenii* 2:347).

29. Toward the end of *Lyubimov* Sinyavsky suggests that Serafima Petrovna also is embodied by several souls from the past. Lenya asks her about having affairs with a number of men, including Handel and Genghis Khan (*Sobranie sochinenii* 1:92–93). Several of my colleagues have indicated that Borges takes the migration of souls further, suggesting that we all may be emanations of one person.

30. An article in *Izvestiya* (12 January 2000: 7) warned of the danger of falling icicles in Moscow. In fact in 1999, fifteen people were struck by falling icicles in the Russian capital. Given this threat, fines were given to the owners of buildings

who allowed icicles to grow to dangerous proportions. Nets were placed below ice-accommodating roof lines, and 250 brigades were sent out to look for "icy killers" (*ledyanye ubiitsy*).

31. Dalton claims that the title of this story is Sinyavsky's rejoinder to Ehrenberg's novel *The Thaw* (*Andrei Siniavskii and Julii Daniel'* 73).

32. At the end of volume 1 of *Dead Souls* Gogol speaks of Russia's progress, using the following words: "other nations and governments yield the road to her" (*I dyut ei dorogu drugie narody i gosudarstva*) (*Izbrannye proizvedenia* 360).

33. In his final plea to the court, Sinyavsky gives many examples of how the prosecution "blackens character" by conflating the words of a character with the words of the author (Ginzburg 301–6).

Chapter Eight

Beauty and the Beast: An Allegory of Self and Other

In the Russian national character Sinyavsky finds a fierce patriotism and a mistrust of all foreigners. He claims:

> The concepts of "one's own" and "other," of "ours" and "not ours," are deeply embedded in the Russian psyche. Probably, this arose from the patriarchal-tribal past, which enforced a conception of human relations dominated by patterns of kinship. ("Russian Nationalism" 483)[1]

He argues that in Russian fairy tales there is a clear division of dramatis personae into "ours" and "not ours," the latter associated with darkness and evil (*d'yavol*, *chert*: devil), Teuton (*nemets*: mute), and Mongol (Tatar: from Tartarus or Hades).[2] He maintains that xenophobia among Russians is also bound up with their feelings of impoverishment and inferiority and, therefore, envy (484). Fanned by the revolution and Sovietization, the hunt for class enemies put searchlights upon cultural, economic, religious, and ethnic differences. According to Sinyavsky, "everyone was occupied with routing out, identifying and exterminating the class enemy, on whom had been placed the stigma of otherness" (485). To stand out in some way, he maintains, signaled not so much a class enemy as a national enemy such as "kulaks" (wealthy peasants) or "cosmopolitans" (Jews).

Sinyavsky witnessed a growing anathematization of the other, resulting in a ludicrous proscription of legal Marxists, vulgar Marxists, socialist revolutionaries, Trotskyites, Vlasovites, Tikhonites, the bourgeois intelligentsia, left-wing deviationists, right-wing deviationists, internal émigrés, idealists, parasites, and bystanders. He suggests the magnitude of this proscription when he speaks of an official "criminalization" of many segments of society (*Soviet Civilization* 184).[3] Breaking with the required political correctness of the day, Sinyavsky introduced the other into his fiction without any disclaimers. Moreover, he played against Soviet social, ethnic, and ideological stereotypes, presenting, as it turns out, a gallery of delightful thieves, Jews, artists, and intriguers. Sinyavsky is not the first author to embarrass the authorities with an allegory about outcasts and alleged misfits. This kind of allegory has been a well-used mirror for satirists.[4] In "*Pkhents*" especially, he constructs a very Swiftian account of otherness, born of displacement in time and place.[5] In fact in "*Pkhents*" Sinyavsky tells a tale of alienation that is offset by faith. In this chapter let us consider this extended metaphor about a prickly survivor who emerges following the Bolshevik Revolution.

On the surface "*Pkhents*" belongs to science fiction. To many readers it may seem like an archetypical story about a visitor from outer space.[6] A cactus-like creature from a distant planet crash-lands in the Soviet Union. His ship is destroyed; his fellow travelers perish. Only he survives.[7] In order to blend in with earthlings, he puts on a disguise: an anthropoid sac, a wig, India-rubber ears, false teeth, and a few straps to constrict his extra limbs into a hump upon his back.[8] After thirty-two uneasy years, he contracts an unlikely malady: dehydration. As a result, he grows weak, returns to the site of his crash-landing, and prepares to incinerate himself so that no one will have an opportunity to exhibit him in a laboratory or a zoo.[9] Without an interpretation of the word "*Pkhents*," the story ends here, or in speculation about fantastic elements, de-familiarization, a search for transcendence, or the plight of an artist or an intellectual.

But before suggesting how a synthetic word fits into the allegory of this story, it would be in order to provide a few details about the place that "*Pkhents*" occupies in Sinyavsky's writing as well as in his final statement to the court on February 12, 1966. Moreover, it would also be in order to point out that the creature in "*Pkhents*," a member of a long line of outsiders in Sinyavsky's fiction, is, according to Sinyavsky's testimony, very autobiographical. In his otherness and his echoes of Sinyavsky's life he resembles *Kroshka Tsores* (Little Jinx), the tragic protagonist of the 1980 novella published under the name of Terts. Of the nine works which Sinyavsky published abroad, only three were cited in the official indictment at his trial: *Chto takoe sotsialisticheskii realizm* (*What Is Socialist Realism*), *Sud idet* (*The Trial Begins*), and *Lyubimov* (*The Makepeace Experiment*). His *Fantasticheskie povesti* (*Fantastic Tales*), among which

"*Pkhents*" has been placed, did not play an important role in the proceedings. Since "*Pkhents*" did not appear in print until Sinyavsky's trial, it did not figure directly or indirectly in the charges brought against him under Section I, Article 70 of the Criminal Code of the RSFSR. Even when Elena Dokukina, one of the witnesses for the prosecution, admitted that she had read "*Pkhents*" in manuscript form, no questions were raised regarding its contents (Ginzburg 257).[10] At the conclusion of three days of examination and cross-examination, Sinyavsky suddenly referred to "*Pkhents*," citing, by memory, a passage regarding otherness that he considered on point: "Just think, if I am different from others, they immediately start to swear at me. Well, I am different" (Ginzburg 306).[11] It is surprising that Sinyavsky should cite this passage in this story, for it could have been sequestered as additional evidence for the prosecution. Although it is unusual for an author to explain himself in terms of his characters, it is more unusual for a Russian author, who is on trial for his intent, to provide additional corpus delicti and to suggest a link between himself and an obvious misfit. He could have quoted once again from his works on hand in the courtroom to draw attention to passages that did not support the case against him. Instead, in his final defense, he chose this one. He chose the angry words of an alien to explain his own identity, an identity that consists of being different.

This difference is the central theme of "*Pkhents*," a theme that is explored in much of Sinyavsky's fiction both before and after his imprisonment. It is embodied not simply in anomalous features, but in anomalous features that are fantastic, such as the clairvoyance of the protagonist of "*Gololeditsa*" ("Icy Conditions"), the metamorphosis of the tenants in "The Tenants" ("*Kvartiranty*"), the tricks of the conjurer-manipulator in "*V tsirke*" ("At the Circus"), or the hypnotic power of Lenia in *Liubimov* (*The Makepeace Experiment*). Such features set its bearer apart from others, causing suspicion, envy, and hostility. Although the alien in "*Pkhents*" is singularly different, he represents a model Sinyavskian outsider, possessing rather than lacking enabling capacities and appearing to others as a clear threat.

To examine the semantic field of names in "*Pkhents*" is to discover the first clues to an underlying discourse about difference involving the alien, the author, and Soviet society.[12] For example, the alias of the alien, Andrei Kazimirovich Sushinsky, is a rather bold counterpart to the name of Andrei Donatovich Sinyavsky, who, like the alien, has also adopted another name. What with Sinyavsky's half-Polish parentage, the alien's patronymic is suggestive enough. But when the alien makes a point about his half-Polish, half-Russian ancestry, there is no guesswork about autobiographical allusions.[13] The name of the director of central stationery supplies, Jakov Solomonovich Zak, also signals significance that lies outside the narrative. Although his surname sounds like an invention from Dr. Seuss, it serves as an anagram for "*zek*"—well-known slang for "prisoner" (*zaklyuchennyi*), in this case "a nice little Jew" (*simpatichnyi takoi evreichik*). If the non-Russian name of the hunchback, Leopold, is also taken into account, it becomes clear that Sinyavsky has chosen to amplify the meaning of difference in several ways through several characters.[14] In other words, the author, the alien, a hunchback, and a Jew are linked by semantic subtleties. By association they are alike. By implication they signal what difference may mean in a society built upon uniformity and conformity.

As the image of the alien is outlined by his relationship to Soviet society, the image of Soviet society is outlined by its relationship to the alien. It is, after all, not the tension between the alien and *Homo sapiens*, but the tension between the alien and *Homo sovieticus* that generates the dynamics of "*Pkhents.*" This tension is not only apparent in the alien's struggle with everyday Soviet life, but also in his overall perception of the history of Soviet life. While his observations about cleanliness, food, sex, and anatomy are humorous, his subtle references to the November Holiday, the lack of conveniences in the 1920s, misplaced youth, the Siberian frosts and, above all, the loss of sight in one eye in 1934, are very telling.[15] In fact it is more important how the alien views the past rather than how he lives in the present. To him the present is only about survival. His uneasy relationship with Soviet society is not a result of his immediate circumstances, but the result of the main event of the story, which, as in a Greek play, has taken place offstage in the past.

Without a doubt, the crash-landing of the alien in the Soviet Union is the main event of "*Pkhents*." It is also the core of Sinyavsky's allegory. The alien's description of this event is, therefore, a point of departure into this very core:

> But why here? Namely here? No one planned it. All the way from the other side. Things don't happen that way. We got lost. Back of the beyond. Seven and a half. We fell freely. Well what if it was an accident? The very same trajectory. A deviation from course and the winter time table. The first place we came to. A coincidence? As one pea is to another. (*Sobranie sochinenii* 1:239)

This account is so important that the alien repeats it, this time, in greater detail:

> We did not plan to fly into space, but simply to go, if I may express it crudely, to a resort. Then, on the way—there was an incident, well, let's say it was a meteorite to make it seem more intelligible—we lost buoyancy and fell into the unknown. For seven and a half months—only not your months, but ours—we continued to fall and by pure chance we ended up here. (*Sobranie sochinenii* 1:244)

What appears to be an explanation for the outcome of an accidental voyage into space is, at another level, an interpretation of the outcome of an event which took seven-and-a-half months: the approximate span of time between the February and the October revolution of 1917 (according to the Gregorian calendar, March 15 to November 7). While describing the course of his interplanetary flight, the alien is describing the course of the Russian revolution, complete with ideological innuendos. In his opinion this course was unintentional, accidental, pure chance, a deviation, a plunge into the unknown. What was planned as a trip "to a resort" (*na kurort*) resulted in a disaster.[16]

The alien's twice-told account is the centerpiece of the story's daring analogies, accented in a very telegraphic way. True to the allegorical mode, its "other" meaning is embedded, in this case, in hints, in clipped references to intent, time, space, direction, and mishap. While each account is similar in form and content, the second one contains a clarification of a seemingly unimportant allusion to "seven and a half" (*sem' s spolovinoi)*. Rather than "seven and a half," the second account refers to "seven and a half months" (*sem s polovinoi mesyatsev*), corresponding to the most crucial period of time in the course of the 1917 revolution and the most reckless period of time in the course of the alien's voyage.

It is not the revolution per se, but the loss of the ideals (mission) of the revolution that figures in the alien's displacement, a displacement so great that he refers to the agony of "a fish jerked out of water on a hook" (1:235). This loss accounts for his longing for *Pkhents*, the name for his past, his ideals, his home. According to the alien, *Pkhents* is "sacred" (*svyashchennyi*), a quality which is reserved for the highest ideals. It is the very quality that Sinyavsky attributes to the memory of the revolution in *On Socialist Realism*.[17] This sacred memory is all that remains from the alien's past, a past that has been severed during the unprecedented "voyage" to Soviet Russia. Even after thirty-two years, when the alien's recollections of the past have almost entirely faded, this particular memory lives on. In fact *Pkhents* becomes a code word that the alien uses to test the identity of the hunchback, who, he suspects, is a fellow creature, also hiding extra limbs under his shirt. Above all, *Pkhents* becomes the last reference, the final amen, in the alien's prayer just before his death:

> *O, Rodina! Pkhents! Gogry Tuzheroskip!* I am coming home to you. *Gogry! Gogry! Tuzheroskip! Tuzheroskip! Gutenabend! Tuzheroskip! Bu-bu-bu! Miau-miau! Pkhents!* (*Sobranie sochinenii* 1:250)

Although the alien's uncamouflaged appearance marks him as extra-terrestrial creature, his beliefs mark him as a Christian, indeed, an early Christian. Consider what is suggested by his remark about burying his fellow travelers "in the prescribed way" (*Pokhoronili ix kak polozheno*) or what is spelled out by his many references to suffering, martyrdom, fish, water, and life after death. In fact, owing to this emphasis upon Christian symbols, the alien bears the signs of a Christ-figure, a figure in harmony with the original intent of Communism, that is, the Messianic mission of the revolution. When he speaks of his suffering with reference to Christ, Jan Hus, and Stenka Razin, the link between Christianity, martyrdom, and revolution cannot be disputed. The alien's Christlike gentleness, single-mindedness and ultimate self-sacrifice are fitting to his role as "the only model of that lost harmonious beauty" (*edinstvennyi obrazchik toi utrachennoi garmonicheskoi krasoty*), which is *Pkhents*. In spite of the alien's lofty calling as well as his potential superiority, he lives as "a humble bookkeeper" (*tikhaya professiya shchetovoda*).[18] As in the life of Christ, it is after thirty-two years on earth that he undergoes a trying period, a period that tests his faith in all that *Pkhents* signifies. Most important, throughout his life he resists what he calls "the influence of an alien milieu" (*vliyanie chuzherodnoi sredy*). Realizing that if the truth were discovered about himself and *Pkhents* he would face only misunderstanding, persecution, or grotesque sensationalism, he vows to keep himself and *Pkhents* free from dishonor at all costs:

> And in those two hours, while I was calling for help, I vowed that if I lived I would keep my secret to the end and not let this last lump of my home land, this beautiful body, fall into the hands of my enemies for them to rend and mock. (*Sobranie sochinenii* 1:248)

Christian symbolism is especially apparent in the alien's water ritual, a ritual that recurs throughout the story. At one level, water is a source of nourishment appropriate to the alien's plantlike nature. At another level, it is an *elixir vitae* in a sacramental act not unlike baptism. As in baptism this water is not ingested into the body, but poured over the body. It appears that under ideal conditions the alien actually immerses himself in true early Christian fashion. It turns out that because of the nature of shared apartment facilities, it is not easy for the alien to have access to water, especially in the privacy of his room. Through circumstances beyond his control, he is deprived of a washtub—his sacramental vessel. Without a sufficient quantity of water, he becomes weak. In fact he becomes seriously ill. In agony he calls to Veronika (true image), the only member of Soviet society who blindly accepts him.[19] In a very desperate moment he pleads for water, calling out in scriptural fashion: "Water! Water for Christ's sake!" (*Vody! Khrista-radi vody!*) When he later explains that this extended deprivation of water "not only wrecked his body, but also crippled his soul" (*ne tol'ko slomila telo, no iskalechila dushu*), he is clearly pointing to the literal and symbolic meaning of nourishment.

In "*Pkhents*" Sinyavsky continues an age-old allegorical tradition, encoding issues and events from Russian history into a story about a stranger in a strange land. In comparison to his other short stories, "*Pkhents*" has an Aesopian measure of wit and humor not unlike that of *Lyubimov*. It stands alone, however, in its expression of reverence for the ideals of the Russian revolution. In fact, this kind of expression corroborates our sense of its place in time next to *What Is Socialist Realism*. Not only was it written at approximately the same time as *What Is Socialist Realism*, but it also shares the same concern for a loss of direction. As the narrator in *What Is Socialist Realism* speaks about "not knowing which direction to take" (*My ne znaem kuda idti),* the alien in "*Pkhents*" speaks about "not knowing in which direction to yearn" (*i v kakom napravlenie mne nado grustit' tozhe neizvestno*). In facing a disturbing loss, both grapple with preserving a faith from the past.

We should not overlook that in "*Pkhents*" Sinyavsky refers to Swift's *Gulliver's Travels* and Defoe's *Robinson Crusoe*, providing a well-known context for fantastic voyages and shipwrecked survivors. In *Golos iz khora* (*Voice from the Chorus*) he pauses to discuss the essence of both of these works, explaining their points of convergence and departure.[20] He claims that both authors use an entirely different frame of reference to define the self, Defoe, relying on a confined and stable perspective, Swift, relying on an unstable and unconventional perspective. While Defoe's model exemplifies the conventionalization of what is strange, Swift's model exemplifies the estrangement of what is conventional. There is no doubt that Defoe, showing the transformational capacity of man, is more pertinent to

Sinyavsky's day-to-day struggle in prison. Swift, on the other hand, although mired in relativity, celebrates the transformational capacity of art, the very capacity that Sinyavsky wires into his "exaggerated prose" (*utrirovannaya proza*). It turns out that in "*Pkhents*" he follows a Swiftian satirical path, focusing on contact with the other, relying on an otherworldly point of view to illuminate this world. In fact, like Swift, he puts together an intricate allegory in the very same way, commenting in the same way about the manners of the day.

Estrangement in time and place is a very common platform for fiction, especially fiction with more than one level of discourse. This kind of estrangement sets the stage for another devastating satire of Soviet society: Mayakovsky's *Klop* (*The Bedbug*).[21] In this play, Prisypkin, frozen solid during a fire in the winter of 1928 when firemen inadvertently drown him in a basement, is medically resurrected. After fifty years, he wakes up to a society that has greatly changed, especially in its ideological perceptions. Prisypkin, like the creature in "*Pkhents*," is completely out of place. To everyone in the year 1978 he is no longer worker and party member, but, owing to his taste for wine, women, and song, a different species: *bourgeoisius vulgaris*. Moreover, he draws attention to almost forgotten issues, raising disturbing questions. Like the creature in "*Pkhents*," Prisypkin longs for a lost world.[22] Zoya Berezkina, a factory worker, tells Prisypkin that no one could be found to answer his questions. Only a few old women vaguely recalled what he was talking about (Mayakovsky 264). While the creature in "*Pkhents*" turns to the hunchback to explain what happened, to account for his difference, to accept him, Prisypkin turns to visitors in front of his cage. His plea clearly addresses the issue of belonging, of self and other:

> Citizens! Brothers! My own people! Darlings! How did you get here? So many of you! When were you unfrozen? Why am I alone in the cage? Darlings, friends, have pity on me! Why am I suffering? Citizens! (Mayakovsky 273)

Different and therefore dangerous, Prisypkin is locked up and put on display in a zoo. The creature in "*Pkhents*" escaped this fate only by incinerating himself.

NOTES

1. When Nadezhda Krupskaya met Peter Struve in St. Petersburg in 1895, she spoke of him as "not one of ours" (Tompkins 216).

2. Sinyavsky's etymology notwithstanding, "Tatarus" is Greek and occurs in East Slavic texts before the appearance of the Mongols or the Tatars.

3. Sinyavsky argues that Stalin turned metaphors such as "traitors to the working class," "lackeys of imperialism," "hirelings of capital," "ideological saboteurs," "renegades," "double-dealers," and "literary Vlasovites" into reality ("The Literary Process in Russia" 93).

4. Allegory, which is an important means to satire in a repressive society, has been defined many times. According to Empson in *The Structure of Complex Words*, "Part of the function of allegory is to make you feel that two levels of being correspond to each other in detail and indeed that there is some underlying reality, something in the nature of things which make this happen. . . . But the effect of allegory is to keep the two levels of being very distinct in your mind though they interpenetrate each other in so many details" (346–47). In *Allegory: The Theory of Symbolic Mode*, Fletcher claims that in the simplest terms allegory says one thing and means another; that it is a fundamental process of encoding; that it is based on a parallel between two levels of being that correspond to each other, one supposed by the reader, the other literally presented in the tale (2, 3, 113). What we now refer to as "double-voicedness" (*dvugolosnost'*), is, in fact, a feature of allegory.

It is possible to classify a number of Sinyavsky's works as allegories, especially *The Trial Begins*, *The Makepeace Experiment*, *Kroshka Tsores,* and "*Pkhents*." Through this mode, he revisits highly charged moments in Russian history, while telling a story at once funny and disturbing.

5. "*Pkhents*" first appeared in a Polish translation in the January–February issue of *Kultura*, no. 219 (1966): 67–84. It then appeared in an English translation in the April issue of *Encounter* 26 (1966): 3–13. In the two-volume edition, *Abram Terts*, *Sobranie sochinenii v dvukh tomakh*, published in Moscow in 1992, this short story is dated 1957. In an interview in 1989 Sinyavsky dated it 1956 ("*O sebe*" 242). According to Nepomnyashchy, Sinyavsky delayed the publication of "*Pkhents*" because he was afraid that Sergei Khmelnitskii, who was present when the manuscript was read, would reveal the identity of Terts to the authorities (*Abram Tertz and the Poetics of Crime* 337). When asked about which of his works he valued the most, he named "*Pkhents*" first ("*O sebe*" 242). For further discussion of "*Pkhents*" see Andrew Field, "Prisoner in Fantasy," 17–18; Margaret Dalton, *Andrei Siniavskii and Julii Daniel',* 93–98; Richard Lourie, *Letters to the Future*, 151–54; Deming Brown, "The Art of Andrei Sinyavsky," in *Soviet Russian Literature since Stalin,* 331–51; Edward J. Brown, "Exodus into *Samizdat* and *Tamizdat,*" in *Russian Literature since the Revolution,* 238–50; Michel Aucouturier, "Writer and the Text in the Works of Abram Terc," in *Fiction and Drama in Eastern and Southeastern Europe,* 1–10, passim; Andrew Durkin, "Narrator, Metaphor, and Theme in Sinjavskij's *Fantastic Tales,*" 134–35; Nepomnyashchy, *Abram Tertz and the Poetics of Crime,* 64–75.

6. Sinyavsky was well acquainted with science fiction, developing an interest in H. G. Wells at a very early age. He, of course, provides evidence of his theoretical knowledge of this genre in his article "*Sovremennyi nauchno-fantasticheskii roman*." In an interview (Nepomnyashchy, "Interview with Andrei Sinyavsky" 14), Sinyavsky points out that in "*Pkhents*" he revises both the image of a monster and the image of a hero from outer space, creating instead a creature in an ordinary disguise living in a communal apartment. For a general discussion of the implications of the alien, see Gary K. Wolf's *The Known and the Unknown: The Iconography of Science Fiction,* 102–8, and Hans Jonas, *The Gnostic Religion: The Message of the Alien God and the Beginning of Christianity,* 49–56.

7. Sinyavsky's fiction is, in many respects, about survivors. In the epilogue to *Gololeditsa* ("Icy Conditions"), the narrator immediately establishes the tone of a survivor by comparing himself to someone who has become shipwrecked, telling of his distress (*Sobranie sochinenii* 1:179).

8. In Sinyavsky's fiction the use of disguise is ubiquitous owing to the presence of so many characters with something to hide, including, of course, undercover agents. The extent of people wearing disguises is suggested in "You and I," when the narrator exclaims: "Moscow is swarming with people fit for the stage" (*Sobranie sochinenii* 1:136). It could be argued that the use of a disguise has the same implications as the use of a pseudonym, especially in this allegory.

9. The fears of the creature in "*Pkhents*" regarding medical intervention and public display in a zoo are borne out by what happened to Ivan Prisypkin in Mayakovsky's *Klop* (*The Bedbug*).

10. It was Dokukina who watched over and subsequently burned several of Sinyavsky's manuscripts.

11. Sinyavsky cites these very words once again in "*Chtenie v serdtsakh*," 208.

12. In the manner of Gogol, Sinyavsky uses names to isolate a particular trait, e.g., Tikhomirov (quiet world), Krovatkina (bed), Kostriskaia (bone of leg of beef), Globov (globe or world), Galkin (jackdaw), Proferansov (Fr., to express), Liubimov (beloved). As caricaturist and taxonomist he also uses national, cultural, and ethnic name tags not so much to characterize, but to caricaturize as in Anchutker, Sofia Frantsvan Vinter, Genrikh Ivanovich Grabe, Tatyana Krechet, Straustin, Moisei Yekhelevich, Solomon Moiseevich, Samson Samsonovich, and Rabinovich. Fletcher argues that isolation and reduction of particular traits exaggerates and transforms characters into abstractions through which allegory is possible (*Allegory: The Theory of a Symbolic Mode,* 33–34).

13. Nepomnyashchy underscores the autobiographical links between Sinyavsky and Tsores in *Kroshka Tsores* (*Abram Tertz and the Poetics of Crime,* 248–49).

14. The hunchback draws attention to his name as well as to his appearance. When he identifies himself he says, "As funny as it may seem, my name is Leopold Sergeich. And as you can see I am also a bit of a hunchback" (*Sobranie sochinenii* 2:241). Leopold means "champion of the people." According to leg-

end, it was good luck to touch a hunchback. According to the symbolic logic of dreams, a hunchback is a symbol for happiness.

15. All of these references are either spatially or temporally telling. It is not fortuitous that the alien lost sight in one eye in the year of the first congress of Soviet writers and the assassination of Kirov. Sinyavsky claims that a great patriotic upsurge began in 1934. In his opinion:

> Collectivization was approaching completion in that year, i.e., the dispossession of the peasant landowners and the enserfment of the countryside. The peasantry was deprived of its land and its native way of life. In exchange for this permanently lost ground, there began a cynical play on the national-patriotic feelings of the peasantry, who were acclaimed the greatest, strongest, most fortunate people in the world. ("Russian Nationalism" 478)

16. The rest-and-recreation euphemism "going to a resort" (*ekhali na kurort*) is echoed in *Lyubimov* when a proposed counterrevolution is described as "strolling about in the fresh air" (*progulki po svezhemu vozdukhu*, *Sobranie sochinenii* 1: 45). Since "*Pkhents*" and *Lyubimov* focus indirectly upon the events and issues of the 1917 revolution, they share a great deal. Of particular interest are *Lyubimov*'s references to the advance of the revolution into space, putting "*Pkhents*" in very related territory. In *Lyubimov* the narrator declares: "I was firmly convinced that very soon we would invade the cosmos" (*Sobranie sochinenii* 1:28). The footnote to this declaration on the bottom of the page reads: "History has since proved me right!"

17. *Fantasticheskii mir* 436. It should be recalled that prior to his break with Soviet society, Sinyavsky, like his father, was devoted to the ideals of the revolution.

18. Sinyavsky refers to the alien's profession as a bookkeeper three times. In a very broad sense a "bookkeeper" not only calculates, but also keeps records of human transactions. He is, in this regard, a historian. In *Lyubimov*, which is so focused upon record keeping, Sinyavsky notes that Leonid Tikhomirov is "disguised as a humble bookkeeper" (*pod vidom prostogo uchetchika)* (*Sobranie sochinenii* 1: 910).

19. According to legend, the image of the face of Christ was impressed upon Saint Veronica's handkerchief. Hence, Veronica means true image of Christ. In "*Pkhents*" only Veronika captures the alien's true essence. Only she sees his beauty and dignity. For her this "monster" becomes "man, human, humanity."

20. According to Nepomnyashchy, Sinyavsky puts his prison experience on the same level with the voyages of Gulliver and the desert island of Robinson Crusoe (*Abram Tertz and the Poetics of Crime* 179). For Sinyavsky's discussion of Swift and Defoe, see *Golos iz khora* (*Voice from the Chorus, Sobranie sochinenii* 1:451–54). In "*Grafomany*" ("Graphomaniacs") Straustin is at first disturbed by his son's stories about Lilliputians (*Sobranie sochinenii* 1:162–63). But he has a change of heart. At the end of the story he encourages his son to compose such "fairy tales" (*skazki*) (*Sobranie sochinenii* 1:179).

21. Not only do "*Pkhents*" and *The Bedbug* (1928) share a similar kind of estrangement and a common satirical thread, but Mayakovsky and Sinyavsky admit to creating reflections of their own circumstances. Mayakovsky went so far as to coach the actor who played Prisypkin to mimic very "Mayakovskian" mannerisms. Sinyavsky, on the other hand, confessed to the court at his trial that he and the creature in "*Pkhents*" shared the same identity of "otherness." *The Bedbug*, like Mayakovsky's *Bathhouse* (*Banya*), is a satire on the follies of Soviet society. Both plays were rarely performed, appearing on stage with great acclaim only in the mid-1950s, that is, after Stalin's death.

22. In the foreword to her translation of *Lyubimov* (*The Makepeace Experiment*), Manya Harari compares the reaction of Prisypkin in *Klop* (*The Bedbug*) to *Lyubimov*'s narrator, Savely Kuzmich, who also rejects the "advantages" of a utopia (11–12).

Chapter Nine

Bringing Terts to Paris: New Literary Confrontations

Sinyavsky's preference for writing that violates a prohibition or a taboo signals not just satire, but the provocative direction of satire.[1] He proceeds boldly in this direction not only in his fiction, but also in his criticism. Taking this direction unreservedly, Sinyavsky develops a great measure of playfulness as well as bluntness, which reaches a new level in what he calls "fantastic literary criticism." In an unprecedented way he combines creative writing and analysis, allowing *épatage* to prevail over prudence very much like Vasily Rozanov.[2] It is in Paris that he raises the stakes of this kind of criticism, moving back and forth between literary issues and social issues, challenging widely held opinions among Russians and Russian émigrés. Clearly, Sinyavsky engages in direct satire; he pounces. But he also prods, drawing attention to foolish certainties through a calculated web of exaggeration, outrageous analogies, abruptness, startling assumptions, and tangled expressions. Such is Sinyavsky's calculated web. According to P. K. Elkin, this kind of web taunts and perturbs the reader, entangling his or her sense about what is acceptable and unacceptable, forcing him or her to question convenient beliefs (*The Augustan Defense of Satire* 201). Bearing Sinyavsky's preprison literary instigations in mind, let us examine how he launches a new level of provocation in his writing during and after his prison sentence, especially as he turns his attention from the Soviet literary canon to literary canons in general, not to mention literary politics.

It should be remembered that Sinyavsky made his pseudonymous literary debut with *Chto takoe sotsilalisticheskii realizm* (*What Is Socialist Realism*), one of the most provocative literary assessments in Russian literature. Published under the name of Abram Terts, it created an immediate sensation in the West and outrage in Moscow. No one would have suspected that its author was Andrei Sinyavsky, a mild-mannered scholar.[3] But this same mild-mannered scholar, who also wrote a succession of underground stories, developed a reputation in Moscow literary journals as an extremely witty and thorny critic. From his acerbic reviews in *Novyi mir* (*The New World*), it is clear that he not only candidly assessed, but also ridiculed mediocre writers and ready-made ideas about art. In fact, he spoke out in the same kind of voice as in his fiction. As I said in chapter 5, Sinyavsky not only participated in, but also initiated very heated polemics, taking issue with numerous writers and critics, including A. Sofronov, V. Dolmatovsky, I. Shevtsov, E. Evtushenko, V. Bushin, D. Starikov, S. Smirnov, V. Fedorov, V. Solov'ev, as well as the editorial board of *Oktyabr'*. It is not possible to calculate how many literati and pseudo-literati were waiting for an opportunity to pounce on Sinyavsky, to make him pay for his sharp wit and his disparagement of the official positions of the day.[4]

While Sinyavsky's prison sentence brought an end to his first period as a writer, it did not bring an end to his writing or his irreverence. In fact he survived more than five years of incarceration namely through writing. Given the strict regime of prison censorship, it was not possible for him to continue his double-voiced tales, his unmasking, and his pointed humor. It goes without saying that in prison he was not permitted to write about desperate circumstances, depravation, hard labor, or brutality. Yet it turns out that he incorporated the shared experiences of prisoners, samples of their boiled-down views of life, as well as their unvarnished manner of speaking into a text called *Golos iz khora* (*Voice from the Chorus*).[5] Single-minded as ever, Sinyavsky obtained paper, pencils, and ballpoint pens, not to mention books from fellow prisoners and the prison library.[6] He even managed to hide hand-copied pages of the Book of Revelations in the calf of his boot (Jan Kott 26). Amazingly, he inscribed passages for two-and-a-half books into letters to his wife, Mariya Vasilevna: *Golos iz khora* (*Voice from the Chorus*), *Progulki s Pushkinym* (*Strolls with Pushkin*) and *V teni Gogolya* (*In the Shadow of Gogol*).[7] Right after his release from prison, he put together *Golos iz khora* from these passages, making few changes (Nepomnyashchy, "Interview" 12). Of course, he had ample opportunity between the time of his release in 1971 and the publication of *Golos iz khora* in 1973 to revise his manuscript, to accommodate more structure or perhaps the kind of fantasy that had characterized his previous works.[8] Sinyavsky, it turns out, chose to write in the flamboyant and rambling manner of Rozanov, a manner that he also attributed to Pushkin about whom he was writing at this same period of time. Moreover, it is as if he set out to minimize the darkness of his prison situation not unlike Silvio Pellico, whose book, *Ob obiazannostiakh cheloveka (On the Obligations of Man)*, Pushkin reviewed in 1836. In his *Progulki* Sinyavsky, in fact, underscores Pushkin's comments about Pellico, who, after ten years in prison, published notes, which, against all expectations, were devoid of complaints and bitterness (*Progulki* 54).[9]

Golos is also against expectations. It is an anti–prison camp memoir. What could be further from prison than lively decentered discourse in a vague barracks setting?[10] It has nothing in common with Dostoevsky's *Notes from the House of the Dead*, Koestler's *Darkness at Noon,* or Solzhenitsyn's *One Day in the Life of Ivan Denisovich*.[11] In fact in *Golos*, prison for Sinyavsky is not an endpoint, but a point of departure for other themes. There is a centripetal rather than a centrifugal movement in this work, pulling apart from the center, pulling apart large "literary" structures, fragmenting units of disquisition, as well as a unified self. In so many ways Sinyavsky demonstrates the antithesis of prison through his omission of its trappings, through his free flow of ideas in a boundless space. Sinyavsky's imagination actually soars, establishing a great distance between self and prison, as well as the conventions of prison camp literature. It is in this distance that the reader becomes lost, finding neither a cogent representation of prison experience or, for that matter, the author.[12] What irony there is in *Progulki* when Sinyavsky claims that Pushkin "teased" (*draznil*) rather than developed or carried on the genre of the narrative poem, for it is this very teasing that Sinyavsky puts into the genre of prison camp literature (68). He plays his fragmented meditations, anecdotes, and unvarnished quotations from fellow prisoners against the high seriousness of this genre.[13]

It must be acknowledged that art "as strolling" (*progulki*), which Sinyavsky sees as a dominant feature in Pushkin's work, is exemplified in his own work, especially in *Golos* (*Progulki* 177). Sinyavsky, like Pushkin, strolls among topics from art to literature to history, philosophy, religion, sex, dreams, and folklore. He flits from one thing to another with great anecdotal acumen. But what gives *Golos* additional lightness, additional freedom from structural moorings, is a chorus of polyphonic voices that speaks by and large in aphorisms, a form of expression that Sinyavsky champions in his study of Rozanov. According to this study, these philosophical kernels free an author from the need of expressing ideas gradually and sequentially in conjunction with some kind of system or doctrine

(*"Opavshie list'ya" V. V. Rozanova* 187). Through aphorisms, anecdotes, and meditations Sinyavsky leads the reader far from the locus of the archipelago that Solzhenitsyn envisioned. In this sequel to his *"Mysli vrasplokh"* (*"Thoughts Unaware"*), Sinyavsky once again rejects the idea of building a literary edifice, telling the reader in the end that there is no need for character or plot (*Golos* 327). Instead, he leaves us a construction site with a warehouse of cluttered impressions and observations. At this site, he is content with rummaging around in raw materials, unpackaging a few ideas, and thumbing his nose at readers who only come to look through the prison bars.

In *Golos* Sinyavsky makes a statement of defiance. He demonstrates, above all, that while he was deprived of freedom, his writing and his spirit were absolutely free. In other words, the authorities failed to crush him. Moreover, they failed to "rehabilitate" his expression. Once again Sinyavsky brings together lofty and low language, letting crude references ambush the reader and unexpected analogies shock delicate sensibilities. In fact, the grating of prison speech against topics such as survival, sex, and death gives *Golos* a special ballast. Fabricating a scene in which stool pigeons roast Pushkin on a funeral pyre, Sinyavsky pretends to quote the defiant poet: "Hey, suckers! Tell people I died a thief! (*Golos* 159)[14] Clearly, he provides no quarter to what polite society inflates beyond its value. Using surprise rather than decorum, he urges us to chirp like Chekhov or to buy a nice pair of shoes the way Shakespeare's King Lear did. But most provocative is Sinyavsky's shared experience with prisoners, a positive experience, setting *Golos* apart from the usual prison camp memoirs.[15] Equally provocative is his praise of his circumstances, his exhilaration at finding a special sanctuary for writing. And how unsettling for authorities to realize that in prison, where they sentenced him for what he had written, he discovers that writing is the basis of his existence.

While Sinyavsky's *Golos* may have been offensive to many with preconceived notions about prison camp memoirs, his *Progulki s Pushkinym* (*Strolls with Pushkin*) clearly infuriated readers who had preconceived notions about Pushkin. The path of this fury, which Katharine Nepomnyashchy maps out in the spring issue of *Formations* in 1991, is incredible in its reach and its duration. Not only did *Progulki* create a scandal among émigré critics in 1975, but it also created a scandal in Moscow in 1990 when *Oktyabr'* (*October*) published excerpts from it. In fact, because of the publication of these excerpts, the journal's editor was removed.[16] How was it possible for Sinyavsky to provoke Russians and Russian émigrés with a study of Pushkin that in fact was filled with praise? In an age of postmodern revisions of long-standing notions about literature, Sinyavsky's study should not have caused such outrage. At the sixth meeting of the administrative level of the Russian Writers' Union on the 13th and 14th of November of 1989, *Progulki* was attacked again and again.[17] The uproar in Moscow followed in the wake of what was a growing reaction to Sinyavsky's writing, both old and new, some of which was appearing in Russian journals in Moscow for the first time. *Progulki* was like a bolt out of the blue, a flash point, and, above all, an easy target for critics. What could have been more noble for them than a defense of the shrine of Russia's great poet and, in the process, a tirade against "blasphemy?"

Sinyavsky was well aware of the *épatage* that he built into his study, calling Pushkin lazy (*lentyai*), capricious (*vetrenik*), a womanizer (*povesa*), a parasite (*tuneyadets*), a renegade (*otshchepenets*), a clod (*zdorovyi lob*), a vampire (*vurgalak*), a goldbricker (*shtafirka*), and a deadbeat (*shpak*). He even suggests that Pushkin had a lot in common with Gogol's Khlestakov, a rogue who thrived on duplicity (*Sobranie sochinenii* 2:99). With such exaggerated characterizations, his study was bound to cause a stir. But he did not have any intention of writing a proper scholarly analysis tied to monuments and monument makers. Most important, in this study Sinyavsky reintroduces his bête noire, that is, purposefulness, and how its absence in Pushkin's writing is the basis of genuine art. Having underscored the problems of purposefulness in Soviet ideology as well as Soviet literary policy in *Chto takoe sotsialisticheskii realizm*, sixteen years later in *Progulki* he restates his thesis in the context of the literature of Pushkin and its monumentalization. This time he does not put forward a study of coercive literary policies, but a contentious essay that appears to be "a slap in the face of public taste," especially the public taste regarding Pushkin.[18]

Even while he was writing *Progulki* in prison, he anticipated that the subject of this poet would take the prison authorities by surprise. On one of my visits to Sinyavsky, he laughed for the longest time, recalling how shocked the guards were when they discovered that he was writing about Pushkin. According to Sinyavsky, they expected him to be writing something subversive, something in violation of the guidelines for prison camp correspondence. To their amazement he was not breaking the law. On the other hand, he did break ranks with critics who do not tolerate a departure from decorum when speaking about Pushkin. Actually Sinyavsky dropped this decorum regarding Pushkin in his early fiction, specifically in *"Gololeditsa"* ("Icy Conditions"), *Lyubimov* (*The Makepeace Experiment*) and *Golos iz khora* (*Voice from the Chorus*), where he drags fragments of the poet's biography into fantasies of the most irreverent sort.

There would have been more of an uproar over *Progulki* had critics taken umbrage not only at irreverence, but also at the recontextualization of Sinyavsky's literary positions. Using Pushkin as the most defensible artistic exhibit, Sinyavsky argues, once again, against realism, purposefulness, and genre restraints. This argument, which overarches much of Sinyavsky's literary criticism, gives *Progulki* a rather barbed addressivity and an intertextual link with his past polemics. Moreover, Sinyavsky's view of the composite or fragmented self, which he fleshes out in "*Gololeditsa*," is boldly echoed here. Rather than celebrating a unified Pushkin, Sinyavsky celebrates Pushkin's contradictions (giant/nonentity; fullness/emptiness), his otherness (e.g., tsar, Apollo, Hannibal, poet, and rake), and his imposture both in art and life. In view of this celebration alone, which involves several leaps of the imagination, more than one reader has given up reading Sinyavsky's study beyond the first few pages. In fact, those who have read Sinyavsky's *Progulki* as an attack on Pushkin reflect not only contemptuousness for Sinyavsky's positions, but also quotable examples of a careless reading.

What makes Sinyavsky's *Progulki* so provocative is that it revises the terms of Pushkin's genius and at the same time parades itself as a red herring in the "scholarly" industry. Filled with flamboyance, actually going so far as to flesh out a context for Pushkin's foot fetish, it is meant to disturb, to get a rise out of the reader, as Dora Shturman suggests (*Novoe russkoe slovo* 21). In many respects, *Progulki* is a tour de force, especially in that its idiosyncratic assumptions about art provide the basis for an assessment of Pushkin who, as Sinyavsky knows, represents an "absolute" (*absolyutnyi kriterii*) for Russians ("*Ne bol'she chem pisatel'*" 32). Considering this absolute, especially in the light of entirely new criteria for Pushkin scholarship, Sinyavsky was guaranteed more of an audience than if he had written another art-under-siege exposé. But what is crucial here is that Sinyavsky leads this audience not only to a major revision, but also to a construction of the scandal-making side of Pushkin. Claiming, for example, that *Evgenii Onegin* "was calculated to shock the public" (*Sobranie sochinenii* 1:386), Sinyavsky suggests Pushkin's intent, which, as readers of Sinyavsky know, is, arguably, no different from his own, beginning with *Chto takoe sotsilalisticheskii realizm*.

Sinyavsky thought that his study of Gogol, *V teni Gogolya*, would also evoke sharp disagreement and annoyance, as he explained in an interview shortly after it was published ("*Ne bol'she chem Pisatel'*" 32).[19] Anticipating out-and-out rejection of his interpretation of Chichikov, he pauses in chapter 4 of *V teni* to declare:

> They will say that there is not a grain of truth here, that everything is only the result of fantasy, idle thoughts, feeblemindedness, mixed-up yarns from the village that only mock Gogol, who himself suspected nothing of the sort from Chichikov and who would be amazed if readers took a narrative of anecdotes literally. (*Sobranie sochinenii* 2:255)

True to iconoclastic form, Sinyavsky turns away from previous approaches to Gogol, including claims about realism and romanticism, as well as theories about a mania regarding Gogol's "Nose."[20] In fact, in a footnote, Sinyavsky takes Victor Vladimirovich Vinogradov to task for his theory regarding Gogol's nose (viz., "noseology") as well as his testimony regarding literary style for the KGB, which was used as "evidence" at his trial in February of 1966 (*Sobranie sochinenii* 2:317).[21]

Unlike *Progulki*, Sinyavsky's study of Gogol makes great demands on the reader. It is daunting in its mass, its convoluted passages, and its turbulent flow of ideas. While Sinyavsky makes no scholarly claims about his study, he does say that it is an application of "fantastic realism" to literary criticism. For the reader this application means constant exaggeration as well as drastic repositioning of literary evidence—or what passes for it. It means that the reader is taken for a ride through rearranged territories, such as the chronologically backward construction of this study, which moves from Gogol's death rather than his birth. But by starting with Gogol's death Sinyavsky adds a measure of drama to his study, incorporating Gogol's fears of being buried alive and rumors that his fears were justified. Gogol's death, moreover, provides Sinyavsky with a central metaphor so large that he could easily move in and out of literature, philosophy, anthropology, and folklore. With such a free hand Sinyavsky could put Gogol right where he wanted him—not between Pushkin and Dostoevsky, but between heaven and hell, as well as magic and madness.

What disturbs Sinyavsky and gives his study a seething side is *Vybrannye mesta iz perepiski s druz'yami* (*Selected Passages from Correspondence with Friends*), which immediately followed Gogol's attempts to write volume 2 of *Dead Souls*.[22] Sinyavsky sees it as a retreat from literature caused by Gogol's wish to be "of use" (*po'lza*) to Russia. For Sinyavsky the ultimate stages of this retreat lie in Gogol's mission to save Russia through his writing. Those who have read Sinyavsky's *On Socialist Realism* or his objections to Solzhenitsyn's writing immediately understand that Gogol's artistic purposefulness or any artistic purposefulness is unacceptable. Without mincing words, Sinyavsky says:

> Gogol killed literature with his total approach, creating an ancient epos as a supplement to trash. And perhaps therefore with the completion of the first volume of this narrative poem in front of him, he raised the question about the aim and purpose of all of his writing, switching attention from his exhaustive creative practice to moral problems of art and life. (*Sobranie sochinenii* 2:278)[23]

By killing literature, Gogol himself, according to Sinyavsky, dies. Relating this death to Gogol's text, Sinyavsky explains:

> When the road trembled and a pedestrian standing nearby shrieked in fear, I understood that Gogol's soul had departed: he died at the end of the first volume of *Dead Souls*. (*Sobranie sochinenii* 2:110)

In no other work of literary criticism does Sinyavsky speak with such vehemence, exhibition, and brashness. He is, after all, unveiling something extraordinary: a portrait of Gogol and, allegedly, a spiritual autobiography (TLS, May 23, 1975, 560). While it is not easy to fetter out one from the other, it is possible to sense that Sinyavsky's narrative weaves in and out of erudition and art, inspiration and inference. Combining literary criticism and imaginative writing, *V teni* has the hybridized quality to which Sinyavsky aspired from *Thoughts Unaware* to *Goodnight!* Owing to this quality, the reader constantly faces the interchangeability of earnest arguments, preposterous evidence, and fanciful displays of language linkage. In this study the reader cannot escape "exaggerated prose" (*utrirovannaya proza*)—both Gogol's and Sinyavsky's, which results in arresting images and playful departures at every turn. Sinyavsky clearly exasperates scholars such as P. Pletnev, who goes on at length about Tertsian distortions, false etymologies, and coarseness ("*O zlom suemudrii knigi Abram Tertsa*" 73, 74, 76, 78, 79). Taking a position within the shadow of Gogol, Sinyavsky becomes a part of it. In this shadow he is an extension of Gogol, overwhelming the reader with details about customs and rituals, architecture, space, motion, magic, the damp mother earth, and the healing power of laughter.

When he speaks, for example, of Plyushkin's estate in terms of Gogol's "thick Russian baroque" (*gustorussko barokko*), he displays his own baroque form, turning lengthy trains of thought into sentences, shunting in and out of allusions, piling up references wherever possible, stretching analogies to the breaking point (*Sobranie sochinenii* 2:213–15).[24] One such analogy is built upon the relationship between Chichikov's little traveling box and a music box. Here Sinyavsky argues that Russian literature did not come out of Gogol's "Overcoat," that is, from a seminal work called *"Shinel',"* but from Chichikov's little box (*Sobranie sochinenii* 2:258, 262). Pushing this analogy, Sinyavsky suggests that the mainspring of Gogol's *Revizor* (*The Inspector General*) is a music box (*muzykal'nyi yashchik*) which sets the tone and the tempo for little puppets, dancers on their toes, stepping left and right, artificial figures coming to life with grace and clarity (*Sobranie sochinenii* 2:68). In fact, he calls *Revizor* not a play, but a dance that replaces deeds with "movements of the body, turns of every sort and pirouettes" (*Sobranie sochinenii* 2:97).[25] In fueling such analogies, Sinyavsky no longer writes like a literary critic, but like an artist with Gogol's sensibilities, creating images that are an end in themselves.

With startling positions alone, Sinyavsky turns his study of Gogol into a work that is not simply dramatic, but disquieting. Using alarm and relief, Sinyavsky modulates his narrative, lulling the reader into submission with quiet intimations about Gogol's hypochondria in Rome then suddenly rousing him or her with strident warnings to writers who preach. To pull the reader one way or another, Sinyavsky merely resorts to overstatement, declaring, for example, "Until Gogol there was no prose in Russia" (*Sobranie sochinenii* 2:325). Using this same formula in his study called *"Opavshie list'ia" V. V. Rozanova* (*Fallen Leaves*), he declares that Rozanov became a writer without a program, without a theme, and without a subject (128). After building a head of argumentative steam in the fourth chapter of *V teni*, for example, he flatly announces that the epic, *Dead Souls*, is in fact an antiepic, adding that it is empty, heroless, eventless, motionless, and static (*Sobranie sochinenii* 2:276, 284). Such overstatement, filled with the potential to startle, is also filled with the potential to vex. Enumerating and underscoring Gogol's clumsy language, awkward syntax, poor word choices, etymological gaffs, and faulty punctuation, Sinyavsky may unnerve more than one reader when he explains: "Genius is not the one who writes well, but the one who writes badly" (*Sobranie sochinenii* 2:207).

Sinyavsky generates the most shock value when his overstatement reaches a poetic register in which a void is suggested, such as his characterization of Khlestakov's farewell letter in *Revizor* (*The Inspector General*) as "a Babylonian trash heap" (*Vavilonskaya kuchka musora*) or Khlestakov himself as "a nonentity, a nobody" (Khlestakov—*nichtozhestvo, nikto*). In this register Sinyavsky takes poetic license, explaining, for example, that in the opening of *Dead Souls,* "much is said and nothing is said" (*Sobranie sochinenii* 2:280), or that "from zero millions are obtained" (*Sobranie sochinenii* 2:30). But nothing compares to his treatise on laughter in *V teni* where this peculiar human reaction is given the most privileged link between man and God (*Sobranie sochinenii* 2:110–12). When Sinyavsky exclaims, "Laughter is the disappearance of matter" (*Smekh—eto ischeznovenie materii*), it is some indication of the rhetorical route that he has taken, a route clearly marked by *épatage*. Given so many immoderate statements and the disregard for so many critics, Sinyavsky in *V teni* even outdoes Nabokov's unconventional study of *Gogol,* which ruffled feathers when it was published in 1944.[26]

In keeping with what Dmitry Urnov calls "Rozanov's methodology," Sinyavsky gravitates toward "interlinear" or "parenthetical" issues which, in his analysis, acquire immense importance.[27] He is not only adept at arguing that Gogol is a sorcerer, but at stringing together disparate elements such as singing, laughter, movement, a troika, Russia, and the sky (*Sobranie sochinenii* 2:112). Sinyavsky, of course, is familiar with the standard interpretations of Gogol, but in eccentric fashion he proclaims terms of spirit and flesh, physical and spiritual space, myths and magic, from which a different discourse emerges, simmering in the ebb and flow of its creation. He interprets *Dead Souls* in more than one way, including that of a great rhapsody on the human condition in which Chichikov plays the part of the devil, buying up souls where their value matters only on paper. As if not apart from Gogol, but together with him, Sinyavsky addresses a time and place at once real and unreal, where everything is typical and yet atypical, where a landowner like Korobochka is just as crooked and greedy as her neighbors and at the same time extraordinary in her resemblance to Baba Yaga, a well-known witch from Russian folklore.[28]

With *Golos iz khora* (*Voice from the Chorus*), *Progulki s Pushkinym* (*Strolls with Pushkin*), and *V teni Gogolya* (*In the Shadow of Gogol*), Sinyavsky set the tone for his postprison publications in the West, a tone that did not endear him to all readers. By using his pseudonym once again, he was not adopting a quixotic pose. He was resuming his combative stance. Writing then a number of highly charged essays, he seemed to be setting the stage for more than one polemic with more than one audience. In fact, he fired his first direct postprison salvos at the Soviet literary establishment in an article called "*Literaturnyi protsess v Rossii*" ("The Literary Process in Russia"), one year after emigrating to France.[29] Writing now from his new residence in a suburb of Paris, he was able to give voice to direct satire with relative impunity for the first time. While many of his accusations in this article were carefully calibrated, he went beyond the immediate target of the literary process, striking hard not only at Sovietization, but also at aspects of the Russian national character, including nationalism and anti-Semitism. Certainly, he wanted to embarrass Soviet authorities, showing that their policies backfired and their ideals were riddled with contradictions. Privileging uncensored literature, Sinyavsky also embarrassed Russian writers who did not agree with dissenters or who were afraid of prison. Moreover, he outraged many readers when he figuratively referred to Mother Russia as a "bitch."[30]

Given Sinyavsky's fresh attack upon realism in this article, writers who considered their works "truthful" took umbrage or took cover. In fact part of Sinyavsky's major dispute with Solzhenitsyn begins here in reproaches to writers who "succumb to the temptation of the truth" ("The Literary Process in Russia" 105).[31] Objecting to what he sees as hypocrisy and intolerance in Soviet Russia, Sinyavsky blasts away in a very general direction. With biting irony, he explains:

> Russia, of course, will manage without Jews, just as she has managed without a Church, without a nobility, without an intelligentsia, without literature. ("The Literary Process" 113)

Failing to catch this irony, institutions, entire categories of Russians, including the clergy, descendants of landed gentry, writers, and well-educated professionals cannot but take umbrage. Still under the sway of prison camp language and the guise of Terts, Sinyavsky makes bold to redefine literary language, not considering the repercussions of his blustery remarks or his very personal window of perception:

> The language of literature, if one takes a close look at it, is the language of obscenity. In a broad sense, the language of literature is a string of four-letter words—even when the writer uses it to say: "How lovely, how fresh the roses were!" You think that he means roses? You are wrong; those words are a curse, which the writer (in this case Turgenev) is hurling at the walls of a prison. ("The Literary Process" 84)

He goes on to say that the literary language is a breakaway language, a language that makes ordinary people ashamed or horrified—a language of direct confrontation. Clearly, he could not have made his position more perturbing or his place in the Russian émigré community more precarious.

In Paris, Sinyavsky updates his stormy start in literature, breaking additional taboos, going against the grain of Russian émigré opinion, demonstrating clearly that he was not going to settle quietly into the suburbs. Repelled by the politics of émigré journalism, Sinyavsky began to write articles for *Sintaksis*, a journal which his wife, Mariya Vasilevna, published from the first floor of their home. Some of his most fulminatory postprison writing was first published here. And what could have been more fulminous than a newcomer taking aim at the Russian émigré community? In an article called "*O kritike*" ("On Criticism"), he charges this community with being indifferent to the development of Russian literature, especially when it veers from the "beaten track" "*stobovoi protorennoi dorogi*." He goes on to say that the long-standing problem in this community has been the lack of open debate about literature ("*O kritike*" 152). He finds that here there is not only a dearth of genuine literary criticism and competent literary critics, but also a stubborn fix upon past Russian glory and the "truth" as witnessed by Solzhenitsyn. Above all, he expresses amazement that no one in the community would argue with Solzhenitsyn's definition of the "truthfulness" of Russian literature.[32] Citing G. Ivanov, he puts forward an unattractive portrait of Russian émigré literature and its readership—a portrait of a "nice corpse" (*dorogogo pokoinika*). Picking up on this metaphor of lifelessness, Sinyavsky's wife, Mariya Vasilevna, characterizes the Russian émigré scene as "the most colossal cemetery" (*kolossal'neishee kladbishche*) from which emerges only "vampires" (*vampiry*) (John Glad 164).

Granted, the rejoinders to Sinyavsky's writing in the 1970s and especially the 1980s were vicious—all the more so when he was quoted out of context and his positions were perverted.[33] As in the past, Sinyavsky faced not simply differences of opinion, but vilification, including name-calling and libelous denunciations.[34] But that is the price for breaking with propriety, for irreverence, for plunging into "forbidden" topics, for exposing phony artists and phony ideas, for introducing jokes, hyperbole, word games, and prison camp locations into serious discourse. It is the price for lighting a fire under the Russian intelligentsia. But clearly, Sinyavsky's intentions were never hidden. He spoke openly and consistently; his positions were straightforward, especially when he explained, "*Sintaksis* was founded not to join a chorus in a hymn to copy-book truisms, but to speak out about poignant, contentious and 'forbidden' [Sinyavsky's emphasis] topics" ("*Chtenie v serdtsakh*" 205, n. 2).

But provocation begets provocation. Just as Sinyavsky provoked, he, in turn, was provoked— especially by Roman Gul', Aleksandr Solzhenitsyn,

Vladimir Maksimov, N. N. Yakovlev, Z. Shakhovskaya, D. Mirov, I. Shafarevich, and Vs. Kochetov. Defending himself, he seized opportunities to go public with bitter retorts, even to carry on vendettas very much in the style of the 1920s in Russia when the stakes were high in literary politics. With sarcasm he referred to Vs. Kochetov, the editor of *Oktyabr'*, as the "great Russian humanist" ("*Chtenie v serdtsakh*" 210). He even characterized Maksimov, the editor of *Kontinent*, as the organizer of some kind of mafia, using money and threats, forcing Russian émigrés to conform to his wishes. His wife, Mariya Vasilevna, added her opinion, saying that there was a cult of personality around Maksimov, Solzhenitsyn, and Dmitrii Dudko (John Glad 149, 159). But it is Solzhenitsyn whom Sinyavsky criticizes again and again. In fact, he sees him as a rallying point for a dangerous phenomenon: nationalism, which he considers as the "womb of violence" ("Russian Nationalism" 493).

Not only does Sinyavsky object to Solzhenitsyn's moralizing and notions of Russian "pureness," but also his literary manner which he sees "gravitating toward socialist realism" (*tyagoteyushchii k sotsrealizmu*). While he praises *Odin den' Ivana Denisovicha* (*One Day in the Life of Ivan Denisovich*), *Rakovyi korpus* (*Cancer Ward*), and *Arkhipelag GULAG* (*Gulag Archipelago*), he finds *V Kruge pervom* (*The First Circle*) weak. To him the day-to-day realistic depiction is boring. Moreover, he calls *August 14-go* (*August 1914*) tendentious and filled with fundamental misconceptions regarding the idyllic nature of Russia's patriarchal past (John Glad 150). He even points to the awkwardness of several of Solzhenitsyn's verbal constructs, as well as the awkwardness of his erotic scenes written in the spirit of an ancient Russian text ("*Chtenie v serdtsakh*" 204). He cannot tolerate the "Black Hundred" that follow Solzhenitsyn. Needless to say, he is alarmed by the attraction of Solzhenitsyn's historical interpretations, authoritative prescriptions, and despotic ways ("*Chtenie v serdtsakh*" 209).[35]

Arguably there is no break in the path of Sinyavsky's writing after his arrest and imprisonment. Fiction and literary criticism are still his companions. But turning mostly to the genre of the essay, Sinyavsky seems to sharpen and expand his satire of praise and blame, giving it argumentative form, going beyond the boundaries of literary topics and, above all, putting his lines of assault where everyone could see them—or sense them. The presence of these lines, like the presence of "Terts," antagonized the émigré community. While this community will, no doubt, return to its quiet and conventional ways, Sinyavsky disturbed its unified views on Russian literary matters for about two decades. Intruding on the order of émigré politics, he drew attention to vices and follies in a community that was, in his opinion, not only closed, but also remote from the predications of give-and-take. Sinyavsky provoked, but he also initiated a debate that was unprecedented, drawing Russians and Russian émigrés not necessarily together, but, out in the open regarding a number of issues. As in his first period as a literary scholar, he raised difficult questions—and not only about literature. Moreover, he sounded the alarm about the future of Russia, about the dangers of nationalism, the implications of combining Orthodoxy and Russian statehood, and what he saw as new levels of intolerance. Finally, in his last book, *The Russian Intelligentsia*, which will be discussed in chapter fourteen, he stunned both friends and foes, charging namely this group under Yeltsin with indifference to people's misfortunes. It is a book that David Remnik called "a kind of intellectual version of sensationalism" ("How Russia is Ruled" 14).

NOTES

1. See chapter 2, n. 2 Sinyavsky also claims, " all true writing—even when no clash with authority is involved—is something forbidden, something reprehensible and in this illicit element lies the whole excitement, the whole dilemma of being a writer" ("The Literary Process in Russia," 83).

2. Both Valentin Nepomnyashchy and Dmitri Urnov suggest Vasily Rozanov as the prototype for Sinyavsky's flamboyant literary analysis in "*Obsuzhdenie knigi Abrama Tertsa 'Progulki s Pushkinym,'*" 65, 83.

3. Sinyavsky has made much about the difference between himself and his alter ego, Abram Terts. In an interview in 1986 Sinyavsky gave his most succinct account of this difference (Glad 152–53).

4. Sinyavsky claims that Vsevolod Kochetov, "the great Russian humanist" (*bol'shoi russkii gumanist*), called him a "*pogramist*" for his earlier reviews of the work of Sofronov, Dolmatovsky, and Shevtsov in *Novyi mir* (*The New World*) ("*Chtenie v serdtsakh,*" 210).

5. For further discussion of *Golos* (*Voice from the Chorus*) see Ivask, "'*Golos iz khora'* Sinyavskogo"; Hayward, "Sinyavsky's *A Voice from the Chorus*"; Kolonosky, "Andrei Siniavskii: Chorus and Critic"; Muchnic, "Light from Above"; Tikos, "On Abram Tertz's *A Voice from the Choir*"; Holmgren, "Transfiguring of Context"; Clarence Brown, "*A Voice from the Chorus* by Abram Tertz (Andrei Sinyavsky)"; Gifford, "Andrey Sinyavsky: *The Voice from the Chorus*"; Golomshtok, "Posleslovie"; Kott, "*A Voice from the Chorus*"; "Levitt, "Siniavskii's Alternative Autobiography"; Ruth Mathewson, "Sinyavsky's Mission"; Meerson, "*Progulka s Tertsem*"; Nussbaum, "Literary Selves"; Scammel, "Spec-

ulations of a Captive Monk"; Woronzoff, "Writer as Artist and Critic"; Nepomnyashchy, *Abram Tertz and the Poetics of Crime,* 165–96. My textual citations will correspond to *Golos iz khora*, Izdatel'stvo Stenvalli, London (1973).

6. Helen Muchnic points out that Sinyavsky was allowed to receive books twice a year—books on Greek and Roman history, literature from several countries, art, archeology, anthropology, architecture, and folklore ("Light from Above: *A Voice from the Chorus,*" 8). Sinyavsky indicated that the prison library at Lefortovo was adequate in "*Chtenie v serdtsakh,*" 205 and in John Glad's "Interview," 162.

7. According to Igor Golomshtok, Sinyavsky was allowed to write only two letters a month, but he did so regularly, sending between fifteen and twenty pages of very small and very neat handwriting, that is, twenty four letters a year, yielding approximately one-and-a-half thousand pages during a sentence of five-and-a-half years (afterword in *Golos iz khora,* 331).

8. Sinyavsky's wife, Mariya Vasilevna, maintains that *Golos* was finished in 1968 ("*K istorii i geografii etoi knigi.*" *Voprosy literatury,* 61).

9. Citations in the text will correspond to *Progulki s Pushkinym*. London: Overseas Publications Interchange in association with Collins, 1975.

10. Sinyavsky's wife, Mariia Vasil'evna, was pleased that in the horrible circumstances of prison her husband managed to write "a most cheerful little book like *Strolls with Pushkin*" (Glad 162).

11. For further comment on Sinyavsky's departure from prison camp literature, see Nepomnyashchy's *Abram Tertz and the Poetics of Crime* (351, n. 17).

12. For a discussion of self-elimination, see Levitt, "Siniavskii's Alternative Autobiography *A Voice from the Chorus*"; Holmgren, "The Transfiguring of Context in the Work of Abram Terts"; Nepomnyashchy, *Abram Tertz and the Poetics of Crime,* 102–3, 107, 142–43.

13. When Sinyavsky arrived in Paris he told Hélène Zamoyska that he had nothing to add to what had already been said about prison camps ("Andrey Sinyavsky Arrives in Paris," 65).

14. Sinyavsky adds that he would make Pushkin's words his epigraph, if he considered himself worthy of using them.

15. Sinyavsky maintains that the world of prison was most interesting because he learned more about Russia there than in all of the years prior to his sentence. He points out that the other prisoners, with rare exception, treated him well. For him prison turned out to be an unlikely encounter with his "own people" (*sobstvennyi narod*) (John Glad 155–56).

16. Sergei Bocharov, "A Discussion of Abram Tertz's Book *Strolls with Pushkin,*" 64.

17. Bocharov, "A Discussion of Abram Tertz's Book *Strolls with Pushkin,*" 64, note b, 87.

18. In this study of Pushkin, Sinyavsky follows in the footsteps of Mayakovsky and the futurists who in their literary manifesto, "A Slap in the Face of Public Taste," wanted to shock the bourgeoisie.

19. See Nepomnyashchy's discussion of *In the Shaow of Gogol* in *Abram Tertz and the Poetics of Crime* (223–47).

20. P. Pletnev claims that Sinyavsky disregarded the scholarship of N. Losskii, V. Zen'kovsky, Ermakov, V. Vinogradov, and K. Mochul'sky among others ("*O zlom suemudrii,*" 74, 77).

21. In a footnote Sinyavsky adds:

> Here we meet on a narrow path, dear Viktor Vladimirovich, my late teacher and professor at Moscow University. For your, forgive me, "stylistic expertise" that you rendered to the KGB, where you, against tradition, ascribed criminality to style, having perceived in it "a latent form of politically subversive activity"—even the investigator at that time was taken aback by your academic promptness, getting ahead of the events and the inquiry of the authorities—how I was tormented, how I thought about you, about your "Nose" [his essay on Gogol—WFK] in my cell in Lyubyanka!—and I dare you, dead one, to come forward with such an interpretation today. (*Sobranie sochinenii* 1:317)

22. Gogol's *Selected Passages from a Correspondence with Friends* is another scandal-provoking work. It materialized in 1847 after Gogol's failure to complete part 2 of *Dead Souls*. A work of poor judgment, filled with moralizing and romantic notions about art, it rationalized the status quo in Russian society, justifying a place for serfdom. It outraged both Slavophiles and Westernizers, drawing harsh criticism especially in the form of a widely circulated letter from V. Belinsky, who had lionized Gogol until the appearance of this misguided message regarding salvation.

23. Like Sinyavsky, Bakhtin also criticizes *Dead Souls* in a very frank fashion. In his opinion,

> Gogol could not manage the move from Hell to Purgatory and then to Paradise with the same people and in the same work; no continuous transition was possible. The tragedy of Gogol is to a very real extent the tragedy of a genre (taking genre not in its formalistic sense, but as a zone and a field of valorized perception, as a mode for representing the world). Gogol lost Russia, that is, he lost his blueprint for perceiving and representing it; he got muddled somewhere between memory and familiar contact—to put it bluntly, he could not find the proper focus on his binoculars. (*The Dialogic Imagination* 28)

24. In an interview Sinyavsky speaks about his own style in terms of baroque. He says, "it is especially evident in *The Shadow of Gogol*" (Glad 157).

25. Ironically pertinent to Sinyavsky's musical analogies is Solzhenitsyn's claim that the method of analysis in *Strolls with Pushkin* is "a dance around Pushkin," "an empty jig" ("*Koleblet tvoi trenozhnik,*" 136).

26. Vladimir Nabokov, *Nikolai Gogol* (New York: New Directions, 1944). See especially his extended definition of the Russian word "*poshlost*'" (banality) in chapter 3.

27. Dmitry Urnov, "A Discussion of Abram Tertz's Book *Strolls with Pushkin,*" 83.

28. Sinyavsky is not the first critic to speak about folklore elements in Gogol. He claims, however, that these elements in Gogol's writing were unconscious and therefore unintentional. Given Sinyavsky's interest in folklore, he does not overlook the presence and the possible origins of such elements. Baba Yaga is allegedly a representation of an ancient goddess of death. She appears in a number of Russian folktales, reflecting an earlier practice of cannibalism very much like the witch in "Hansel and Gretel."

29. "*Literaturnyi protsess v Rossii*" was first published in *Kontinent*, a journal that set out to bridge the gap between Russians and Russian émigrés in regard to the development of Russian literature and culture. Sinyavsky was invited to participate in the work of this journal by its editor, Vladimir Maksimov. After contributing several articles, he and Maksimov had a serious falling out.

30. "*Literaturnyi protsess v Rossii,*" 183.

31. For a fuller picture of this polemic between Sinyavsky and Solzhenitsyn, see not only Solzhenitsyn's "*Koleblet tvoi trenozhnik,*" but also "*Nashi plyuralisty,*" as well as Sinyavsky's "Russian Nationalism," "*Solzhenitsyn kak stroitel' novogo edinomyslya,*" "*Chtenie v serdtsakh,*" "*O kritike,*" and "*Otkrytoe pis'mo A. Solzhenitsynu.*"

32. Sinyavsky is especially concerned about Solzhenitsyn's view of the exclusive source and makeup of "genuine" Russian literature, that is, village prose actually written by those who live in a village. Rather than a discussion of this exclusivity, especially in its parallel with Proletcult theory in the 1920s, there is, according to Sinyavsky, a widespread acquiescence regarding Solzhenitsyn's position. He points out that N. Struve, for example, does not approve of taking issue with Solzhenitsyn, who is, in Struve's opinion, not the author of just any book, but of *Arkhipelag GULAG*, the very author who has done so much for the Russian word—for Russian glory ("*Chtenie v serdtsakh,*" 209).

33. Recalling how he was criticized in Moscow, Sinyavsky maintains that censure was worse in the Russian émigré community. He goes on to say that aesthetic conventions and stereotypes also prevail in this community. Anticipating a response, he exclaims: "You will probably take offence, pointing out that in emigration they don't put you in prison for what you write." He adds: "Really?" ("*Chtenie v serdtsakh,*" 208). The attacks upon Sinyavsky reached a high point in 1975 with responses to his publication of *Strolls with Pushkin* and in 1989 with responses not only to *Strolls*, but also to several of his essays and interviews which had appeared in Paris, as well as to those which were appearing in Moscow for the first time. Nepomnyashchy attributes the controversy around Sinyavsky in 1989 to the publication of excerpts of *Strolls* in Moscow in *Oktyabr'* (*Abram Tertz and the Poetics of Crime,* 22).

34. Sinyavsky was accused of many things, including blasphemy, vulgarity, hooliganism, haughtiness, cynicism, mockery, liberalism, pluralism, "pogromism,"

cooperation with the KGB, contempt for Russia and Russian culture, as well as illusions of grandeur. In 1989 Sinyavsky said, " I have been living under constant fire from the leaders of the Russian emigration" ("A Trip to Moscow," 8).

35. Sinyavsky uses the pejorative label "Black Hundred" to recall extreme right-wing groups in Russia in the early twentieth century who advocated nationalism, absolutism, and anti-Semitism. During the 1905 revolution, they established fascist organizations such as the Union of the Russian People.

Chapter Ten

Strolling with Rozanov

In 1973 Sinyavsky, together with his wife and son, immigrated to France. In the academic year that followed, that is, 1974–1975, he offered a seminar on Vasily Rozanov (1856–1919) at the Sorbonne (University of Paris IV), where he had obtained a position as a professor of Russian literature. Seven years later the lectures from this seminar were published in Paris by *Sintaksis* as *"Opavshie list'ya" V. V. Rozanova* (*V. V. Rozanov's "Fallen Leaves"*).[1] They did not attract much attention, but they did suggest further links between Sinyavsky and this turn-of-the-century eccentric. What is most striking in these lectures is Sinyavsky's enthusiastic tone and his high regard for Rozanov's rebellious projects and practices. Given that Rozanov has been anathema in almost every circle both past and present, in these lectures Sinyavsky parts company with most critics.[2] He especially challenges assessments of Rozanov as a "cantankerous obscurantist," or "the petty demon of Russia and Russian writing" ("*Op list*" 6).[3] Clearly these lectures serve to rehabilitate Rozanov's reputation; moreover, they underscore that Rozanov and Sinyavsky do not simply share a discourse, but a barbed discourse. In fact, this discourse, which critics have discussed mostly in stylistic terms, is rooted in a repudiation of what is official, conventional, political, monumental, and expedient.[4] In the following chapter let us bare in mind the question of influence as we discuss Sinyavsky's late exhibit of Rozanov, especially his presentation of the way that Rozanov goes against the grain of both liberal and conservative opinion, and the way that Rozanov makes going against the grain an art form that is as unique as it is damning.

Sinyavsky pauses more than once to explain that Rozanov is a child of the great Russian cultural renaissance that peaked at the beginning of the twentieth century. He places him among the "god-seekers" (*bogoiskateli*), specifically among Russian religious philosophers such as Vladimir Solovev, Nikolai Fedorov, Konstantin Leontev, and later Dmitri Merezhkovsky, Nikolai Berdyaev, Sergei Bulgakov, Pavel Florensky, and Lev Shestov. It is namely these philosophers who implicitly figured in Sinyavsky's exploration of the "bourgeois intelligentsia" in his dissertation in the early 1950s. There is no doubt that Sinyavsky got acquainted with the writing of Rozanov during his research into this milieu, the results of which he was unable to share until he was free of censorship. What should not be overlooked is that even among these "god-seekers" Rozanov is an anomaly, for he carried on a lifelong polemic with the teachings of Christ, namely in regard to sex. Sinyavsky hastens to point out that Rozanov's curious negation of Christ is only one facet of his rebellion against traditionally accepted beliefs, as well as fashionable convictions of the day such as positivism and materialism. According to Sinyavsky, Rozanov was more of a "free-thinker" (*vol'nodumets*) and a "trouble-maker" (*smut'yan*) who exemplified Lev Shestov's notion of living one's philosophy with sarcasm, derision, alarm, confrontation, doubt, despair, and hope ("*Op list*" 12).

Peter Struve accused Rozanov of moral insanity for his political indifference; Nikolai Mikhailovsky suggested that Rozanov be banished from Russian literature; Vladimir Solovev called him Porfiry Golovlev, after the hypocrite in Saltykov-Shchedrin's novel, *The Golovev Family*.[5] Sinyavsky, on the other hand, maintains that the development of Rozanov's ideas was like the development of a tree, sprouting branches in different directions, "twisting, winding and meandering." While he challenges Rozanov's theory of the link between evil and the dark appearance of old icons, he does not take issue with his numerous contradictions. Building a case for the independence of Rozanov's thinking, Sinyavsky does not consider it unusual that Rozanov published radical points of view in *Russkoe slovo* (*The Russian Word*) under the name of V. Varvarin and conservative diatribes under his own name in *Novoe vremya* (*New Time*). Certainly Rozanov signaled that he was up to something when he picked a pseudonym for his radical posture that was rooted in "barbarian." But Sinyavsky is also up to something when he underscores opinions that place Rozanov's legacy "in a garbage heap or a toilet, as well as in the deepest layers of the culture of the ancient world of Egypt and Babylon" ("*Op list*" 6). By viewing Rozanov as genius, heretic, immoralist, reckless logician, honest Christian, family man, and defender of people of no consequence, he can put some very unprepossessing traits in the fascinating attire of paradox.

Rather than minimizing the importance of efforts to stop publication of Rozanov's *Uedinennoe* (*Solitaria*) because of alleged pornographic subject matter, Sinyavsky explains how central sex is to Rozanov's religious philosophy. In this way, he not only links Rozanov's sexual fixation with serious discourse, but he also emphasizes one of the important themes of his Sorbonne lectures: Rozanov was a taboo-breaker. Sinyavsky traces Rozanov's theories about sex to his interest in the paganism of ancient Greece, Rome, Assyria, Babylon, and Egypt. In Rozanov's opinion, sex is central to all of the ancient religions. It is the sun, energy itself, warmth and light, the beginning of life, the projection of God. "Sex," for Rozanov, "is not a thing or a place, but a wave of emotion which bespeaks the very essence of man—what is in his blood and, moreover, in his soul" ("*Op list*" 30). Rozanov's arguments regarding the importance of sex have been entirely misunderstood, in the opinion of Sinyavsky. Rozanov did not advocate free love, but he did insist on the singular place of sex in creation and, therefore, in God's creation. Sinyavsky maintains that outrage over Rozanov's notions about phallic cults or sex with the deacon's wife obscured his up-to-date observations about theological givens. In line with his theories, Rozanov looked to the monastery, for example, not as a place for the disappearance of sex, but a supply depot for passion that is transferred to another territory, to the sphere of the soul, the sphere of God. Taking further steps down this Freudian path, Sinyavsky explains that for Rozanov the holiness of holy men is the radiance that radiates outward as a result of sexual sublimation.

Sinyavsky argues that Rozanov's quarrel with Christ stems from the replacement of a religion of life with a religion of death, which, in its antisexual foundations, has a deep-seated dread of women. In the words of Rozanov, "all of the teachings, parables, images, analogies, promises and precepts of The New Testament may be reduced to one thing: avoid women" ("*Op list*" 51). According to Sinyavsky, Rozanov's quarrel with Christ is so serious that he boldly refers to the Son of God as the "devil" (*d'yavol*) and as "a shadow over the whole history of the Christian church" (*ten' na vsyu istoriyu khristianskoi tserkvi*). Sinyavsky shows that Rozanov's quarrel continued in regard to the ideals of religious institutions, surfacing with attacks on the church hierarchy for insisting that sex was shameful and sinful. Rozanov believed that through monasticism the church not only rejected the flesh, that is, the world, but also marriage, sanctioning and regulating it only as a concession to "man's weakness" (*slabost' cheloveka*). This concession notwithstanding, the institution of marriage and the family were looked upon as subordinate to a life of celibacy—the "official" path to salvation.

Faced with Rozanov's troubled acceptance of Christ and his eleventh-hour reconciliation with fundamental Christian teachings, Sinyavsky argues that life's final hardships brought Rozanov to his knees. Of particular importance, however, is Sinyavsky's point about Rozanov's enduring contradictions. In fact, he sounds the alarm about concluding that old Rozanov became a new Rozanov, embracing Christianity and thereby rejecting his well-digested positions. According to Sinyavsky, these contradictions should be viewed as the cadences of a person's life balanced on "the scales of the morning and evening" ("*Op list*" 73). These cadences, made more acute by the high and lows of a tumultuous era, not only maintain Rozanov's offensive and defensive disunities, but also make alienation almost inevitable for such a sensitive soul. Rather than resolving any serious conflicts, Rozanov turns more and more inward, focusing, in Sinyavsky's opinion, "on what goes on in one's soul" (*chto delaetsya v dushe cheloveka*), not mitigating differences, but constructing a new genre of personal discourse filled with stream-of-consciousness utterances.

Unwilling to construct even a partly conciliatory Rozanov, Sinyavsky insists not only on Rozanov's uncompromising nature, but also on his final unrepentant position regarding paganism. Although Rozanov called for an Orthodox priest to administer rites before his death, Sinyavsky points out that Rozanov did not exhibit any willingness to repent or express any pangs of conscience regarding his paganism. He, in fact, views the claims about Rozanov bowing down to pagan gods before his death as hearsay ("*Op list*" 89). Sinyavsky wants to be certain that Rozanov is seen in a serious light, namely as a genuine iconoclast, one who distanced himself from the radical intelligentsia as well as the bourgeois intelligentsia, and above all the church, not to mention many conventions of the day. In response to claims that Rozanov had few followers, Sinyavsky argues that Rozanov did not aspire to popularity or prophesy. He, according to Sinyavsky, took on the contradictory task of both confirming and denying the common ground between religion and philosophy, between the church and the intelligentsia.

Sinyavsky especially admires Rozanov's *Opavshie list'ya* (*Fallen Leaves*), viewing it as writing that "overcomes literature" (*preodelyaet literaturu*), that is, the traditions and inertia of existing genres. In fact, he compares its uniqueness to that of Pushkin's *Evgenii Onegin* (*Eugene*

Onegin)—a novel in verse. He claims that it does not represent a diary, a memoir, or a confession, but "fallen leaves," as Rozanov says, which brings us back to the analogy of Rozanov as a tree with many branches, "twisting, winding and meandering."[6] According to Sinyavsky, Rozanov composed this remarkable antiliterary work by writing down scraps of thoughts on scraps of paper wherever he was, gathering them finally into a pile from which came three "books": *Uedinennoe* (*Solitaria*), two "koroby" (baskets) of *Opavshie list'ya* (*Fallen Leaves*), and the *Poslednie list'ya* (*Last Leaves*) of the apocalypse. Startling the reader with Rozanov-like expression, he asserts that these books are right out of the "waste basket" (*iz musornoi korziny*), "devoid of any core idea, path or purpose" ("*Op list*" 112). He goes on to characterize them as a "running account" (*beglaya zapis'*) of what is going on in the soul at a given moment. Openly claiming to speak in Rozanov's language, Sinyavsky calls them "secretions of saliva from a saliva gland" (*otdelyaetsya slyuna iz slyunnoi zhelezy*), suggesting not what is expectorated, but what is very closely, that is, organically, connected, to the author ("*Op list*" 113).

Given the "involuntary" (*neproizvol'nyi*) and "offhanded" (*bestseremonnyi*) nature of *Opavshie list'ya* (*Fallen Leaves*), Sinyavsky objects to its published format, suggesting that one aphorism per page would better reflect the spirit and the intervals in the making of the manuscript. In fact, he insists on the "manuscriptness" (*rukopisnost'*) of Rozanov's writing, underscoring the original meaning of "manuscript," that is, "handwritten," for Rozanov's writing was direct evidence of the author's hand—something personal and tangible. Sinyavsky goes so far as to call this handwritten work a polemic with the printed word, a polemic with Gutenberg. He argues that Rozanov's handwritten text is something to be seen and examined, for its cursive entries include signatures, dates, times, notes, comments in the margins, abbreviations, and a wealth of parentheses and quotations. It has an unfinished, which is to say, unpolished quality, which Sinyavsky ranks above mainstream literature. Unlike mainstream literature, with its cut-and-dried qualities, Rozanov's *Opavshie list'ya* (*Fallen Leaves*) sets a new standard by means of its half-raw material grounded in spoken words, unceremonious turns, reproachful asides to adversaries, and chaotic movement in and out of very personal experiences.

Sinyavsky argues that Rozanov refused to write a standardized work with a social agenda. For Rozanov literature in general was a questionable enterprise. But what irony there is then in Rozanov's apprehensions about literature when he, in fact, devoted his life to writing. According to Sinyavsky, Rozanov was contemptuous of his possible "literariness" (*literaturnost'*). He was offended by what he saw in writers and yet he became one, turning his trials, tribulations, and polemics into literature. Rather than sympathizing with Rozanov's sense of committing a "sin" (*grekh*), for turning his life into literature, Sinyavsky expresses awe over Rozanov's independent path, writerly leap forward, and expansion of the boundaries of literature.

Readers who are familiar with Sinyavsky will not fail to recognize that many of the literary peculiarities that he identifies in Rozanov's work apply to him as well. Clearly, there are few discrepancies between what he "finds" in Rozanov's mode of writing and what he incorporates into his own work. Most important, Sinyavsky's lifelong objections to programmed or useful art resound in Rozanov's rejection of conventional writing and lofty literary goals. It turns out that both Sinyavsky and Rozanov are motivated to "overcome literature" (*preodolet' literaturu*), especially literary traditions that have been co-opted to serve a purpose. It is also possible to say that Sinyavsky and Rozanov share a territory of literary mischief—especially in their inclinations for genre sabotage, aphoristic liberties, narrative obfuscation and, of course, polemical satire. Moreover, such mischief, demonstrated clearly in both authors' disturbing topics and mixture of high and low language, is also paralleled in their revisionist assessments of Russian authors. Sinyavsky's *V teni Gogolya* (*In the Shadow of Gogol*), for example, is, arguably, an extension of Rozanov's pioneering study, "*O Gogole*," from the 1890s. In fact, Sinyavsky follows in Rozanov's footsteps, rejecting, once again, a wealth of Gogol criticism, arguing, like Rozanov, that Gogol is a puppeteer and a magician rather than a realist.

More than once Sinyavsky expresses concern that Rozanov's erotic themes mislead readers into making assumptions about Rozanov's libidinous energy—that he was preoccupied with sex. Addressing Rozanov's racy references the way he addresses his own, Sinyavsky underscores the important place of challenging well-worn conventions, of getting the reader to rethink generally accepted rules of propriety ("*Op list*" 223). Echoing what he said about his own fiction, Sinyavsky argues that Rozanov chooses such themes namely because they are "forbidden" (*zapretnye*).[7] But, he adds, Rozanov chooses other themes that may also be considered inappropriate. He suggests that Rozanov's writing is like a lyrical newspaper, for it contains, among other things, a wealth of documentary material and a stream of consciousness regarding the self ("*Op list*" 138). In Rozanov's writing, Sinyavsky maintains, it is necessary to recognize inventories (*opisi*) and other forms of documentation, including correspondence, a "fetishism of details" (*fetishizm melochei*), grocery lists, and accounts of the most routine events in the Rozanov household.[8] It is necessary to recognize Rozanov, the journalist, with his sense for shock value, quick reportage and evidence, not to mention strong words for settling scores with opponents, as well as Rozanov, the secret poet, unraveling his experiences and feelings, becoming the center of a very personal journey within his text.

Sinyavsky declares that in *Opavshie list'ya* there is a close connection between prose and poetry, that within the montage of documentation Rozanov steps forward not just as author-narrator, but as a lyrical hero. Sinyavsky makes much of the presence of Rozanov's "I," viewing it as a reliable index to an emotional reality. In fact, he speaks about Rozanov's expression of self in surges of emotion analogous to what is found in the poetry of Pushkin or the prose of Gogol ("*Op list*" 150). But, placing Rozanov in the context of the poetry of the avant-garde, Sinyavsky associates him more with the antimaterialists of the era who replaced systematizations of nature with the modulations of delight and despair. For Sinyavsky, Rozanov's circle of experiences in his writing suggests the life of a poet where laughter, tears, love, and pain are lifted from within and allowed to flow, collide, and become entangled with external issues. But Rozanov, according to Sinyavsky, does not follow his muse into a conventional poetic realm. In fact, in his fleeting intimations, his so-called "webs of thought" (*pautinki mysli*), he strays further from the camps of poets than the polemics in which he was embroiled.

Sinyavsky is quick to point out that in spite of all of the "poetry" in *Opavshie list'ya*, Rozanov does not poeticize himself. Instead, according to Sinyavsky, he projects himself not only as ordinary and humble, but also as unattractive and disagreeable. Sinyavsky goes so far as to say that Rozanov puts on a cynical mask, a mask that provokes many readers. It is a mask that we recognize in Sinyavsky's badgering and disparaging literary persona called Terts. Sinyavsky explains that what readers sense as rude and obscene in *Opavshie list'ya* is rooted in such expression—including Rozanov sticking out his tongue at the sight of himself in the mirror ("*Op list*" 128). Nurturing such expression, Rozanov dwells on his alleged shortcomings, for example, his family name, appearance, clothing, and fate. Like Dostoevsky's underground man in *Zapiski iz podpol'ya* (*Notes from the Underground*), Rozanov, according to Sinyavsky, not only degrades himself, but he also creates a discourse of "*oblizyvat'sya*" "licking one's wounds." Arguably, in

Rozanov's references to his unsightly appearance, his clammy skin and shabby clothes, and his uncombed, lice-infested hair lies the raw material for Sinyavsky's *Kroshka Tsores*.[9] Such unsavory details, Sinyavsky claims, constitute a thorny cover for deeply felt suffering. In fact, he considers such an unsettling focus on the exterior to be not so much a cover, but a doorway to the pain and horror of the interior ("*Op list*" 172–73).

Sinyavsky laments that Rozanov's display of unattractiveness and disagreeableness is not seen as calculated. It is through this display that Rozanov eliminates the usual literary affectation, sentimentality, and sincerity. Moreover, Sinyavsky argues that in Rozanov's projection of self-debasement lies the image of a "freak" (*urod*) as a "holy fool" (*yurodivyi*), that is, one who seeks "purification" through a most unsavory, unhygenic, and maniacal way of suffering.[10] In this manner, not only is pride thwarted, but one's very being is exposed, hence, Rozanov's claims to "nakedness" (*golyi*) ("*Op list*" 218). Arguing that in such self-debasement Rozanov is a disciple of Dostoevsky, Sinyavsky points to Rozanov's introduction of a gumboil (*flyus*) into his text as an analogue to the well-known tooth-related abscess in Dostoevsky's *Notes from the Underground*. Expressing the same kind of spitefulness as Dostoevsky's underground man, Rozanov, no doubt, offends readers. But Sinyavsky is quick to remind readers about Rozanov's way of masking and unmasking without decorative stuffing, loud and lofty notes, or poetic effusion—his way of capturing the rawness of self.

While Rozanov's writing is easily dismissed because "it is devoid of any core idea, path or purpose" (*bes zamysla, bes predvaritel'nogo syuzheta, bes tseli*), Sinyavsky considers this very "formlessness" (*besformennost'*) to be its primary asset.[11] Moreover, Sinyavsky considers Russian prose to be characterized by formlessness and hybridization, citing the work of Gogol and Pasternak as examples. He even considers Rozanov's aphorisms, that is, his recognizable prose units, to be a departure from the usual definition: a succinct statement of truth. In fact, he finds Rozanov's aphorisms so fragmented that he calls them "scraps of thought" (*klochki mysli*). He goes on to compare these scraps to a street under repair with rough and uneven surfaces exposed. He traces this kind of work in progress to what Rozanov called his "embryos" ("*Embriony*") in the 1890s. One of the examples, namely a "sprout" (*zachatok*), is as follows:

> "What is to be done?" asked the Petersburg youth impatiently. "What do you mean?" "If it is summer, clean the blueberries and make jam." "If it is winter, enjoy the jam with your tea." ("*Op list*" 195)

It captures a village response to a well-known utopian inquiry as well as the characteristic unexpectedness of Rozanov, who is capable of moving suddenly from a ventilator shaft to eternity or from galoshes with holes to thoughts with holes ("*Op list*" 207). It is the kind of semantic vaulting that Sinyavsky underscores in Rozanov's writing—the kind that he cultivated in his own fiction.[12]

It is when Sinyavsky discusses Rozanov's polemical practices that he is very much at home, for his own practices have the same kind of sharp edges and the same kind of targets. He stands together with Rozanov especially when there is anger vented at Russian officialdom, at lofty language, clichés, at stereotypes, attention-getting patriotism, and eagerness to get on the right side of the issue. Showing Rozanov to be an outspoken social critic, Sinyavsky draws attention to how this critic was capable of upbraiding Russia in "the most obscene language" (*samye grubye i nepotrebnye slova*) ("*Op list*" 253). What Sinyavsky calls obscene, however, is not far from his own language, especially in his reference to Russia as a "bitch" (*suka*).[13] One of Sinyavsky's principal exhibits of Rozanov's misgivings about Russia is a letter to Peter Struve. In this letter, Rozanov expresses sweeping criticism, admonishing Russia and the Russian people, who, he maintains, do not have a sense for history, a sense for their past or future, their continuity, culture, or self-worth, who, he goes on to say, are at heart anarchists unfit for anything ("*Op list*" 253).

Not wanting to paint Rozanov as a conservative counterpart to Chaadaev, Sinyavsky reminds readers not only about Rozanov's contradictions, but also about his refusal to defuse explosive predicaments of his own making.[14] In fact, he argues once again that Rozanov is a disciple of Dostoevsky, assuming an irrational posture as a counterpoint to that of the revolutionary intelligentsia. Like Dostoevsky, Rozanov insists on the boundlessness and, therefore, the measurelessness of man's soul, the condition, according to Sinyavsky, for becoming an independent person, someone not stamped out from a standard mold ("*Op list*" 260). It is such independence, not unlike that of Sinyavsky's Terts, that leads to Rozanov's admission: "I am contemptuous only of what is proper, correct, monotonous and attributable to everyone" ("*Op list*" 161). With these words Sinyavsky clearly conveys the tenor of Rozanov's rebellion, a rebellion further expressed in the Rozanovian equivalence of saints, thieves, lechers, and swindlers ("*Op list*" 272).

It is not with a straight face that Sinyavsky shares Rozanov's attack on Semen Vengerov, a well-known literary scholar with populist sympathies. Not only does Rozanov speak of him as fat and sinister, "like a bloated cockroach" (*kak bryukhatyi tarakan*), but also as a breed of proper and colorless people ("*Op list*" 266). But more poignant are Rozanov's objections to Vengerov's scholarship, the kind of scholarship that Sinyavsky especially derides.[15] Pointing to "professorial pedantry," Rozanov maintains that in Vengerov's scholarly editions, Pushkin, for example, becomes tedious. In terms that echo his own regarding Pushkin scholarship in *Progulki s Pushkinym* (*Strolls with Pushkin*), Sinyavsky claims: "Vengerov killed Pushkin with his countless explanations, references and examples" ("*Op list*" 266). Factoring in Rozanov's initial misgivings about Vegnerov, Sinyavsky adds that Vengrov's stomach was bulging because he had devoured Pushkin. Sensing a link between "still other cockroaches" and Peter Struve, Sinyavsky points to a tirade about middle-of-the-road politics, for when Rozanov slings mud in the direction of Peter Struve, it thickens namely around the issue of moderation. Moderate Westernization, moderate nationalism, moderate rationalism, and moderate idealism, Sinyavsky says, "drove Rozanov crazy" (*vyvodila Rozanova iz sebya*). Rozanov, in Sinyavsky's succinct declaration, called Struve a brick wall covered with empty words such as "politics," "party spirit," "legality," and "proper procedure" ("*Op list*" 268).

In these lectures Sinyavsky does not attempt to portray Rozanov as inexplicably defamed; nor does he hide damning details such as the reasons behind efforts to expel Rozanov from membership in the Religious-Philosophic Society in 1914. In fact, in his concluding lecture he declares that *Opavshie list'ya* secures Rozanov's reputation as an "obscurantist" (*mrakobes*). In the final analysis, what Sinyavsky maintains is that Rozanov is marked not by "truths," but by bristles, which he extends in a unique way. With great flare, Rozanov shows these very bristles to the Decembrists, nihilists, positivists, liberals, and socialists. With great vehemence he shows them to Herzen, Belinsky, Chernyshevsky, Dobrolyubov, and Pizarev—the founding fathers of the "progressive" intelligentsia. Even Spencer and Darwin were not out of the range of Rozanov's sharp points ("*Op list*" 287). According to Sinyavsky, Rozanov turned out to be a master of the weapons of a satirist—lampoons, caricatures, and parodies—taking them deep into scandalous territory, for example, when he asked the very dignified Dmitry Merezhkovsky in print what kind of woman he preferred to take to bed.[16] It is this kind of territory that sets off alarms and that sets off Rozanov's writing from other religious philosophers.

Sinyavsky could have called his lectures on Rozanov "*Progulki s Rozanovym*" ("Strolls with Rozanov"). With such enthusiastic focus on independence of expression, on breaking with tradition and propriety and, above all, lofty purpose, they are close to *Progulki s Pushkinym* (*Strolls with Pushkin*), which, incidentally, Sinyavsky published in 1975, during the second semester of his seminar on Rozanov.[17] Writing about Rozanov, however, Sinyavsky did not have to exaggerate any scandals. To Sinyavsky, Rozanov is a more striking rebel than Pushkin, so striking, in fact, that the fate of many authors who are intractable and outspoken about what and how they write is implicitly raised. Clearly Sinyavsky's treatment of *Opavshie List'ya* (*Fallen Leaves*) forces us to look once again at his positions in *Strolls with Puskin* and his manner of discourse in "*Mysli vrasplokh*" ("*Thoughts Unaware*") and *Golos iz khora* (*Voice from the Chorus*), for Rozanov's influence seems to loom large. It turns out that Rozanov is a model for Sinyavsky in more areas than the development of prose. In his life and in his writing, Rozanov provides Sinyavsky with another example of an extraordinary person who is in conflict with society, moreover, who occupies a zone of disputation both inside and outside of his texts—a zone coveted by Sinyavsky.

These lectures not only suggest the many territories that Rozanov and Sinyavsky share, but they also draw our attention to the place that they occupy in Sinyavsky's new lease on writing in Paris. It is here in 1973, not long after his arrival, that he renews his life in print, publishing *Golos iz khora* (*Voice from the Chorus*), a sequel to his earlier and somewhat meager Rozanovian meditations, "*Mysli vrasplokh*" ("*Thoughts Unaware*"). In this sequel, Sinyavsky carries on Rozanov's example of discontinuous and often unvarnished utterances, pieced together in open intervals and free from almost all literary conventions. But not only does Sinyavsky reassert Rozanov's model of writing and then offer lectures about this model, but he also rejuvenates the kind of polemical satire in which he engaged when he wrote for *Novyi mir* (*The New World*). In fact, during the course of his years in Paris, he becomes a polemicist very much like Rozanov, entering one scandal after another. While he does not abandon fiction, he devotes a substantial amount of his time to polemics, going beyond attacks on "*Literaturnyi protsess v Rossii*" ("The Literary Process in Russia"). In fact, he assails the literary process in general, the literary canon, politics in the émigré community, Russian nationalism, Solzhenitsyn, anti-Semitism, and government corruption. His life becomes defined by polemics, culminating in his lectures at Columbia University in 1996, where he takes up one of Rozanov's fundamental causes—condemning the Russian intelligentsia.

NOTES

1. References to page numbers in the body of my text will correspond to "*Opavshie list'ya" V. V. Rozanov*, Paris: Sintaksis, 1982. In these references I will shorten this title to *Op list* for the sake of brevity and for the sake of distinguishing it from Rozanov's work.

2. After the Bolshevik Revolution Rozanov's reputation suffered a further blow. In spite of his brief enthusiasm for the revolutionary movement after the 1905 revolution, he became, in official Soviet accounts, somewhat of a non-person.

3. *Petty Demon* (*Melkii bes*) is the title of Fedor Sologob's "decadent" novel of 1907 that suggests the presence of Satanism in Russian society.

4. Only Sinyavsky's "*Mysli vrasplokh*" ("*Thoughts Unaware*") and, to a certain extent, *Golos iz khora* (*Voice from the Chorus*) have been discussed in regard to Rozanov's influence. On the other hand, the influence of Rozanov on Sinyavsky has been suggested many times. For commentary in this regard, see Edward Brown, *Russian Literature since the Revolution,* 247; Dalton, *Andrei Siniavskii and Julii Daniel',* 129; Field, "Abram Tertz's Ordeal by Mirror," 33; Lourie, *Letters to the Future*, 97–116 passim; Gul', "Abram Terts: '*Mysli vrasplokh,*'" 276; Holmgren, *First-Person Liberties,* 143–45; Nepomnyashchy, *Abram Tertz and the Poetics of Crime,* 150–55; Ivask, "Rozanov v izobrazhenii Sinyavskogo," 308–13; Bakhrakh, "Vechnyi Rozanov," 16–18.

5. Peter Struve (1870–1944) was a leading theorist of Marxism in Russia in the 1890s. But he left the circle of social democrats and became a member of the liberal intelligentsia. Before he emigrated from Russia, he served the monarchists under General Wrangle in the capacity of minister of foreign affairs. Nikolai Mikhailovsky (1842–1904) was a literary critic and leader of the populist movement. Valdimir Solov'ev (1853–1900) was one of Russia's foremost philosophers and poets. He is known for his religious philosophy and especially his theories regarding "holy wisdom" or "Sophiology."

6. Following this analogy, Sinyavsky focuses on Rozanov's "*Luchinka*" (kindling wood), a short account written shortly before his death ("*Op list*" 123–26). Here Sinyavsky suggests that kindling wood is yet another feature of the author as a tree with its branches, leaves, and finally chips of wood.

7. In an interview with John Glad, Sinyavsky declares that his writing is linked with violating what is forbidden in terms of subject matter and style ("*Pisatelstvo vsegda dlya menya svyazano s narusheniem zapretov i syuzhetnykh i stilistcheskikh*" 153).

8. Rozanov's first wife was Apollinariya Suslova, with whom Dostoevsky had an affair in the 1860s. After three years, she decided to leave Rozanov. He then took up with Varvara Rudnev with whom he fell passionately in love. He could not marry her, however, for, in the eyes of the church, he was still married to Apollinariya, who refused to grant him a divorce. He, nevertheless, made Varvara

his common-law wife. They apparently had a very happy relationship through which a daughter, Tat'yana, was born. Rozanov was so taken up with his wife and daughter that, according to Sinyavsky, he incorporated more of the details of their lives into his writing than the details of his own.

9. The protagonist, Tsores, is built namely upon the ugly-on-the-outside/beautiful-on-the-inside formula. But what especially gives Tsores a Rozanovian basis is Sinyavsky's emplotment of his autobiographical circumstances into this novella, including the projection of misunderstanding, suffering, and guilt.

10. There are a number of references to "holy fools" in Russian history. Although the famous cathedral in Red Square in Moscow was officially named *khram Pokrova* (The Cathedral of the Veil), it came to be known as *khram Vasiliya Blazhennogo* (St. Basil's Cathedral) after the holy fool who lived in its shadows. Basil lived in extreme poverty, in rags and filth, and behaved like a madman. But beneath his unprepossessing exterior was a wise and holy man. Miracles were attributed to him as well as the prediction that Ivan the Terrible would murder his own son.

11. In his *Progulki s Pushkinym* (*Strolls with Pushkin*) Sinyavsky again and again emphasizes Pushkin's formlessness, claiming, for example, that *Eugene Onegin* was a novel about nothing (*Sobranie sochinenii* 1:382).

12. The writing of Sinyavsky contains a wealth of semantic vaulting. His sentence fragment, "From a dead duck to a living lute" (*Ot mertvoi utki k zhivoi lyutne*) is a good example, for it displays a sound relationship (alliteration), linking the duck with the lute (*Sobranie sochinenii* 2:564). It follows a discussion of relationships in which Sinyavsky talks about "things coming together, parallel and incongruous."

13. It is possible to say that Sinyavsky's language incorporates many elements from the street, including a few vulgar words, colloquialisms, and prison camp slang. He discusses these elements in "*Literaturnyi protsess v Russii*" ("The Literary Process in Russia"), which was published during his lectures on Rozanov.

14. Petr Chaadaev (1794–1856) also condemned Russia in very harsh terms. In fact, for his criticism of Russia in *Lettres philosophiques addressées à une dame* he was declared insane. Like Rozanov, he maintained that Russia was a backward country without any worthy traditions and no legitimate claims to a place among Western nations.

15. It is possible to say that Sinyavsky's *Progulki s Pushkinym* (*Strolls with Pushkin*) is an attack on stodgy scholarship, the kind that merely serves to monumetalize Pushkin and earn a place in the poet's radiance.

16. Rozanov is not begging the question about Merezhkovsky's genuine or imaginary impotence, but about his siding with Struve and the "sexless" rationalists ("*Op list*" 270). Dmitry Merezhkovsky (1865–1941) was a religious philosopher and a prominent literary critic who showed leadership in the promotion of the Symbolist movement in Russia.

17. In the conclusion to his *Progulki s Pushkinym* (*Strolls with Pushkin*), Sinyavsky succinctly underscores the problem of Pushkin scholarship. He says that the reader has the choice between two Pushkins: one related to conflict with the world, a break with morality and society, and the other related to the almost saintliness and blessedness that give people in art uncanny influence and social authority (*Sobranie sochinenii* 1:435).

Chapter Eleven

Metafiction with Barbs

Published in 1984, *Spokoinoi nochi* (*Goodnight!*) is the quintessence of Sinyavsky's prose, a seamless splicing of fact and fiction and a worthy successor to his experiments with genre.[1] It not only contains experiences that Sinyavsky considers worthy of fiction, but also striking portraits of family, friends, academic acquaintances, and members of the KGB. Like most of Sinyavsky's nonacademic writing, *Goodnight!* is filled with disclosures regarding surveillance, arrest, interrogation, prison and, in general, the game of cat and mouse that marks his fiction and his life. It bristles with satire on institutions and individuals, with focused derision of Stalin.[2] It also bristles with the features of metafiction, what Patricia Waugh calls "a celebration of the power of the creative imagination together with an uncertainty about the validity of its representations" (*Metafiction* 2).[3] These features stem from Sinyavsky's lifelong objections to realism, culminating not only in writing that pits fantasy and realism against each other, but also in toying with the conventions that allegedly set them apart. In the following chapter let us follow Sinyavsky into a Nabokov-like territory, where he zigzags between confession and fabrication, emplotting his past into fiction and fiction into his past, disputing again and again what passes for make-believe and certainty.[4]

Anyone who has read Sinyavsky is struck by telltale signs of metafiction. Narrators, for example, don't know their place. In fact, given the opportunity, they speak out against the author. Characters discover that they don't exist or turn up in a context outside the story in which they are embedded. Sometimes they address the reader, anticipating what he or she is thinking. In *Goodnight!,* where events from Sinyavsky's life are at issue, there is no attempt to keep fact and fiction apart. Narratives develop on their own to such an extent that a fantasy of *Alice-in-Wonderland* proportions actually splinters away in the writing of *Goodnight!*, emerging as a novella that was published as *Kroshka Tsores* (*Little Jinx*).[5] Two people are making love in chapter 4 and suddenly Tolstoy's voice booms, telling them to stop disgracing themselves (*Sobranie sochinenii* 2:509). It is but one of many voices in *Goodnight!*, which is made up of numerous accounts, a play, letters, a newspaper article, poems, songs, folktales, historical tracts, literary quotations, ruminations on art, and crisp dialogues. In fact, the many texts that give *Goodnight!* its eclectic character deny its stability. This very character endows this novel with what geologists refer to as "plate tectonics." *Goodnight!*, in other words, is not a solid mass, but an accumulation of self-differentiating texts whose relativity, it turns out, is largely satirical.

Sinyavsky takes a major step toward metafiction when he fabricates Terts as author, narrator, and occasional character.[6] Sinyavsky takes Terts seriously, relating to him not unlike Dostoevsky related to his characters (Bakhtin, *Problemy* 43).[7] In other words, Sinyavsky approaches Terts as a fully fledged persona separate from himself.[8] Accordingly, Terts has his own consciousness and personality, his own motivation; moreover, he speaks in a language distinct from Sinyavsky's. Acknowledging the brusque manner and the prison camp jargon in *Strolls with Pushkin*, Sinyavsky reminds everyone that it is Terts who is speaking ("*Chtenie v serdtsakh*" 205, 209). More than once, Sinyavsky declares that his postprison writing was meant to demonstrate that Terts was still alive. Through his recontextualization of a legendary Jewish bandit like Terts, Sinyavsky not only scoffs at the establishment, but he also problematizes the voicing in his fiction. The reader must put up with a fictional construct that straddles the world of Sinyavsky—the person and the writer. The reader knows that Terts does not really exist, yet it is impossible to deny his presence not only inside Sinyavsky's texts, but also in the paraliterary space around them.

Sinyavsky does not stumble into metafiction in *Goodnight!* He plunges into its theoretical essence at the end of *What Is Socialist Realism* where he advocates not just an indeterminate being, but an indeterminate domain, a domain that is constituted by fantastic realism—the very domain of metafiction.[9] Balking at the dictates of socialist realism, Sinyavsky preferred to hedge between fantasy and realism. Privileging neither one nor the other as an end in itself, he, as I have said, plays one against the other, just as he plays Terts against a construct of himself. In stories such as "*Ty i ya*" ("You and I") and "*Kvartiranty*" ("The Tenants"), where he clearly emplots Terts and a construct of himself, Sinyavsky prepares the stage for high metafiction. In this emplotment he not only suggests Terts's consciousness, but he also creates that sought-after territory that is hypothetical yet incontrovertible, a territory that is sure to baffle many readers. From this territory he can confirm or deny almost anything, bending what is straight and straightening what is bent. From this "in-between" territory he can make a solemn confession or cast aspersions in the most brazen manner.

Sinyavsky suggests the "in-between" quality of *Goodnight!* when he claims that it is essentially a novel, but, in some respects, an autobiographical novel in that it is based on a "real canvas" (Nepomnyashchy "Interview" 10). Given that this "real canvas" is displayed in a fictional gallery, that is, in a novel, Sinyavsky clearly puts the reader in a metafictional bind. Caught in this bind, the reader, in fact, may throw up his or her hands, especially in the light of Terts whose designated authorship of *Goodnight!* should technically turn the facts of Sinyavsky's life into a biography. In *Goodnight!* Sinyavsky seems to share a number of experiences. Yet, he scatters them in a vaulting and zigzagging narrative, denying a measured account of childhood, boyhood, and youth.[10] He seems to authenticate his past with specific details, with anecdotes, impressions, asides, and disclaimers. But while he lards his narrative with texts that seem to document his past, these texts take on a life of their own, providing entertainment rather than evidence. No reader could overlook how this purposeful patchwork of texts vies with the seriousness that *Goodnight!* promises in regard to recounting Sinyavsky's past—his home life, his university days, his friends, his arrest, and his prison experience.

If, at an abstract level, *Goodnight!* is the story of how Sinyavsky became a writer, then the culminating moment in this novel is his epiphany in the forest when he was with his father in Rameno, a Russian town approximately six hundred miles south of Moscow (*Sobranie sochinenii* 2:496–98).[11] Here, two mysterious events come together: his father's sensation of the workings of a brain implant and the sudden seething of trees in the forest. On this day Sinyavsky senses "the stamp of damnation and happiness on his forehead," that is, he comes to understand his father's destiny as his own (arrest, prison) and his calling to be a writer (*Sobranie sochinenii* 2:497). Amazed at the effects of a whirlwind on a stand of trees, he suddenly realizes that everything that he had witnessed that day converged:

> Inwardly I said to my father, or to opponents yet to be. To myself. . . . Look, see for yourself. This is the reality that you ignore, disdainfully calling it "fantasy." Here it is! There is no need to fantasize, it is enough to see it, and

> it does not matter in the least what you call it. You can call it a tree or a human being. Whatever you like! The tree is me in an imagined dream. The tree is my father. It swirls; you look closer; it seethes, as you and I do, like the universe in an abyss of hypotheses and hyperboles. (*Sobranie sochinenii* 2:497)[12]

In fact, it converged for Sinyavsky namely as a man destined to be a writer. In this revelation, he no longer speaks about the promise of fantasy as he did in *Chto takoe sotsialisticheskii realizm* (*What Is Socialist Realism*), but about its shared territory with reality. In fact, here Sinyavsky addresses the central issue of metafiction, suggesting "the universe in an abyss of hypotheses and hyperboles" (*vselenniya v bezdne gipotez i giperbol*), reminding the reader of the tenuous nature of all things and the arbitrary names that we assign to them.

At another level, *Goodnight!* is a farewell to Stalin's Russia, to what Sinyavsky calls a "deep, deep August night" (*gustaya-gustaya avgustovskaya noch'*). Clearly, Stalin belongs in Sinyavsky's autobiography—in the very layers that make it metafiction. Arguably, he is Sinyavsky's dark muse, rousing him to write satire on the abuses and follies of the day, especially the most deceptive activity on the part of a national leader: promoting what is false in the name of what is true. Sinyavsky, in fact, blames Stalin for creating a fictive epoch ("The Literary Process in Russia" 95).[13] In *Goodnight!* he turns to the very issue of fictiveness, seeing Stalin as its source and its product. But instead of unmasking the myth and the mythmaker, Sinyavsky seems to add more myths, putting forward both "hypotheses and hyperboles." Leaving aside spoofs of "newspaper lyrics" (*gazetnaya lirika*) in which Stalin is referred to as "the bright-eyed falcon" (*sokol yasnoglasnyi*), "our own" (*rodnoi*), "beloved" (*lyubimyi*), and "the master" (*khozyain*), Sinyavsky posits a fantastic Stalin.[14] Turning to the reader regarding Stalin's capacity to be all-knowing and all-powerful, he expresses what could pass for either trepidation or hyperbole:

> I won't hide it—I am afraid to write about Stalin. No sooner do I sit down and start to write than a little magic ensues. Fear, confusion. Some kind of bee stings me like a needle in an infected area. My hand falters. I get weak in the knees, as they say. I throw up in the wastebasket. My pulse speeds up. My urine reeks of acetone. My mind is turned upside down. (*Sobranie sochinenii* 2:508)

Rather than adding to the list of commonplace images of Stalin, Sinyavsky calls him a mystery, an invisible force, a magician, a poet, a film director, and a choreographer. He underscores Stalin's abilities not as leader or monster, but as an artist.[15] Setting the stage for a bizarre portrait, he refers to Stalin as an "old wolf" (*staryi volk*), a "werewolf" (*oboroten*), and a "dragon" (*drakon*). Moreover, he goes so far as to describe the atmosphere around Stalin as "that of a black mass, a witches' Sabbath, howling from the grave." (*Sobranie sochinenii* 2:537).

Sinyavsky constructs an extraordinary Stalin in keeping with his extraordinary characters, as well as with the quasi folklore that he shares about him in *Soviet Civilization*.[16] Realizing that these amazing stories about Stalin raise questions about the fantasy/realism equation, he explains, "It does not matter so much whether it is truth or invention, since conjecture can contain more of reality than the facts" (*Soviet Civilization* 100). In *Goodnight!* The fantasy/realism equation is at the heart of Sinyavsky's calculations when he introduces a folktale (*skazka*) which he claims was based on actual events, on facts, he adds, whose authenticity could not be doubted (*Sobranie sochinenii* 2:505). To further authenticate this folktale and at the same time pass through the gates of fiction, Sinyavsky introduces a storyteller called Alla into the narrative who, as it turns out, suffered in no small way at the hands of Stalin. By coincidence, Alla is a medium (*posrednik*) with a good standing in the occult community, competent to make contact beyond the grave. Her story within a story conveys how Stalin appears to her on the night before his death in bone-chilling coldness, in a gaseous state comparable to methane or nitrogen, asking for forgiveness before his departure into the next world. Such forgiveness is, of course, denied.

Sinyavsky puts all of the ingredients of metafiction into this folktale/factual account/dream—the same ingredients that are attributed to fantastic realism. He prepares the groundwork for a ghost story with a historical platform, leaving the door slightly open to the possibility of a dream, or, more specifically, a nightmare. He then relies on the reader to figure out the implications of this fascinating tale in the light of its alleged source and its hypothesis, not to mention its motif of retribution. Not only is Stalin shown in the same kind of desperation in which he placed his victims, but he is also linked, albeit intertextually, to the fate of the wandering Jew, doomed to spend an eternity, not wandering, but seeking forgiveness from each and every one of his victims.

The reader is reminded once again about what is real and what is not, when Sinyavsky also speaks of a false-Stalin, a phenomenon rooted in Russian history as well as in metafiction. After a bit of comic relief regarding the proliferation of Russian pretenders to the throne, Sinyavsky turns to the false-Dmitry, constructing a historical analogy between the time of Stalin's death and the time of the death of Ivan IV's son, Dmitry, in 1591, an analogy that gains further depth if rumors about the poisoning of Stalin are taken into account. Adding grist to the sixteenth-century side of this analogy, Sinyavsky inserts passages from an allegedly rare old text, *Skazaniya inostrantsev o smutnom vremeni* (*Foreign Accounts of the Time of Troubles*), passages that reveal just enough twentieth-century references to bring a smile to the reader's face. He, moreover, increases the intertextual mass of this analogy by interrupting these alleged historical associations with his personal recollections of March 5, 1953.[17] Going back and forth between the sixteenth and the twentieth century, Sinyavsky creates the same kind of inter-temporality as in Bulgakov's *Master i Margarita*, which also hinges on a satire of Stalin.[18] Obtaining a good narrative position to carry out one of his metafictional ploys, he plants a telling anachronism: when the tsarina Marfa confirms that the pretender is, in fact, her son, the Politburo, rather than the Boyar duma, applauds (*Sobranie sochinenii* 2:519).[19]

When Sinyavsky includes a text from the Time of Troubles that focuses on the work of a torturer following the investigation into the death of Dmitry, the reader cannot but make his or her own analogies.[20] The cutting off of tongues of those who blaspheme the state is certainly a reference to Stalin's brutal measures regarding free speech. Yet there is no explicit connection here—just juxtaposition. It is the kind of juxtaposition that pervades *Goodnight!*, setting the stage for potential rather than absolute meaning—for the assumptions of the reader whose complicity in making Stalin into a text is a given. In fact, Sinyavsky argues that Stalin's image was a product of discourse not simply from above, but from below, from the Russian people, whose expectations fed upon myths and the variants that they invited (*Sobranie sochinenii* 2:540). It turns out that Sinyavsky's Stalin is more fiction than fact. Ironically, Sinyavsky posits the most dominant historical figure of the era as more thematic than factual, a subject for stories, for accounts that are filled with what he calls "hypotheses and hyperboles."

Sinyavsky's juxtapositional links with Stalin are compelling because they touch upon what is historically recognizable, yet they are built upon fantasy. These links, in fact, have little in common with reality, yet they are cited and repeated as if they were from a common text familiar to a vast community. Such is the common text regarding Stalin's sexual magnetism, which a Georgian relates to Sinyavsky in the basement of the Lenin Library. Actually the Georgian boasts about his own sexual escapades, which, at first, seem to have little import. But it turns out that the Georgian is irresistible to women because of his resemblance to Stalin

(*Sobranie sochinenii* 2:540). While he has many conquests, there is, in compliance with the tradition of storytelling, an extraordinary episode involving an extraordinary woman. Carried away by the Georgian's tobacco-scented moustache in the heat of passion, this woman, who had been Stalin's lover, suddenly fantasized herself as an adolescent. Moreover, she imagined herself a daughter, searching for someone else in the Georgian, someone whom she loved like no one else. In her metamorphosis into daughterhood, she exclaims: "I am Svetlana! I have come to you, Light of my life! At Last! Father! Father!" Sinyavsky merely adds: "What can you say here? It looks like incest" (*Sobranie sochinenii* 2:539).

What is striking about this text about Stalin as well as the many texts that make up *Goodnight!* is that they demonstrate a theatrical quality—the very inside/outside quality of metafiction. They represent a different kind of make-believe, setting themselves apart from the main narrative, unfolding as separate realities on a separate stage—sometimes in another era. Not satisfied with description, Sinyavsky stops his narrative to introduce events that are transcribed or acted out. The play, *Zerkalo* (*The Mirror*), in chapter 1 is a case in point.[21] It has five scenes with extensive stage directions and is inserted into the novel to convey the experience of prison, which, according to Sinyavsky, can only be grasped in the symbolic realm of the theater (*Sobranie sochinenii* 2:341). It, in fact, reorients the reader's perception, putting him or her not directly in front of a scene in a novel, but in front of the panoply of the stage. Explaining that theater and reality are the same in prison, Sinyavsky decides to use the conventions of the stage to tell his story. Turning to the reader with a metafictional caveat, he says: "Please do not confuse it [the play] with the actual story of my arrest which I will relate at the same time" (*Sobranie sochinenii* 2:341). As playwright, director, and actor, Sinyavsky takes the reader into that metafictional territory where the "facts" are projected in a dimension that is clearly illusory, but completely captivating.[22]

Zerkalo suggests Sinyavsky's talent as a playwright. It also suggests his inclination to subordinate the narrative to theatrical strategies that contribute to making a spectacle in more than one sense of the word.[23] This inclination, which culminates in *Zerkalo*, is also evident in the role that Sinyavsky assumes in introducing so many "outside" texts. In doing so, Sinyavsky becomes a master of ceremonies rather than a narrator. He, in fact, comes to occupy that important metafictional position as clown and impostor, constantly interrupting the narrative flow, surprising the reader with "outside" evidence or "inside" remarks. What could be more theatrical than Sinyavsky's citation of his early poetry, especially when he immediately dismisses it.[24] Or his reproduction of the signatures of Semichastnyi, the Head of the KGB, Volkov, the Chief of the Bureau of Investigation of the USSR, and Pakhomov, Investigator on Cases of Special Importance. (*Sobranie sochinenii* 2:392).[25] These signatures are only for effect—as is much of the alleged "documentation" in *Goodnight!*

In considering what is and what is not for effect, the reader will certainly pause upon Mariya Vasilevna's notebook, the text of which shows lines of ellipses as in *Evgenii Onegin* or *Tristram Shandy*, signaling that some information is missing (*Sobranie sochinenii* 2:408). It is a notebook that she brings with her on one of her visits to her husband in prison. In her conversation with him, it becomes clear that still other words are written down in this notebook—fragments of information constituting a husband-and-wife code. Not unlike a character in a metafictional novel, Mariya Vasilevna cuts the text from this notebook into little strips, puts them into a saucepan, adds hot water, stirs and then pours the mixture down the toilet, laughing to cover the sound (*Sobranie sochinenii* 2:409). An extraordinary letter that Sinyavsky cites from his days in prison may have had a similar fate. In fact, in its very first line Sinyavsky declares that it would never get past the censors (*Sobranie sochinenii* 2:428). Given the fascinating account that follows about rumors of his death at that time, readers may not pause to question how this "letter" survived censorship, prison security, and the ravages of time. Its authenticity under suspicion, this "letter" is nevertheless effective in its "physical" representation, making the reader think that he or she is on the trail of something that has documentary value.

What with all of the texts that appear to document events, Sinyavsky seems to fulfill his promise of building his novel upon a "real canvas." Actually he fulfills his role as a writer, using whatever conventions that work. Above all, he fulfills his inclination for the theater by making a theater world, getting his many props into position, staging his memoirs with sufficient alarm and relief, shamelessly playing to the audience, going so far as to use the conventions of the nineteenth-century novel, the kind of novel that he saw as contrived. In other words, he turned to set pieces for effect, telling us, for example, that his "aerial companion" disappeared, possibly having entered a monastery, or having joined a persecuted sect, or having gone down the drain with drink (*Sobranie sochinenii* 2:528). Likewise, in speaking about the fate of the Georgian, whom he met in the Lenin Library, he waxes in the same manner, telling us that the Georgian also disappeared, possibly having been run over by a truck, or having been arrested or having departed for the Caucasus in order to seek his fortune and keep a low profile (*Sobranie sochinenii* 2:540).[26]

Exploiting the conventions of "authentic evidence" and "sincere asides," Sinyavsky not only follows a well-trodden departure into metafiction, but a well-known position in the theater—right on the edge of the stage between the audience and the spectacle. From this position he can speak in a parenthetical manner, creating a separate discourse—one than can agree or disagree with the principal narrative.[27] From here Sinyavsky can play a part, feigning a special relationship with the reader as when he makes a disclaimer regarding a woman who attempts to flush a mouse down the toilet: "Forgive me, reader. Don't be too hard on me. And don't be frightened. I made it all up. There was no such woman with those fingernails. None of it happened" (*Sobranie sochinenii* 2:443). Sinyavsky even turns to the reader in the sentimental fashion of Karamzin, asking with tongue in cheek: "Dear reader, did you ever happen to spend any time in a prison's public house?" (*Sobranie sochinenii* 2:401) Feigning deference to the most delicate sensibilities, especially when he is about to enter the Rabelaisian territory of sex and death, Sinyavsky specifically addresses the "dear female reader" (*dorogaya chitatel'nitsa*) and "nice young ladies" (*milye baryshni*) (*Sobranie sochinenii* 2:403).

Working the melodramatic scale of emotions, Sinyavsky cannot but be an impostor, looking over his shoulder, winking, holding back his laughter as he proffers texts and extraordinary yarns. Owing to this imposture, even Sinyavsky's portraits of family and friends are subject to some degree of theatricalization, that is, some degree of hypothesis and hyperbole. One such portrait is that of Seryozha, Sinyavsky's companion from boyhood and youth, who contributes to the roman-à-clef side of *Goodnight!* In fact, his resemblance, vis-à-vis the "facts," to Sergei Khmelnitsky led to a heated controversy regarding the accuracy of these "facts" after *Goodnight!* was published.[28] Making one of many asides about the construction of his novel and, in this case, about the construction of Seryozha, Sinyavsky explains:

> To be on the safe side and avoid entanglements, you designate them by their first name or with a single letter. You slip in some little detail as a reference point—and that does it. But you are sadly aware in advance, no matter how much you outline and sketch, any character, even the most hopeless case, will elude hypothesis, true description, even his own photograph. Like smoke from a chimney. (*Sobranie sochinenii* 2:575)[29]

It turns out that Sinyavsky introduces a most extraordinary Seryozha, so extraordinary, in fact, that he resembles a literary type. Endowed with features from the Dostoevskian tradition of romantic realism, he is very much like Stavrogin, that is, possessing both brilliance and dark shadows.[30] True to type, Seryozha dares "to cross the forbidden line" (*perestupit' zapret*), showing very early in life that he had a capacity for almost any undertaking. Whatever Seryozha's qualities may have actually been in "real" life, his embodiment in fiction has a certain familiarity, especially in his contradictions where, for example, his erudition, original outlook, and taste are played against his disdain for the crowd, his collaboration with the KGB, and the "monstrous" (*chudovishchno*) way that he teases a classmate who stuttered (*Sobranie sochinenii* 2:559). Sinyavsky underscores Seryozha's extraordinariness, whetting the reader's appetite with hints about him being "an exception to morality, psychology and even biology" (*Sobranie sochinenii* 2:568).

Like Dostoevsky's Stavrogin, Seryozha suddenly behaves in a way that astounds everyone. At a gathering of students, he seizes someone called Irina and, in front of everyone, attempts to kiss her. But instead of a kiss, he bites her lip, then looks at everyone's reaction, enjoying the scene that he had created (*Sobranie sochinenii* 2:567).[31] Exclaiming "What effect!" (*Effekt!*), Sinyavsky gives Seryozha a theatrical side, actually adding the language of the theater to the narrative. Thus, he compares Seryozha's bravado to someone who steps up to and over the "ramp of the stage" (*rampa*) (*Sobranie sochinenii* 2:569). He, moreover, pauses to explain Seryozha's "need for an audience" (*potrebnost' v auditorii*), his performance of a "dazzling vaudeville" (*osleppitel'nyi vodevil'*), and a "jolly harlequinade" (*veselaya arlekinada*), which did not elicit a "bravo." In keeping with theatrical metaphors, Sinyavsky even refers to Irina's role in regard to Seryozha as a "pretty walk-on" (*khoroshen'kaya statistka*). When he cites Evreinov's *Teatr dlya sebya* (*Theater for Its Own Sake*), he, of course, underscores the reflexivity and self-reflexivity of the stage.

It is Sinyavsky's father, however, who is placed in the most dramatic context, so dramatic that one senses not only the unraveling of a tragic flaw, i.e., an uncompromising nature, but also the denouement of the novel. Through his father, Sinyavsky discovers not only a common destiny, but also the stuff of fiction: surveillance, a house search, arrest, trumped-up charges, exile, mind-reading devices.[32] This destiny, with its fictional proportions, led namely to writing, which, for Sinyavsky, meant survival.[33] Considering the possibility that his father's thoughts were being monitored through a brain implant, Sinyavsky places his father right on the border of fantasy and reality, where fiction and fact can easily change places. It is here that Sinyavsky can introduce "hypotheses and hyperboles," characterizing his father as a truly encyclopedic man, an inventor, fearless in all things, but, at the same time, a complete failure, unusually stubborn and quirky.

Sinyavsky builds a case for uncertainty regarding the image of his father, especially in regard to his state of mind after an alleged brain implant in prison. But in this very uncertainty lies the deepest link between father and son. As his father becomes uncertain about what is real and what is not, so Sinyavsky arrives at the same dilemma, making it a central issue in his writing. Sinyavsky's revelation in the forest regarding seething trees is echoed in his father's revelation about the KGB listening in on his thoughts. Sinyavsky's father, like Sinyavsky, faces what is most troubling, declaring: "I can not be sure of anything. It is possible that I was seeing things, I admit that. But what if I weren't? And it was all real . . . ?" (*Sobranie sochinenii* 2:490). The reader, of course, will never know.

Above all, Sinyavsky's epiphany in *Goodnight!*, which resonates with his manifesto on art in the conclusion to *Chto takoe sotsialisticheskii realizm* (*What Is Socialist Realism*), reconfirms his suspicions about what may or may not be hypothetical and hyperbolic in the world around him. In other words, Sinyavsky insists on uncertainties, the very uncertainties with which he defies Marxism and celebrates metafiction. Rejecting what could make *Goodnight!* a crude winnowing of "the facts," he constructs versions of make-believe and reality that play against such winnowing. In fact, it is possible to argue that Sinyavsky's *Goodnight!* is a counter-measure to what is expected from a memoir. But such a measure does not mean that he holds back on the "facts" regarding his past or the abuses and follies that shape it. It means that he does not present so much a record or a recollection, but a spectacle of events and characters that bleed into history and fiction. For Sinyavsky, *Goodnight!* is no more and no less than a spectacle in which his life is both reflected and constructed and then mediated by Tertsian maskings and unmaskings. He understood that *Goodnight!* could not be a review of his life without being a fabrication of it and, vice versa, that it could not be a fabrication of his life without being a review of it. As review or fabrication it illuminates an incredible stage on which horror and humor stand close together and the trappings seem real.

NOTES

1. It is also the best source for Sinyavsky's thoughts on his prison experience. For further discussion of *Spokoinoi nochi*, see Nepomnyashchy, *Abram Tertz and the Poetics of Crime,* 261–319; Gachev, "Andrei Sinyavskii-Abram Terts," 235–66;

Holmgren, *First-Person Liberties,* 227–313 and "Transfiguring of Context," 965–77; Richard Lourie, introduction to *Goodnight*! vii–xiv; S. Maksudov, "*Spokoinoi nochi,*" 93–96; Matich, "*Spkojnoj noci,*" 50–63; Nussbaum, "Literary Selves," 238–59; and Tatarinov, "Andrei Sinyavskii i Abram Terts," 20–22.

2. Stalin becomes *the* principal target for satire during the Soviet period. Long after his death, satirists continued directly and indirectly to unmask his abuses and follies. Sinyavsky makes sport of Stalin whenever he can. While he tells a number of Stalin jokes in *Soviet Civilization*, for the most part he comments on the dictator's behavior and its effect upon the people with feigned awe. In *Goodnight*, his approach to Stalin is both fanciful and humorous and not without a measure of the grotesque. Rosalind Marsh considers Sinyavsky's satirical treatment of Stalin very much like that of Voinovich, Iskander, Aleshkovsky, and Zinoviev (*Images of Dictatorship* 212).

3. For further discussion of metafiction in regard to Sinyavsky's writing, see Erika Haber's "In Search of the Fantastic in Tertz's Fantastic Realism."

4. In my reference to Nabokov, I take my cue from Sinyavsky who considered him a most interesting contemporary writer ("Exile and Writer," 18). Nabokov always brings literary games to mind, especially through allusion and parody. Sinyavsky too enjoyed taking the reader for a ride. He acknowledges that he incorporated "many games" (*massa igry*) into *Progulki s Pushkinym*, purposefully attributing, for example, the quote regarding the obligation to be a citizen first and a poet second to Lomonosov rather than Nekrasov (John Glad 161).

5. *Kroshka Tsores* (*Little Jinx*) is built upon the same autobiographical and fictional mix as *Goodnight!* In it the narrator seems to recall episodes from his childhood, boyhood, and youth. We discover how he comes to be called "little jinx"; we also discover that his last name is Sinyavsky. So that the reader is not tempted to take everything seriously, the narrator reminds him or her that he is making it all up. With its independent development and richness of magic elements, *Kroshka Tsores* is more like a satellite rather than an appendage of *Goodnight*. It was first published in Paris by *Sintaksis* in 1980. The first chapter was translated in 1984 by Nepomnyashchy. The rest of the novella was translated by Larry P. Joseph and Rachael May in 1992. For further analysis see Nepomnyashchy, *Abram Tertz and the Poetics of Crime,* 248–57; Nussbaum, "Literary Selves," 238–59 and Vera Dunham, "Serenity," 110–17.

6. In "*Kvartiranty*" ("The Tenants"), for example, Terts plays a central part in the story, not only providing a narrative voice, but also looking out after a writer who seems to represent Sinyavsky. In "*Ty i ya*" ("You and I") he emerges very confessionally, explaining his awkward position on the border of Sinyavsky's consciousness. In *Lyubimov* (*The Makepeace Experiment*) he plays a very self-effacing role, deferring to the entertaining accounts of Savely Kuzmich and Professor Proferantsov. In *Spokoinoi nochi* (*Goodnight!*) he breaks into the text, making a cameo appearance, defining himself in his relationship with the narrator, who, in the context of this autobiography, is Sinyavsky.

7. Speaking about the sovereignty of any given character, Sinyavsky explains:

> No person fits the category assigned to him. And just what are the limits? And, who knows, maybe yesterday's traitor will accept the cross on the barricades tomorrow. And the day after tomorrow he will become a Buddhist monk or pull some other quirky, unpredictable stunt that eludes all definition. How am I supposed to create characters, paint portraits after that? What, have I lost my mind? Every character has a frighteningly vast range and can go flying off at any second. *Bon voyage*! (*Sobranie sochinenii* 2:575)

8. At a conference at the University of Nottingham during the summer of 2000, Galina Belaya, a scholar who was acquainted with Sinyavsky, insisted that when he was drinking he became Terts.

9. Nepomnyashchy traces the concept of fantastic realism to Dostoevsky (*Abram Tertz and the Poetics of Crime,* 321, n. 1). The terms "fantasy" and "realism" are, of course, problematic. More problematic is the notion of realism with a fantastic quality, or, vice versa, fantasy with a realistic quality. Clearly, a discussion of "fantastic realism" leads to a discussion of the jurisdiction of such concepts inside and outside fiction. Above all, these terms, because they are in a muddy contradiction, cannot clearly qualify each other. To use them together, nevertheless, is to hedge between them, that is, to hold on to the denotation of one and the other.

10. In regard to vaulting and zigzagging, Sinyavsky's narrator explains with tongue in cheek:

> In my own defense, I should add that all this hopping about in telling the story of my life is not the result of a weakness for diversion or an innate penchant for chaos, but, on the contrary, an unquenchable desire to write as precisely, bluntly and thoughtfully as possible. (*Sobranie sochinenii* 2:351–52)

11. Sinyavsky's epiphany is set in the most extenuating circumstances in 1951, when he was finishing his dissertation, shortly after his father's release from prison. Not only is the forest in Rameno, his father's place of exile, a special place for father and son, but also, on the day of this epiphany, Sinyavsky had planned to tell his father about Terts namely there. As Sinyavsky explains, his father never found out about Terts, just as Sinyavsky's mother never found out about her husband's brain-wave phenomena.

12. There is a similar pasage in *Lyubimov* (*The Makepeace Experiment*) where the narrator, Savely Kuzmich, pauses to describe the play of shadows and light at dusk on a summer day. Instead of ghosts and astral bodies, he draws attention to particles of dust, fabric, and threads that hang in the air and to something that moves from one corner of the ceiling to the other with the flick of a tail. As if dismissing any hint of supernatural phenomena, he assures the reader that what people mistake for ghosts are the shapes of ordinary

thoughts which all inanimate objects exchange with each other (*Sobranie sochinenii* 1:73).

13. Nina Muravina, like Sinyavsky, claims that her generation was imbued with the most fantastic representation of reality (*Vstrechi s Pasternakom* 18).

14. The epithets that are cited are gleaned from Sinyavsky's *Sud idet* (*The Trial Begins*).

15. We should not overlook Sinyavsky's view of an artist as sorcerer. In Gogol's case, unlike Stalin's, the sorcery is good. To compare Sinyavsky's "portraits" of Stalin, see his "*Stalin—geroi i khudozhnik stalinskoi epokhi*" ("Stalin—Hero and Artist of the Stalin Epoch"), which also appeared as a chapter in *Soviet Civilization,* 93–113.

16. In *Soviet Civilization* Sinyavsky recommends that written and oral tales about Stalin should be put together in a book called *Historical Legends and Anecdotes about Comrade Stalin* (99).

17. Sinyavsky turns to Stalin's death in fiction for the first time in chapter 7 of *Sud idet* (*The Trial Begins*).

18. See Sinyavsky's discussion of *The Master and Margarita* in *Soviet Civilization,* 105–7.

19. Sinyavsky's construction of historical links to tragedy, treachery, and Stalin end with passages, as if from another source, which depict and interpret an artistic representation of Christ, the Virgin Mary, and John the Baptist. These passages, which, like others, are interrupted by the main narrative, seem to have an ecclesiastical loftiness from the past, yet, in the playfulness of metafiction, the genuinely lofty is betrayed by very obvious twentieth-century references. This loftiness is further compromised, moreover, when Christ, the Virgin, and John the Baptist enter into dialogue with rather earthly emotions. Their dramatic dialogue has a direct bearing on the problem of Dmitrii's death; it has an overall bearing on the problem of evil in Russia down to Stalin's time. In a Menippean disquisition John the Baptist calls for punishment, enumerating Russia's sins: alcohol, tobacco, the shaving off of beards, and murder. On the other hand, the Virgin pleas for mercy—for the return of Dmitrii to his mother, in accordance with her own experience. Given the intersession of the Virgin, John the Baptist forgoes his objections. In the same way, Christ, although annoyed by his wounds at the hands of man, is moved by the tears and the entreaty of his Mother. He agrees to mercy. But the matter is not settled. He does not act.

To punish or to show mercy is one dilemma; to intervene divinely is still another. Besides, John the Baptist is driven by his suffering and death at the hands of man; the Virgin by her role as eternal intercessor. Christ, with his limitless power, contemplates putting an end to the violent turn of events in Russia, scrapping everything and starting anew. His Mother is the only one who considers how much faith would be gained by the resurrection of Dmitrii. Moved by his Mother's reasoning and her love of man, Christ gives in to her request, in spite of his sense of futility, for he foresees further bloodshed in Russia. His prediction for Russia is put in meteorological terms: "There is bad weather ahead," he says (*Sobranie sochinenii* 2:544).

In the interplay of texts, Sinyavsky lays out philosophical issues with universal as well as Russian connections. Moreover, he establishes a contrapuntal discourse, consisting of voices in marked and unmarked passages, a feature of his writing that becomes more and more pronounced in his postprison publications. While the marked passages are expressed in the manner of a monastic illuminator, the unmarked passages actually illuminate the issues, especially in the light of modern Russia. Even one of the marked passages telescopes ahead to the death of Lenin and Stalin, equating one Time of Trouble with another, while exposing the artificial age of the text. In a subtle way, the notion of progress in the development of Russia is put into question. In fact, a regression to a primitive state is suggested by Christ's "protuberant gorilla-like brow" (*vypuklye, budto u gorilly, nadbrov'ia*) and John the Baptist's eye "covered with a dull film like that of a lizard falling asleep" (*podernulsia mutnoi plenkoi, budto u zasypaiushchei iashcheritsy*). This regression is further suggested by the changing quality of Christ's place on high: from a "light-blue throne" (*goluboi prestol*) to a "golden chair" (*zolotoi stul*) and finally to a "cyprus seat" (*kiparisovoe siden'e*).

20. Torturers and executioners play an important role in Sinyavsky's discourse, especially in connection with their past life as revolutionaries in which they directed all of their hatred to hangmen and jailers. Not only does he attempt to show their contradictory nature, but also their unexpected side. He sees, for example, an ironic similarity between Derzhinsky and Christ (*Soviet Civilization,* 126).

21. Actually Sinyavsky does not call *The Mirror* a "play" (*p'esa*), but a "fairy play" (*feeriya*). It is worth noting that Mayakovsky also did not call *The Bedbug* (*Klop*) a play but a "fairy play comedy" (*feericheskaya komediya*).

22. The play turns out to be a parody of an interrogation, a cat-and-mouse game filled with innuendos and doublespeak. Arguably, the actual story of Sinyavsky's interrogation is implicit in the moves of the game that on one level are humorous and on another treacherous. To make the metafictional picture complete, Lieutenant Colonel V. A. Pakhomov, Sinyavsky's interrogator, appears in a dream much later in Paris, spattering saliva all over Sinyavsky's manuscript of *Goodnight!* (2:391).

23. Sinyavsky's image of prison is not only stated in terms of a theater, but also in terms of a "circus tour" (*tsirkovoe turne*), "carnival-theater" (*teatr-karnaval*), and "commedia dell'arte" (*komediya del'-arte*).

24. Sinyavsky cites four poems: one in imitation of Mayakovsky and three in the style of the imagist movement. After he cites the latter three, he explains: "The only interesting thing about these poems is that they do not at all correspond to who I am" (*Sobranie sochinenii* 2:585).

25. The copies of the signatures of the Chairman of the KGB, the Chief of the Bureau of Investigation of the USSR, and the Investigator on Cases of Special Importance are included in the translation of *Spokoinoi nochi*: *Goodnight!,* 69.

26. Accompanying Sinyavsky's promise about building upon a "real canvas," is his insistence on the freedom "to disregard the facts in order to elucidate them more fully . . ." (*Sobranie sochinenii* 2:341).

27. Parenthetical comments, which play such an important role in metafiction, are more widespread in *Goodnight!* than in other work by Sinyavsky.

28. See Nepomnyashchy's interesting analysis of Seryozha (*Abram Tertz and the Poetics of Crime,* 307–10, 313–14. Sergei Khmelnitsky, who let everyone know that he was the source for Seryozha in *Goodnight!*, disputed the facts in the novel. Furious about how he was depicted, he accused Sinyavsky of collaborating with the KGB to get revenge, "*Iz chreva kitova*," *Dvadtsat'-dva*, no. 48 (June–July 1986): 151–80. The appearance of Sergei Khmelnitsky as a witness for the prosecution at the trial on February 11, 1966, astounded both Sinyavsky and Daniel (Ginzburg 262–63). Under questioning, Khmelnitsky claimed that he suggested the idea for "*Govorit Moskva*" ("This Is Moscow Speaking") to Daniel. Daniel, however, denied that he built his story on Khmelnitsky's idea.

29. Sinyavsky is serious about designating an "actual person" with an initial or with a first name. At first he refers to Sergei as "S," but later in the narrative he spells out "Sergei." More often than not, he does not camouflage names. In fact, his novel is filled with references to contemporaries, including former coworkers whom he satirizes, such as Shcherbrina, Khrapchenko, and Ovcharenko.

30. I refer here to Dostoevsky's Nikolai Stavrogin in *Besy* (*The Possessed*) who could be called one of the most fascinating of Dostoevsky's doubles.

31. In *Besy* (*The Possessed*) Stavrogin suddenly bites the provincial governor's ear.

32. In 1951, thirty years after the fact, Sinyavsky's father was accused of spying for the United States because of his role in the distribution of food and supplies from the American Famine Relief Society in 1922. According to Sinyavsky he presented documentary proof that he was not engaged in espionage. The authorities nevertheless charged him with anti-Soviet agitation under Article 58 (10). He received the minimum sentence—five years exile to Rameno, where he was born (2:476).

33. Sinyavsky says that the twenty-one-hour search and the KGB operative's question regarding an unofficial definition of socialist realism served as a starting point for *Chto takoe sotsialisticheskii realism* (*What Is Socialist Realism*), which was completed in 1956.

Chapter Twelve

Fantasy and Folklore

While it is customary to speak about fantasy in the writing of Sinyavsky, it should also be customary to acknowledge that much of this fantasy is rooted in Russian folklore. Sinyavsky turned to folklore in the same way that Picasso or Chagall turned to primitivism.[1] In fact, a number of modernists found a great richness in the forms of expression of the common people from the past. For Sinyavsky, Russian folk beliefs and customs pointed to an entirely different world, one quite indifferent to Soviet reality. In this world, Sinyavsky saw a simplicity and integrity that was at odds with his era, validating not a scientific history, but a "spiritual history" expressed in rituals, decorative art, tales, and proverbs.[2] In the preface to his published lectures on Russian folk beliefs, Sinyavsky claims that folklore was not just a topic of research, but a passion and a great personal discovery. Moreover, he goes so far as to say that it gave him aesthetic orientation (*Ivan-Durak* 8).[3] In view of the Soviet "struggle with the past," Sinyavsky's satiric appropriation of folklore was tantamount to a countercultural declaration. In the following chapter let us consider how Sinyavsky uses folklore in his fiction; how he incorporates its images and especially its magic core into his stories, turning Russia, its history, and its institutions upside down.

For Sinyavsky fantasy was never an end in itself, but a means, a satirical means, as in the allegory about the otherworldly faith of the displaced creature from *Pkhents*. But while bearing this isolated work of science fiction in mind, let us not overlook the reoccurring spirits from Russian folklore in his writing, especially in "*Kvartiranty*" ("The Tenants"), *Lyubimov* (*The Makepeace Experiment*), and *Kroska Tsores* (*Little Jinx*). Their appearance in these works is more than fantastic stuffing.

They, after all, have a history of playing a part in narratives that mock the establishment—initially the church and the aristocracy. These spirits, namely water nymphs (*rusalki*), wood spirits (*leshi*), witches (*ved'my*), house spirits (*domovye*), devils (*cherti*), as well as creatures that suddenly grow feathers and fly away, wield magic that is in opposition to the agenda of the state. Living outside of physical and social laws, they can cast a spell. More important, they can break a spell, even if it is sustained by the power of authorities.

It is the Russian fairy tale that Sinyavsky considers not only a receptacle for fantasies, but also the wisdom of the common people.[4] In *Spokoinoi nochi* (*Goodnight!*) the narrator, allegedly Sinyavsky, pauses to praise the fairy tale, especially for its depth and clarity. It is the fairy tale, he claims, that grounds us in reality, that provides, for example, a corrective to clichés about the behavior of one or another class (Marxists, take note) (*Sobranie sochinenii* 2:504). Moreover, for Sinyavsky, the fairy tale is an archetypal narrative model. In the conclusion to "*Grafomany*" ("Graphomaniacs"), Straustin, after much soul-searching about what and how to write, urges his son to write "fairy tales" (*skazki*): "Paul, you write fairy tales about your funny dwarfs. And I'll write about mine" (*Sobranie sochinenii* 1:179). In "*Kvartiranty*" ("Tenants") the narrator (Terts) refers to the stockpile of narratives that he relates to Sergei Sergeevich (Sinyavsky) as "fables" (*basni*).[5] He adds that with his fables—enough to fill five volumes—and Sergei Sergeevich's writing skills, they could outdo the Brothers Grimm (*Sobranie sochinenii* 1:151–52).

In "*Kvartiranty*" ("The Tenants") Sinyavsky establishes a major exhibit for spirits from Russian fairy tales. Moreover, he includes an embodiment of Terts in this exhibit, putting him in a narrative role close to an embodiment of himself, that is, Sergei Sergeevich, as well as embodiments of water nymphs, witches, demons, house and wood spirits. Speaking about the nature of his embodiment and his lack of separateness vis-à-vis the author, Sergei Sergeevich, the narrator says:

> The main thing, Sergei Sergeevich, is to stick together. I'll never get out of here in all eternity without your help, that is human help. I can walk around in here to my heart's content—on the walls and the ceiling, if I wish. But I can't get beyond the threshold. It is physiologically impossible. (*Sobranie sochinenii* 1:151)

It is possible to assume that the narrator is also a spirit, for he is not only capable of walking on the walls and the ceiling, but also of transforming himself into a glass. On the other hand, we should also consider that all of these spirits may be no more than the narrator's subject matter. He is, after all, a storyteller and his stories are rooted in Russian folklore.

Early on in "The Tenants" the narrator laments the disappearance of spirits:

> Before long there will only be water nymphs left. And even they . . . . You know: the encroachment of industry upon natural resources. The march of technology! Streams, rivers and lakes smell of chemicals. Methylhydrate, toluene. (*Sobranie sochinenii* 1:146)

Going on about the countless number of wood spirits and witches that have perished, he sighs: "Farewell, my homeland, my primordial place!" (*Sobranie sochinenii* 1:147) When he speaks about the difficulties of a house spirit without a house, he hints, of course, at the difficulties of communal apartments. But rather than taking further aim at Soviet housing conditions or appealing to environmentalists to take action, the narrator lets the trickery of the spirits put contemporary Russian life into a humorous perspective. It is what the writer, Sergei Sergeevich, wants to hear. It is what he writes down and therefore what we are reading. What a metafictional declaration of fantasy—and comedy—on the part of Sinyavsky/Terts and what updated yarns about spirits of yore who once inhabited the imagination of the common Russian people. Now, it seems, these creatures from the preindustrial age can barely maintain their essence. In the new Soviet order they must improvise. Sofya Frantsevna Vinter, for example, in spite of what her passport says, is a water nymph who does aquatic exercises every day, splashing around in the bathroom for hours on end, or sitting in a basin, singing songs about the Lorelei in German (*Sobranie sochinenii* 1:147).[6] And Ninochka, who drove her husband insane with her reckless spending, turned completely into a witch and even learned to fly at night on a lavatory pan. What with intestinal gas, she was like a rocket engine (*Sobranie sochinenii* 1:152).

It is in "At the Circus" ("*V tsirke*") that Sinyavsky draws attention to the coexistence of Christian and pagan beliefs among the common Russian people. To illustrate this coexistence, he points to the line that both unites and separates tricks (*fokusy)* and miracles (*chudesa*). For example, the protagonist, Konstantin Petrovich, who is a stranger to Christian tradition, is struck by a painting of Lazarus. In his opinion, Lazarus was not raised from the dead; a magician (*fokusnik*) assumed the guise of a corpse and then jumped out of the grave and astonished everyone (*Sobranie sochinenii* 1:119). Pondering this kind of claim regarding magic or supernatural intervention, Solomon Moiseevich, a Jewish intellectual with a weakness for alcohol, explains: "the church originated from the circus and nothing was more important to the Russian people than tricks and miracles" (*Sobranie sochinenii* 1:120). In fact "At the Circus" is, at one level, about tricks and intervention that is hardly divine. Through the tricks of a magician (*fokusnik*) at a circus, Konstantin Petrovich, a thief, is inspired, in this case, darkly influenced, to do his own tricks. While he is not a magician, he finds out that he is also capable of demonstrating that the hand is quicker than the eye. He picks someone's pocket in the most magical way, as if some supernatural agency were guiding him (*Sobranie sochinenii* 1:116).[7] With this success, his life takes on a new meaning. But while looting an apartment, Konstantin unintentionally shoots someone. To his surprise, it is the magician. Most important, right up until his final moments in prison, he imagines himself performing tricks, including a somersault on a high-wire rope. While Sinyavsky leaves us with a metaphor that links art with crime, resulting in a prison sentence, he also revitalizes the image of a thief (*vor*) from Russian folklore.

Konstantin, in fact, illustrates what Sinyavsky says about the thief in *Ivan-Durak* (*Ivan the Fool*) (44–59).[8] Touched by magic, he is thrown in the original fairy-tale role of a thief as hero, a beloved hero—far from the contemporary calculations about his picaresque nature. His stealing, drinking, and womanizing are subordinate to his generous ways with money and his devil-may-care attitude. But everything is subordinate to the trickery that his "profession" requires and, according to Sinyavsky, that lies at the heart of the fairy tale (*Ivan-Durak* 50). This trickery (*fokus*) is rooted in sorcery (*koldovostvo*), which, for Sinyavsky, links theft (*krazha*) not simply with resourcefulness, but with the supernatural (*chudo*).

> For us, the supernatural turns into trickery and trickery turns into clowning. And this process makes for a type of carnival sorcery and buffoonery, signifying the kinship and the likeness of these aspects of the fairy tale. (*Ivan-Durak* 57)

Strengthening Konstantin's association with carnival is Solomon Moseevich's remarks about Leoncavallo's opera *I Pagliacci*, for the Pagliacci were wandering performers not unlike the Russian mummers (*skomorokhi*).[9] By association, Konstantin is a mummer (*skomorokh*)—performer, artiste, clown, and trickster—who in a drunken stupor imagines himself on stage with everyone's eyes on him. From within, that is, "in the very depths of his soul," he feels the need to perform, to do an amazing trick—some kind of "somersault" (*salto mortale,* literally a "mortal leap") (*Sobranie sochinenii* 1:117). In fact, he takes a mortal leap when he does a somersault toward the gate in the prison camp. Like Canio in *I Pagliacci*, who also comes to have blood on his hands, he must perform, he must laugh and play the buffoon no matter what fate awaits him. Like Terts's infamous past (theft) and magic partnership in art with Sinyavsky, which acquire no small token of mythology in "At the Circus," Konstantin's art (tricks) and resourcefulness (theft), born as if "from another world" (*potustoronnyi*), predicate his demise.

Lyubimov (*The Makepeace Experiment*), arguably Sinyavsky's best satire, does not just include folklore elements; it is comprised by them. Posited in events that burlesque the Bolshevik Revolution and the theory and practice of building socialism, these elements suggest that Russian folklore and Marxism-Leninism share the same kind of myths, cults, wordy formulas, prohibitions, and fantasies. To give *Lyubimov* storytelling authenticity, Sinyavsky puts the narrative in the hands of Savely Kuzmich who is guided "from above" by Samson Samsonovich Proferansov very much like an author guides his or her narrator. Ironically, the extraordinary events that Savely describes are about Lenya's "scientific revolution," which turns out to be most unscientific. By implication, the very notion of a "scientific revolution" is a fairy tale.

This novella's fairy tale status is signaled in a number of ways, including accounts of omens, spells, incantations, witches, and forest spirits (*leshye*).[10] One way, of course, is the reference to Arina Rodionovna, who, we are told, is Samson Samsonovich's German housekeeper (*Sobranie sochinenii* 1:78). But most readers know that she was, in fact, Pushkin's nanny from whom the young poet learned a wealth of Russian fairy tales. Based on these tales Pushkin wrote *Ruslan i Lyudmila*, a narrative poem, which Savely mentions at the end of chapter 5. It is here that Savely tries to soothe Lenya, telling him that he would not betray him, that he was standing guard, that he was counselor and nanny, that is, Arina Radionovna (*Sobranie sochinenii* 1:84).

Fairy tale magic begins in the very first chapter, right after Lenya is elected as supreme ruler of Lyubimov. According to the old women, whose account contributed to a legend fully in agreement with the imagination of the local people, Comrade Tishchenko, Secretary of the Town Party Committee, spun around and fell from the tribune like a toppled idol (*Sobranie sochinenii* 1:23). His head hit the ground and he vanished. But from the indentation in the ground a black crow materialized, squawking and flapping. Immediately Lenya threw himself down on the same spot.[11] While everyone watched, he was transformed into a hawk—a hawk in pursuit of Tishchenko. Then, when Tishchenko turned himself into a fox, Lenya turned himself into a borzoi. And when Tishchenko turned himself into a bicycle, Lenya turned himself into a motorcycle.[12] Without warning, another voice intrudes upon the narrative, explaining that this incident was not grounded in facts, but was made up by the local people and should be considered on the same level as that of the folk epics about Ilya Muromets (*Sobranie sochinenii* 1:24–25).[13]

It is possible that Savely's description is rejected by Samson Samsonovich who, allegedly, is the author "behind" him. In chapter 2 he reprimands Savely: "Well how, for example, did you present your Lenya? As a wise man, a magician? After all he only played a role, a talented one, but a role nevertheless. You know that it was not by his own power that he seized the city" (*Sobranie sochinenii* 1:38). Savely asks him, "Who else's power could it have been?" Samson Samsonovich answers, "Mine" (*Sobranie sochinenii* 1:38). The difference of opinion about how Lenya came to power and how he dealt with opposition (Tishchenko) is telling, for each side has its own etiological claims. This difference of opinion becomes the axis of the story, but with a twist, for both the point and the counterpoint share degrees of fantasy. This kind of point and counterpoint is further reflected in the divergence between Savely Kuzmich and Lenya. The latter is inclined to science, while the former to art, yet they share common roots (*Sobranie sochinenii* 1:31).

At the heart of the fantasy in *Lyubimov* is the ironic parallel between the socialist-realist model of the incredible success of a blue-collar worker and the folktale model of the incredible success of Ivan the Fool. Like Ivan the Fool, the one most unlikely to succeed, Lenya becomes the town hero—in fact he becomes the "supreme ruler" of Lyubimov, acquiring, like Ivan the Fool, magic power. To consider this magic power, which appears to be a type of hypnotism, is to consider ironic parallels regarding its effects, that is, between raising consciousness, controlling people, and creating illusions. To those who do not understand hypnotism, Lenya is thought to be casting spells. Because of this power, he is both exalted and vilified. On the one hand, he is called tsar, leader, chief, Hercules, and Generalissimo. On the other, he is called magician, devil, sorcerer, Antichrist, and purveyor of black magic. To the old women of Lyubimov, he is Lenya the Beatified, Lenya, Fool-in-Christ (*Sobranie sochinenii* 1:46).[14]

When Savely Kuzmich finds out that Lenya is studying a book from India called *The Psychic Magnet*, he becomes alarmed: "Be careful Lenya, I am worried by the sound of that foreign word. Watch out that you don't fall under the influence of an alien ideology. Doesn't that book contain some sort of sorcery contrary to the laws of nature and scientific progress? (*Sobranie sochinenii* 1:34) To ward off any suspicion, Lenya quotes Friedrich Engels's *Dialectics of Nature*, showing that it supports several positions in *The Psychic Magnet*: for example, that the mind is the highest product of matter and that everything in life is flow and change. Not convinced by Lenya's quotes, Savely attempts to burn the book. But when he touches it, he receives an electric shock. To change Savely's way of thinking, Lenya turns Savely upside down—or he makes him think that he is upside down.

On the wedding day of Lenya and Serafima Petrovna, Savely pauses to explain several folk traditions, pointing out that the wedding dress is a symbol of chastity, and that the offering of bread is a symbol of abundance. He quickly underscores, however, that what Lenya and Serafima wore was not in keeping with Russian tradition: she did not bother to wear a wedding dress and Lenya only marked the day by wearing mouse-colored gloves and a paper chrysanthemum in his buttonhole (*Sobranie sochinenii* 1:47). In an ironic parallel to the biblical account of the wedding feast at Cana (John 2:1–11), Lenya decides to perform a miracle, that is, demonstrate his power of mass hypnosis. Thus, he turns mineral water from Kharkov into alcohol and the water from the Lyubimovka River into champagne. In fact he creates the illusion of a feast with fine cuisine and music when all provisions in Lyubimov were in low supply. But suddenly he becomes confused, trying to sort out what had really taken place:

> It is possible that the hasty drinking of these weak, ignorant and backward people has affected me. Perhaps I have become a victim of my own hypnosis and they are all healthy and sober. Perhaps I am intoxicated by a crazy dream about rows of tables around the city, the exclamations of people down by the river, this wedding escapade and my easy victory over a woman who was so indifferent to my love. (*Sobranie sochinenii* 1:52)

This kind of sorting out runs throughout the novella, especially in regard to what may or may not be magic, for a socialist utopia and a fairy-tale world are dialogically locked in a Menippean contest that shows both polarities and ironies, such as the perception of tanks as "brontosauri" (*brontozavry*), an "armor-plated herd of cattle" (*bronirovannoe stado*), and "monsters" (*chudovishcha*). What Savely calls a pterodactyl,

Almazov calls a bird with an oversized head, a well-fed toad, a crocodile, a monster with the eyes of a snake (*Sobranie sochinenii* 1:59). Speaking about frightening noises in the forest, Almazov argues that a village elder could distinguish the sound of wind or mice from some other sound. He cautions, however, that the devil was another matter—beyond one's knowledge of mice or logarithms. This differentiation of knowledge (mice/logarithms) is further reflected in Lenya's tirade about "fables" (*basni*) regarding the existence of God. In anger he tells his mother that God does not exist, that they shot the Prophet Elijah, that thunder, contrary to what people believe in Lyubimov, is caused by electricity (*Sobranie sochinenii* 1:71). But Lenya himself is not free of doubts and, therefore, contradictions. He wonders if Lyubimov will be "carried into the future" or "fall into the hands of swinish devils." He also wonders: "Would the sorcerer's white potion that has eaten away the soul of nine tenths of the nation be of any help?" (*Sobranie sochinenii* 1:76) Moreover, he is troubled that in a moment of high anxiety he uttered a "superstitious proverb" (*suevernaya pogovorka*) in keeping with the habits of the people of Lyubimov, habits that he considers savage, ignorant, weak, and foolish.

What should not be overlooked in *Lyubimov* is that one of the principal characters is a witch: Serafima Petrovna Kozlova. To heighten the mystery around her, there is much speculation about who she really is. Although the narrator argues that she is of Jewish rather than Russian descent, Lenya claims that there is something Spanish about her. Serafima, however, points out that she is Russian, that her mother was Russian and her father was half-Greek and half-Jewish (*Sobranie sochinenii* 1:31, 92). It appears that she agreed to marry Lenya because of his power, that is, because of his promise to lay Lyubimov at her feet. In this way she would become "mistress of the realm" (*khozyaika gosudarstva*). The narrator, Savely Kuzmich, provides some background, saying that Serafima, who had come to Lyubimov to teach foreign languages, immediately created a sensation. At gatherings, after one glass, she would squeal, spin around and go into a Caucasian dance with a knife between her teeth (*Sobranie sochinenii* 1:14).

Lenya underscores her last name, Kozlova, which he says comes from the Russian word "goat." It is the very word that Sinyavsky focuses upon in his article on Zoshchenko: "*Mify Mikhaila Zoshchenko*" ("The Myths of Zoshchenko"). Looking into both its Latin and Greek roots, he suggests that "goat" is related to "caprice" as well as "tragedy." Moreover, in ancient religions, myths, and folklore, a goat is the embodiment of fertility and is connected with a host of rituals and games ("*Mify*" 55). Owing to this intertextual burden regarding the meaning of "goat," Serafima is not without links to significant "ancestral forces" (*rodovye sily*). Kept under hypnosis for much of the time after exchanging vows with Lenya, she suddenly shows another side. From behind her porcelain visage, she reveals another embodiment: a former Serafima Petrovna. In the twinkling of an eye, this embodiment appears, measures Lenya with a annihilating look, and then retreats behind the porcelain cover (*Sobranie sochinenii* 1:92). Using hypnosis, Lenya probes her memory to find out more about her past only to discover that she had had a string of lovers. To Lenya's surprise, these lovers reach far back into history, indicating that Serafima is a timeless creature not limited to a single unified identity.[15]

Meanwhile, Serafima tries to tempt Vitya Kochetov, Lenya's loyal lieutenant, but he steels himself to her advances. Savely Kuzmich sounds the alarm, telling the reader of her potential to bring chaos to Russia. Suddenly, Serafima shows herself as a "witch" or "she-devil" (*chertovka*) with a broom on which she rides high above the rooftops. Before she vanishes, she calls out to Lenya with a fragmented message, urging him to run away with her to Leningrad, calling him "a cross-eyed devil, a pet-devil," as she did before (*Sobranie sochinenii* 1:106). What with Lenya's hasty departure on a freight train, life in Lyubimov returns to its former patterns, becoming once again "old Russia" with old women, in the words of Savely Kuzmich, "spread across the floor of the church like old mushrooms" (*Sobranie sochinenii* 1:109).

Buried in *Lyubimov* is a germ, something that will grow and develop into another fantastic story rooted in folklore. It is contained in a Jewish word, the only such word that Savely's previous lover, an extraordinary Jewish woman, knew: "*tsores*" (*Sobranie sochinenii* 1:32). Meaning "sorrow" or "trouble," this word becomes the basis of the title of Sinyavsky's novella *Kroshka tsores* (*Little Jinx*), which is dedicated to E. T. A. Hoffmann and recalls the German storyteller's fantastic tale, *Klein Zaches* (*Little Zaches*).[16] With dwarfs, fairies, and wizards, Hoffmann's tale acts as the same kind of catalyst for Sinyavsky as it did for Gogol. Moreover, it provides the mainspring of a plot: a magic spell that suddenly affixes positive qualities to a repulsive dwarf who has no merits whatsoever. Sinyavsky, however, reverses this situation, presenting a spell that affixes negative qualities to a worthy but unattractive person. In *Zaches* the spell is finally broken by a second wizard and followed by a humorous twist. In *Tsores* the spell is broken by the one who cast it: Dora Alekandrovna. In fact, through her dance, which reaches the high art of poetry, she breaks the spell of fear and death (*Sobranie sochinenii* 2:646–47).

Before discussing the spell and the "sorceress" (*volshebnitsa*), Dora Aleksandrovna, who also appears as a "fairy" (*feya*), a "fairy-witch" (*feya-ved'ma*), a "pediatrician" (*vrach-pediatr*), and a "sales clerk" (*prodavshchitsa*), a few words about supporting folklore elements are in order. The narrator, as expected in Sinyavsky's fiction, pauses many times to share observations that are not in keeping with "scientific thinking." He, for example, points out how Dora puts yeast into a paper cone behind the counter of a Moscow department store, explaining that yeast, since the time of ancient Greece, presupposed baked goods, a great feast, drunkenness, and, most important, a wedding (*Sobranie sochinenii* 2:645). He also describes a dream in which he sees a slender girl or a beautiful dog who escapes from a cruel master only to cast off a dress, climb a tree, and fly from the top, wings flapping, into the sky (*Sobranie sochinenii* 2:639). Paying close attention to the gestures that accompany Dora's dance movements—her winks, nods, periphrastic allegories and symbols—the narrator tells the reader that through song and dance everyone is purified; they part with what is known as the self, leaving the body, which is subject to decay, reaching a higher plane, as they did in ancient times (*Sobranie sochinenii* 2:646).

Recalling the motif of many folktales, *Tsores* is built upon a devil's bargain, or, more specifically, upon a fairy's bargain.[17] In place of stuttering, the narrator, whose name is Sinyavsky, begs Dora Aleksandrovna, a fairy in the guise of a pediatrician, to give him the gift of an orator, a writer, or a fable maker.[18] In exchange for this gift, he is prepared to give up being loved. After all, at age five, he did not know the meaning of love. Looking back, he admits: "So, not suspecting, I sold myself to the devil" (*Sobranie sochinenii* 2:613). He came to understand very soon that without love there is only sorrow. His appearance, moreover, contributed to this sorrow, for it turns out that he is bowlegged, dwarfish, melancholy, and grubby. The trade-off is his newly found language abilities, especially his writing, which evokes envy and mistrust rather than admiration.

Not only is Sinyavsky not loved, but he is held in contempt.[19] In school and at home he is looked upon as a jinx—someone who brings bad luck or misfortune. People avoid him. His mother calls him "the devil" (*chort*), accusing him of being responsible for the death of his five brothers: Nokolai, Pavel, Vasily, Yakov, and Vladimir. While he did not kill his brothers, in his fictional account of them, which is where they existed, he did include their deaths. But as a writer, he takes responsibility, especially for the death of Vasily, explaining that he wrote with haste: "this death is my doing. Yes, I actually put my brother in front of a bullet. One is always in a hurry" (*Sobranie sochinenii* 2:626). In chapter 3 he says: "What, from the beginning? For you it is something to read. But I am the one who must answer for it" (*Sobranie sochinenii* 2:621). Sinyavsky is, of course, reminding the reader that he was and is still held responsible for what he writes.

While this devil's bargain and its consequences are easy to follow, they are accompanied by satirical references to the course of Russian history under the Soviets (the increasing loss of life: five out of six brothers) and events in the real Sinyavsky's life (attacks on him because of his writing). Moreover, at an abstract level, the entire story raises philosophical questions about the burden of suffering, sin, and guilt.

It turns out that Dora Aleksandrovna, the ambiguous fairy-witch, is the magic agency that cuts across all levels of this fantastic story. Associated with both heaven and hell, she has no equal on earth. Not only does she guide the destiny of Sinyavsky, but also, in the manner of Bulgakov's devil in *The Master and Margarita*, the destiny of Moscow, for the police, the city council, and the courts are under her sway (*Sobranie sochinenii* 2:646).[20] Through her, Sinyavsky obtains his talent and, therefore, identity as a writer, an identity not without a high price, especially under the Soviets. Moreover, she reappears to him after many years, offering what the devil's bargain excluded: love. In his trip with Dora to the netherworld, he comes to understand that his brothers are alive and that it is he who has died. What he thought was a wedding feast turned out to be a wake—his own. Most important, it is Dora who lets him know that his father was a writer. Before she disappears, she bequeaths to him the magic little cabinet with the bookcase which symbolizes not only his father, but also E. T. A. Hoffmann and the tradition of fantastic tales. From this magic little cabinet emerges the writer Andrei Sinyavsky who is embodied in *Kroshka Tsores*.

With the wealth of supernatural elements in the Russian folktale, Sinyavsky did not have to look far and wide for examples of fantasy. Renouncing what he called "excessive verisimilitude" (*izlishnee pravdopodobie*), he turned not only to writers such as Hoffmann, but also to Hoffmann's sources—folklore, the very sources that he celebrated in his study of Gogol, *V teni Gogolya* (*In the Shadow of Gogol*). While he focused on contemporary life, he seemed to allow not the future, but the past to encroach upon it and, in fact, to undermine its order. It turns out that as a satirist Sinyavsky pictured modern Russia haunted by old Russia in both a playful and a serious manner. While the new Soviet man was busy building socialism, witches and demons were still on the prowl and some of them were up to their old tricks.

NOTES

1. Sinyavsky and I. N. Golomshtok point to Picasso's focus on primitivism and especially black folk sculpture in *Pikasso* (31).

2. Sinyavsky always speaks with great reverence about Russian folklore. In *Golos* (*Voice from the Chorus*), for example, where he ruminates about many of his favorite subjects, he praises folktales for their "purity" and their "truthfulness to the facts" (*Sobranie sochinenii* 1:487, 549).

3. In this preface he adds that his numerous trips to Pereslavl'-Zalesskii with his wife in the 1950s and his experience in prison (1966–1971) were the important stages in his life which led to writing about Russian folk beliefs (8).

4. In *Ivan-Durak* (*Ivan the Fool*) Sinyavsky claims that the fantasies of the common people are fully expressed in fairy tales. In *Mysli vrasplokh* (*Thoughts Unaware*) he speaks about the wisdom of the peasant and his closeness not simply to seasons, fasts, and holidays, but also to eternity. In his simplicity the peasant was at one with heaven and earth, with the past and the future (*Sobranie sochinenii* 1:323).

5. "*Basnya*" can also be used in a figurative sense to refer to a cock-and-bull story.

6. The narrator draws our attention to the water nymph's need for water and her long periods of time in the bathroom (*Sobranie sochinenii* 1:147). The cactus-like creature in "*Pkhents*" also needs water. Like the water nymph he spends long periods of time in the bathroom immersed in water while others in the communal apartment wait in line outside the door.

7. The narrator pauses to underscore the supernatural character of Konstantin's theft of this wallet. In fact, the wallet is described as flying like a bird and winding up under Konstantin's shirt. He adds that this "trick" was in fact a "fairy-tale transformation," reminding us about the words of a song: "What was your money is now ours" (*Sobranie sochinenii* 1:116).

8. In "*Otechestvo*: *Blatnaya pesnya*" ("The Fatherland: A Thieves' Song"), Sinyavsky gives an example of how the image of a thief is restated in a song (95).

9. After exclaiming "Thou shalt not kill! God! Devil!" Solomon Moseevich quotes from the opera: "Pagliaccio, in su tu amor infranto" "Laugh, clown, at the love that has been shattered" (*Sobranie sochinenii* 1:121). Sinyavsky mentions the wandering performers (*skomorokhi*) in an interesting discussion, culminating in associations between sorcerers, fools, thieves, and buffoons (*Ivan-Durak* 55). Nepomnyashchy speaks about mummers (*skomorokhi*) in *Abram Tertz and the*

Poetics of Crime, 246, 355, n. 16. She quotes Sinyavsky's great reverence for *skomorokhi* in *V teni Gogolya,* 335–36, and *Ivan-Durak,* 58–59; Sinyavsky also discusses *skomorokhi as well as* fairy tales, magicians, buffoons, and sorcerers in "*Literaturnaya maska Alekseya Remizova*," 110–11.

10. The narrator pauses to define the forest spirit (*lesha*), calling him the wizard (*volshebnik*) who rules over the local bogs and who keeps people running in circles to keep them away from his lair (*Sobranie sochinenii* 1:58).

11. Such transformations are frequent in Russian folktales. For a specific example, see Afanas'ev's "*Perushko-Finist Yasnyi Sokol*." Transformations involving birds may be traced to the Egyptian phoenix.

12. Such transformations, excluding the bicycle and the motorcycle, are common in the *biliny* (epic folk songs), especially in regard to strategies in the battles of heroes such as Volga Buslaevich, Ilya Murumets, and Dobrynya.

13. Ilya Muromets is one of the great knights (*bogatyr*) from the early epic folk songs (*bylina*) of the Keivan era (circa 978–1015). Both human and superhuman traits are attributed to him. He plays an important role in the tale that brings him together with Ivan the Fool in Afanas'ev's collection.

14. Initially a holy wanderer (*skitalets*), a fool-in-Christ or holy fool (*yurodlivyi*) was revered for his ascetic way of life and uncanny prophesies. Not only did he suffer in imitation of Christ, but at times he exhibited anarchistic and masochistic tendencies.

15. Sinyavsky develops the notion of the "transmigration of souls" in his short story "*Gololeditsa*" ("Icy Conditions").

16. For further discussion of *Little Jinx* see Nepomnyashchy, *Abram Tertz and the Poetics of Crime,* 249–59; Edward Brown, *Russian Literature since the Revolution,* 246–47; Nussbaum, "Literary Selves," 238–58.

17. Consider, of course, the witch's pact in Grimm's "Rumplestiltskin," *The Blue Fairy Book*, ed. by Andrew Lang (London: Longmans, Green, 1889).

18. Sinyavsky is being most autobiographical here, for writing, in his opinion, seemed to be a devil's bargain. In *Abram Tertz and the Poetics of Crime*, Nepomnyashchy suggests that Tsores's stutter casts aspersions on the impact of socialist realism (251). A writer who did not participate in this system faced what Tsores faced: sorrow and misfortune.

19. Once again, Sinyavsky gets very autobiographical, pointing out that from the beginning to the end of his career as a writer he was under attack.

20. Bulgakov's devil in *The Master and Margarita* is also ambiguous, that is, he wills evil, but does good.

Chapter Thirteen

The Wit of a Literary Scholar

Although wit and humor are associated with laughter, quite often the same measure of laughter, they are not anchored in the same substance. The former has its origins in intellectual matters; the latter in joking matters easily recognized by a broad community. Sinyavsky values both for their departure from the dominant discourse, for their wily penetration into delicate as well as proscribed territories of communication.[1] For him all exchanges that are driven by political proprieties, conceit, or decorous banalities invite laughter, if not derision, as in the case of Karlinsky's "original idea" in *Sud idet* (*The Trial Begins*). Thinking that it would be possible to increase the food supply by extracting human embryos and biologically engineering them into species of fish, this self-serving lawyer explains: "it is cannibalism on a more refined and altogether higher level" (*Sobranie sochinenii* 1:264). Clearly Sinyavsky anticipates a strong response to this burlesque, relying on the reader's recognition of the soft peddling of Machiavellian science. In the following study let us consider how this kind of burlesque is a part of Sinyavsky's intellectual buffoonery, the kind of buffoonery that turns his narratives into a linguistic and literary game board governed by allusions, parodies, and puzzles, appealing, in the final analysis, to a select circle of readers.[2]

If wit is a product of the intellect, then Sinyavsky has the wherewithal to produce it in abundance. First of all, he is not just a well-educated man, but an academic, a published scholar and a writer of fiction. Given his predilection for playfulness, he is well positioned to make those connections that we associate with wit. In fact he does not miss an opportunity to play the informed jester in his fiction and literary criticism, building in opportunities for evoking what could be called "a knowing response" to striking references. In his ruminations about the human condition he raises the stakes of these responses, pouncing on old adages and modern assumptions. In "*Mysli vrasplokh*" ("*Thoughts Unaware*") especially, he puts his wit to work, not simply sharing aphorisms (e.g., "We make ourselves secure with the knowledge that we are predestined"), but also broaching unwieldy topics such as free will, sex, death, women, God, and Russian culture.[3] Instead of philosophizing, in the strict sense of the word, Sinyavsky makes pithy observations followed by illustrations that play against widely accepted notions. He does not simply make a point, but an unsettling point, suggesting, for example, "Freedom is always negative and presupposes an absence" (*Sobranie sochinenii* 1:325).

His remarks in "*Mysli vrasplokh*" ("*Thoughts Unaware*") about paradoxes in sex and in religion not only recall the topical and tonal domain of Rozanov, but they also remind us that quips exclude the mincing of words. When he, like Rozanov, turns to characterizing "Russianness," some readers may miss such mincing. True to aphoristic form, Sinyavsky gives cunning definitions, reducing the behavior of Russians, for example, to drinking and stealing. "Together with theft (the absence of a firm belief in what is actual and concrete), drunkenness gives us a vagabond's undue familiarity and makes such coarseness suspicious in the eyes of other nations" (*Sobranie sochinenii* 1:322). He goes on to say that old class hierarchies were replaced in Russia by an amorphous equality and a devious nature, which resulted in a stamp of inconstancy and frivolous irresponsibility. Without ceremony but not without a grin, he dismisses any lofty notion of "Russianness."[4]

Given such measured cultural commentary, Sinyavsky was not out to attract a mass audience. Although he did not exclude street humor or commonplace themes, he subordinated most of what he wrote to issues and innuendos rather than everyday events, realistic accounts, or romance. Nature almost disappeared from his fiction—as well as what we understand as traditional heroes and villains. Like Dostoevsky, he raised the stakes of his narratives, focusing on dilemmas, leading us to threshold moments, ideological battles, and desperate choices. While other authors go into detail about the cut of a character's clothing, the items on a menu, or the view from a window, Sinyavsky raised questions about teleology, identity, ontology, and literary theory. But Sinyavsky did not always raise these questions in a serious forum. In fact part of his strength as a satirist lies in his ability to consider such questions with a mischievous levity. Herein lies his central platform for wit which, of course, calls upon the mindfulness of the reader, the very mindfulness that is needed to sense, for example, that Terts is more than Sinyavsky's literary mask. On this very platform Sinyavsky parades his metaphors, teasing us about the fundamental predicament of both his era and his life in the most outrageous narratives.

It goes without saying that wit is a part of the one-upmanship that literary scholars like Sinyavsky practiced as a matter of course. Anyone who has read Sinyavsky's literary criticism from any period cannot but be struck by his ambushes, smoke screens, cunning arguments and, above all, repartees. He shares one of these repartees in *Spokoinoi nochi* (*Goodnight!*). Seeking to characterize Leonid Sobolev's destruction of the careers of many writers, Sinyavsky comes up with the metaphor "*plavuchaya literaturnaya Tsushima*" (a seagoing literary Tsushima) (*Sobranie sochinenii* 2:347). While it is an awkward mix of naval history and literature, it does recall the Straits where the Russian fleet was annihilated by the Japanese in May of 1905 and thereby links the sinking of ships with the sinking of writing careers. Sinyavsky torpedoes Sobolev with wit. At the same time, he slyly draws attention to the risks that were involved in literary scholarship, risks that even included one's record of book borrowing from the library. Recalling his "strategic-borrowing" days, he makes sport of so-called literary evidence. Using his literary wiles, he fantasizes about a game of cat and mouse, seeing himself checking out volumes of literature for window dressing, including the widely regarded realism of Turgenev, Sholokov, and Alesei Tolstoi. When the KGB was looking for "decadent" literature, he would be reading Abelard and Fadeev. If they were looking for Pasternak, he would be reading Herodotous whom, if necessary, he would replace with Darwin (*Sobranie sochinenii* 2:422).

It may be argued that literary scholars like Sinyavsky who write fiction are never free of the baggage of literature—baggage filled with encyclopedic details, often, with amusing twists. From his many bold and beguiling literary references, it is apparent that he builds his narratives conscious of the reader, ahead of whom he stays, engaging his or her knowledge and memory of writers and their works. Put simply, for Sinyavsky the terms of his fiction are not without a large measure of literary correlatives. Consider, for example, these correlatives when he comments on the cold war in the verbal exchange between a prisoner (Sinyavsky's very embodiment) and an interrogator (Viktor Aleksandrovich Pakhomov) in *Zerkalo* (*The Mirror*), a play embedded in *Spokoinoi nochi* (*Goodnight!*). This exchange begins when the interrogator claims that the prisoner's irreverent reassessment of Pushkin, *Progulki s Pushkinym* (*Strolls with Pushkin*), was ordered by the Pentagon. He goes on to say that the imperialists want to steal Pushkin's literary heritage and replace it with a "rotting cocktail lounge and a would-be Conan Doyle" (*Sobranie sochinenii* 2:381). Their witty point and counterpoint is as follows (prisoner=2; interrogator=1):

> (2) *The Three Sisters* call upon the fraternal peoples of New Guinea—to Moscow! to Moscow! Lobbing a grenade, Vanka Zhukov shouts to the imperialists, "Epikhodov Has Broken His Cue"—that's for you, but "The House With the Mezzanine" and "The Diamond Sky" belong to us.
>
> (1) Let me make some comparisons too! *The Captain's Daughter* is like a mobile machine gun.
>
> (2) Chekhov's "Kashtanka" is the cavalry. Forward, Kashtanka, hurrah!
>
> (1) Heavy artillery never misses: *Boris Godunov*, *Boris Godunov*. . . .
>
> (2) Did you forget *The Seagull*? The air force! (1) Intelligence and counterintelligence—*Mtsyri*, *Mtsyri*.
>
> (2) Let's play fair! Lermontov wrote *Mtsyri*!
>
> (1) What do you mean Lermontov? Lermontov indeed! You and your "Kashtanka." You are missing what is important! You forgot *Eugene Onegin*. *Eugene Onegin* is an intercontinental missile aimed at the heart of America. (*Sobranie sochinenii* 2:381–82)

In this duel of martial means, the prisoner chooses the works of Chekhov; the interrogator—the works of Pushkin. Emulating the arms race, both men ratchet up their literary "weapons," winding up with *Eugene Onegin*—an ICBM. On the one-upmanship side of this contest, the interrogator scoffs at the idea of the cavalry vis-à-vis Chekhov's "Kashtanka"—a dog. Likewise, the prisoner cries "foul play" when the interrogator proposes *Mtsyri*, for it is from Lermontov's rather than Pushkin's "arsenal." Actually the prisoner points to the best cold war strategy when he proposes the propaganda potential of *Tri sestry* (*The Three Sisters*). If Ol'ga, Masha, and Irina are drawn to Moscow, so might the people of New Guinea. Moreover, in suggesting a title such as "Epikhodov Has Broken His Cue," he hints at the implications of playing a game, in this case, a cold war game. In this echo of Chekhovian "byt" (everydayness) from *Vishnevyi sad* (*The Cherry Orchard*), however, something rings false. Chekhov, of course, did not write "Epikhodov Has Broken His Cue." On the other hand, in *Vishnevyi sad* one of the pieces of this cue becomes Varya's playful weapon which she uses to threaten first Epikhodov and then, by accident, Lopakhin.

Sinyavsky's wit actually reaches a level of puzzle making and puzzle solving, bringing reader and author together in a task that has potential not only for laughter, but also for reducing the distance between one consciousness and another. This task, which may involve putting a spin on words and, in response, recognizing this spin, clearly gives wit its highly corporate quality. Placing, for example, well-spun phrases such as "the logic of the international struggle" (*logika mezhdunarodnoi bor'by*), "capitalist encirclement" (*okruzhenie kapitalistov*), "necessary sacrifices" (*neobkhodimye zhertvy*), or "glorious aim" (*velikaya tsel'*) into an unexpected context, Sinyavsky relies upon the reader to recognize not simply their disconnection from the dominant discourse, but their musty smell. Only an outsider to Soviet Russian culture would miss such parodic recontextualization. Sinyavsky, of course, does not spell out such connections and disconnections. He does not explain, for example, that his novella, *Lyubimov* (*The Makepeace Experiment*), is, among many other things, a mock epic about the Bolshevik Revolution; nor does he discuss that his use of fantasy is a way of mocking the notion of a well-ordered Soviet utopia. It turns out that Sinyavsky's writing needs cultural decoding right down to puns such as "*gumanyutsiya*" (a combination of "humanism" and "revolution"), "*Chushkin*" and "*Pekhov*" (Pushkin and Chekhov) as well as "figurative phonetics" (*izobrazitel'naya fonetika*), linking the sound of "Stalin," for example, first with "steel," "slag" and "Stella," then with "Satan," "stalactite," "stability," and "staple" (*Sobranie sochinenii* 2:508–9, 518).

Actually, word play, the first step toward witty connections, is ubiquitous in Sinyavsky's writing, indicating a focus upon language itself—its denotative, connotative, poetic, and emotive potential. Sinyavsky, in this regard, becomes a mimic—not just of words in Old Church Slavonic, German, French, Italian, and English, but also of words in well-marked patterns of expression, including clichés. Through highly contrived and often highly entertaining patterns of speech, he can provide not just ironic declarations, but clever deformations, as in the sequence of suffixes *ksizm-sizm-sizm* and *matsiya-katsiya-zatsiya-natsiya*. The astute reader can easily guess what kind of words from "the commonly accessible language" (*obshchedostupnyi yazyk*) are likely to be built upon "-ism" and "-tion" (*Sobranie sochinenii* 1:292). The same reader can figure out that an aside about "Venus de Medici" is in fact a fractured reference to "Venus de Milo" (*Sobranie sochinenii* 2:643). Not all of Sinyavsky's verbal high jinks, however, are easy to decipher. Certainly the words of the creature in *Pkhents* (*Pkhents*) such as "*gogry*" (?) and "*tuzheroskip*" (?) may require a cryptographer. But even a cryptographer may not puzzle out the string of names that are attributed to the narrator's wife in *Goodnight!* (*Spokoinoi nochi*):

Mariya, Tatyana, Linda, Yulenka, Gertrude, Barbara, and Paulina (*Sobranie sochinenii* 2:441–43). Who is to say that they are not projections of the paradigmatic aspect of language, that is, substitutions for one kind of signifier rather than "genuine" references?[5]

If we follow the trail of Sinyavsky's word play, we will come across more than striking signals, sly non sequiturs, or rhyming associations. We certainly would not miss his witty misquote of a sentence from Tolstoy's *Anna Karenina*: "*Vse smeshalos' v dome Oblomovykh*" (All was confusion in Oblomov's home) (*Sobranie sochinenii* 2:383).[6] What should catch our attention immediately, however, is the abundance of literary allusions, which not only thicken the puzzle-making and puzzle-solving substance of wit, but also the overall parodic measure of Sinyavsky's satire. Herein lies one of Sinyavsky's most developed territories where the stamp of writers, as in "*Grafomany*" ("Graphomaniacs"), is placed in both high and low comic correspondences. It turns out that Sinyavsky takes every opportunity to playfully illuminate his fiction with authors and citations from their works, pausing, for example, in *Spokoinoi nochi* (*Goodnight!*) to discuss the vicissitudes of prophesy in the Russian medieval tale of Oleg the Wise and Shakespeare's *Macbeth*, and to press the reader about metaphors such as "a man not born of a woman" and "the movement of Birnam Woods" (*Sobranie sochinenii* 2:424).

It is clear then that a large part of Sinyavsky's wit is bound up with references to authors and their works, such as to Dostoevsky in *Sud idet* (*The Trial Begins*), *"Gololeditsa"* (*"Icy Conditions"*), *"V tsirke"* (*"At the Circus"), and Lyubimov* (*The Makepeace Experiment*). Following this wit, therefore, means following titles, quotes, and paraphrases, concluding, for example, that Gogol turns up more often than Pushkin in both a pointed and nonsensical way, but bearing in mind that aspects of both of these writers playfully germinate in Sinyavsky's fiction for many years, blossoming finally into the undeniably idiosyncratic studies, *Progulki s Pushkinym* (*Strolls with Pushkin*) and *V teni Gogolya* (*In the Shadow of Gogol*). While Pushkin the man and the artist becomes Sinyavsky's occasional intertextual companion, passages from Gogol's *Dead Souls* become an intermittent theme delivered with a wink to the reader. It is possible that Sinyavsky was living in the shadow of Gogol long before his *pieza bravura* on this satirist was published.[7] He does not simply allude to Gogol's troika passage in "*Grafomany*" ("Graphomaniacs") and "*Gololeditsa*" ("Icy Conditions"), but he places it on the table for the reader's reconsideration: "*O Rus'! Kuda nesesh'sya ty?*" (Oh Russia!

Where are you headed?) (*Sobranie sochinenii* 1:171, 206) It is with wit that he parades Gogol's civic rhapsody, that is, the dreamy image of Russia's singular progress—the image that was revived under socialism. He places it, after all, in the context of his own satire, muting any dreaminess. In a clever way Sinyavsky intertwines Gogol's satire with his own, enticing the reader to sense a number of possible connections, including a replay of earlier laughter in the darkness of oppression and earlier questions about the future of Russia.

As Sinyavsky's references to Gogol become more figurative, his narratives develop a sideshow effect worthy of Gogol himself. In Sinyavsky's earliest witty reference to Gogol, Tolya, a low-level KGB operative, calls *Mertvye dushi* (*Dead Souls*) *Mertvye dushat* (*The Dead Stifle*) (*Sobranie sochinenii* 1:297).[8] Here Tolya reveals his ignorance about the title and the content of this Russian classic, attributing literal meaning to "the dead." Ignorance notwithstanding, he laments that the second half of this classic will never be known because Gogol destroyed it. He argues that by putting a sieve in the drainage pipes of buildings, plans, surveys, love letters, drafts of literary works, and even finished literary projects would be saved (*Sobranie sochinenii* 1:297). What should bring a smile to the face of the reader is that Tolya associates intercepting written material with preserving it. This comedy of associations reaches a high point, however, when Tolya and his partner, Vitya, who recall Bobchinsky and Dobchinsky's paired presence in Gogol's *Revizor* (*The Inspector General*), realize that an invention such as the psychoscope would not only read the thoughts of others, but also their own.[9]

There is, of course, much teasing in Sinyavsky's allusions to Gogol, for teasing is an important part of wit. At times, it is as if Sinyavsky were conducting a scavenger hunt for the reader, leaving clues—cagey clues, such as the name of the protagonist in "*Ty i ya*" ("You and I"), which corresponds to the first name and patronymic of Gogol: Nikolai Vasilevich. Making sure that such clues are not missed in "*Grafomany*" ("Graphomaniacs"), he piles them up, creating, for example, a catalogue of references to birds, such as Straustin (ostrich), Galkin (jackdaw), and Ptitsin (generic bird), who are lightheartedly linked with Gogol (duck) and ultimately his "bird-train" (*ptitsa-poezd*).[10] Such cataloging in and of itself is one of Sinyavsky's many Gogolian hints, as is the humiliation scene, recalling Akaky Akakievich in "*Shinel'*" ("The Overcoat"), which he constructs in "*Grafomany*" ("Graphomaniacs") (*Sobranie sochinenii* 1:160). In this laughter-through-tears scene, Straustin describes his miserable existence, pointing out that his shoes are full of holes, that he has known only rotten cutlets and an apartment inundated by the din of a blaring trumpet. He did not have a study or even a desk. He explains that when he was writing *In Search of Joy*—a veiled reference to Fedin's novel, *Early Joys*—he plugged his ears with cotton and covered his eyes in order not to hear the trumpet or see the depressing marks on the wall: traces of bugs and greasy patches (*Sobranie sochinenii* 1:161).

In *Kroshka Tsores* (*Little Jinx*), Sinyavsky teases the reader with descriptive catalogues that are Gogolian in thematic focus and intensity, rambling manner, and measure of exaggeration. In this parody of E. T. A. Hoffmann's *Klein Zaches* (*Little Zaches*), Sinyavsky's narrator suddenly enumerates like a nineteenth-century author, displaying both a zest for details and a measure of playfulness.[11] He leads us into an entirely un-Sinyavskian discourse on food, a "panaroma" of food in the grocery section of a Moscow department store, prefacing his description with: "I do not know whether you have had the good fortune, ladies and gentlemen, of seeing anything like the mountains of food and spirits." (*Sobranie sochinenii* 2:641). He then describes:

> a fairy-tale abundance behind glass and along the walls that reaches to the sky in the shape of columns, mausoleums, eastern grottoes, porticos, castles, Carthages constructed with slabs of creamery butter, jars of jam, vanilla rusks, cinnamon, eggs and other spicy things. (*Sobranie sochinenii* 2:641)

For more than two pages the narrator strings together foodstuffs, drawing attention to rolls, cheese, meat, fish, and the aroma of ground coffee, adding with Gogolian hyperbole: "—you could shop for a hundred years and still not buy everything—" (*Sobranie sochinenii* 2:642). But the crowning moment in this gastronomical inventory belongs to tea—not simply "Georgian Extra," "Krasnodar Type II," "Chinese," "Indian," or "Ceylon," but:

> Aromatic tea, medicinal tea, forbidden tea, vitamin C-fortified tea, antitubercular tea, astringent tea for the gingiva, tea that takes possession of your soul with red, hot, oily fat that makes your heart beat nonstop like a clock, tea whose strength rivals that of rum, with the consistency of the thickest jam which, I must confess, is best with a little salted herring, tea, like the felt boots, quilted pants, riding boots and sweaters that are delivered to a prison camp in the casual way that Adenauer exchanged his equipment—for five packages of tea, tea generating the funds to make or

> break a career, tea made available to people in unlimited quantities at an incredibly low price. (*Sobranie sochinenii* 2:643)

Through such delights and this tisane profusion, Sinyavsky eases the reader into a half-magic, half-comic territory—a most suitable territory for Dora Aleksandrovna, who is embodied as pediatrician, fairy godmother, witch, salesclerk, and enchantress. The reader, of course, is expected not to overlook that shortly before Dora's unexpected appearance as a clerk in the department store, she is foreshadowed by a dream about a *sirin* (harpy), a half-woman, half-birdlike creature from Russian folklore. In keeping with this lore, which occupies an important place in Gogol's early stories, Dora prances, twirls, and leaps about behind the counter, speaking in riddles, using a dance step to signal agreement to the marriage proposal from Little Jinx, whose last name, in witty intertextuality, happens to be Sinyavsky.[12]

Just when the reader is busy figuring out this puzzling intertextual crossroad, the narrator introduces "an unimaginable little cabinet" (*nevoobrazimyi shkafik*) recalling, in so many ways, Chichikov's "little box" (*shkatulka*) in *Dead Souls* (*Mertvye dushi*), into which much has been implicitly and explicitly placed. As Gogol's narrator takes a whole paragraph to describe the little box, Sinyavsky's narrator takes a whole paragraph to describe the little cabinet, each pointing out the various compartments and their contents. Gogol's narrator underscores the internal arrangement:

> in the very middle, a soap dish; behind it six or seven very narrow partitions for razors; then, square compartments for a sand-shaker and an ink-pot; between these two was an oblong hollow space for quills, sealing wax, and any other rather long items; then there were all sorts of compartments, with and without lids, for shorter items, and in these there were visiting cards, funeral announcements, old theater tickets and other such things, stored away as souvenirs. The entire upper tray with all its partitions was removable and under it there was a space occupied by bundles of papers; then, there was a little secret money drawer that could be pulled out discreetly on one side of the box. (N. V. Gogol, *Izbrannye proizvedeniya* 3:256)

Sinyavsky's narrator does the same:

> Imagine a book cabinet in walnut wood on four legs. But what construction and design! Books behind glass in gilded bindings glittered in the hollow of a tall, elegant structure pressed against the wall. And lower, below its waist, just jutting out half a meter, there is a slanting desk with a lid and two horizontal

> compartments beneath for paper or, if you wish, manuscripts—rough and final drafts. A desk with shelves is perfect. Still lower—and this is important—are twisted legs, rather long and unusual for a cabinet, but seemingly stubby in relationship to the whole frame. (*Sobranie sochinenii* 2:647)

Elevating the significance of this little cabinet, Sinyavsky's narrator, like Gogol's narrator, exhibits a great fondness for it, making sure, moreover, that he always knows its whereabouts.[13] At one point he calls it his "idol," explaining that it is "the embodiment of E. T. A. Hoffmann" (*sam Ernest-Teodor-Amadei Gofman*) who, of course, also inspired Gogol.[14]

In *V teni Gogolya* (*In the Shadow of Gogol*) Sinyavsky focuses on Gogol's "little box," comparing it to a "magic box" (*volshebnyi yashik*) in which a whole army or the entire kingdom of a wandering tsar may be contained (*Sobranie sochinenii* 2:259). In his opinion, out of Chichikov's "little box" emerges a motley procession of people and lives rich with omens of destiny and freedom, a swarm of load-bearing species (*Sobranie sochinenii* 2:258). As Chichikov's "little box" is a magic source, so is the "little cabinet" that Dora bestows upon Little Jinx. Moreover, given Sinyavsky's brazen reference to his own name, this little cabinet is more than a link with folklore or the fiction of a fellow satirist. In one of his most witty entanglements, Sinyavsky has combined the most pithy and the most far-fetched elements. Put simply, he has engineered a complex amalgam of references, parading, once again, a codependency of autobiography and fiction. Putting together this codependency, Sinyavsky becomes a master puzzle maker, giving the reader much to think about in regard to pieces of fiction and reality. In fitting these pieces together, right down to Dora's metaphorical connection with yeast, the wit begins.

Sinyavsky's path to wit is not simply a path to parody, for he does not always satirize the substance or style of an author. In fact, in many cases he exhibits an author, not because of his or her follies, but because of his or her quirks and haunting issues. Like a postmodern architect he incorporates these quirks and issues into the body of his narratives, letting the reader discover their playful connections. After the laughter of recognition dies down, the reader realizes that the work before him or her is also a literary intimation—as in the correspondence between the "little box" and the "little cabinet." In addition to behaving like a satirist, Sinyavsky behaves, as I have said, like a jester who not only has skills in mimicking and masquerading the word, but also who has scholarly credentials. His allusions to authors ultimately indicate his abiding interest in writing, in pulling together old and new elements of illusion and reality in a manner in which he can maintain a serious level of satire and, at the same time, carry on a game of cat and mouse with the reader.

NOTES

1. Sinyavsky puts forward his positions regarding the importance of the joke/anecdote/funny story in "*Anekdot v anekdote,*" 77–95.

2. On the second day of his trial, February 11, 1966, Sinyavsky explained that his writing was not intended for a mass audience. He goes on to say that publishing what he had written was a way of preserving it for himself and a small circle of people (Ginzburg 241–42).

3. "*Mysli vrasplokh*" ("*Thoughts Unaware*"), a collection of aphorisms and meditations, was one of the last items that Sinyavsky smuggled out to the West in the early 1960s. Aphorisms, the fundamental units of Vasilii Rozanov's prose, are, of course, associated with wit. Sinyavsky considered these units a breakthrough in the development of a new genre of literature. For a detailed discussion about Rozanov and his influence on Sinyavsky, see chapter 10.

4. Both Sinyavsky and Rozanov were criticized for their lampoons on Russia. At his trial Sinyavsky was accused of slandering the Russian people.

5. Holmgren explains this enumeration of names as "the artistic transformation of reality," permitting a metamorphosis and a multiplication of images of both wives and mice (*First-Person Liberties* 256). Nepomnyashchy, on the other hand, explains this enumeration as "the free play of the sign in a literary work: names become interchangeable and tropes self-generating" (*Abram Tertz and the Poetics of Crime* 359n).

6. Sinyavsky substitutes the name of Ivan Gonchorov's hero, Oblomov, for Tolstoy's Oblonsky.

7. In an interview, Sinyavsky called *In the Shadow of Gogol* "an attempt at a spiritual autobiography" (Pomerantsev 560).

8. In *The Trial Begins* and *On Socialist Realism*, 96, Max Hayward translated *Mertvye dushat* as "*Dead Scowls*." In his *V teni Gogolya* (*In the Shadow of Gogol*) Sinyavsky names chapter 3 "Mertvye dushat" ("The Dead Stifle").

9. Vitya and Tolya have a nonfictional side. Sinyavsky is lampooning Anatoly Sofronov and Vitaly Kochetov, two establishment writers. He also refers to them in *Lyubimov* (*The Makepeace Experiment*).

10. "*Ptitsa-poezd*" is from Sinyavsky's "*Gololeditsa*" ("Icy Conditions") where he modernizes Gogol's means of transportation, "*ptitsa-troika*," while maintaining its birdlike flight (*Sobranie sochinenii* 1:206).

11. Links to Gogol in a parody of E. T. A. Hoffmann's story should not be surprising. Like Sinyavsky, Gogol was well acquainted with and inspired by the

works of this German storyteller who set an influential example for the literature of the fantastic.

12. In his emphasis upon the movements of the dance, going so far as to call Dora Aleksandrovna a "ballerina," Sinyavsky foreshadows his analogies in *V teni Gogolya* (*In the Shadow of Gogol*) regarding the dance as well as the music box metaphor in Gogol's play, *Revizor* (*The Inspector General*) (*Sobranie sochinenii* 2:68, 97).

13. Sinyavsky's narrator (Little Jinx) points out that he had treasured the cabinet ever since the day that he received it from Dora. As if looking back, he confesses that he had moved twenty times and that many changes had taken place in his life, but the little cabinet was still with him. In fact its presence is underscored in the very last scene of *Kroshka tsores* (*Sobranie sochinenii* 2:647, 652). The little cabinet's books and desk are, of course, the central treasure, linking everything with writing and literature, but specifically with the inspiration of E. T. A. Hoffmann, Gogol, and Sinyavsky's father.

14. It should be recalled that in the conclusion of *Chto takoe sotsialisticheskii realizm* (*What Is* Socialist *Realism*) Sinyavsky names E. T. A. Hoffmann together with Dostoevsky, Goya, Chagall, and Mayakovsky as models of a phantasmagoric art that would replace realistic description (*Fantasticheskii mir Abrama Tertsa* 446). Hence, the intertextual importance of this little cabinet cannot be overstated. When Dora Aleksandrovna refers to Little Jinx's, that is, Sinyavsky's father, she points to the little cabinet, which then stands up on its hind legs (*Sobranie sochinenii* 2:649). In *Abram Tertz and the Poetics of Crime*, Nepomnyashchy speaks of *Little Jinx* as being "fathered" by E. T. A. Hoffmann (249). In the same way, through Dora's conflation of Sinyavsky's father and the little book-filled cabinet, it is possible that the "fathering" of the character, Sinyavsky, and, by implication, the writer, Sinyavsky, is also suggested.

Chapter Fourteen

The Final Polemic: Targeting the Russian Intelligentsia

In spite of its broad-beamed topic, Sinyavsky's *The Russian Intelligentsia* has rather scanty footings.[1] Above all, it does not define the term "intelligentsia," nor does it walk us through the perceptions of this group and its convoluted evolution since the nineteenth century. Readers who are not familiar with Russian history cannot imagine the implications of claiming a link between the intelligentsia under Yeltsin and the old intelligentsia, to say nothing of the politics of terms such as the "revolutionary," "bourgeois," "professional," or "artistic" intelligentsia. There are, of course, many readers both inside and outside of Russia who believe that the intelligentsia lost its identity in 1917, after the Bolshevik Revolution, that it was absorbed by the outcome of its efforts. Even during the growing opposition of the 1960s, the term "dissenters" was used instead of "intelligentsia" to refer to the conscious stricken who spoke out against government policies. Certainly Sinyavsky could have made a distinction between an *intelligent* and an intellectual. Instead, he leaps to the attack, condemning high-placed supporters of Yeltsin, aiming salvos at Russians with professional, scholarly, and artistic profiles in both recent and past decades. But, it must be argued that Sinyavsky's topic is not unworthy, that stripped of evocative ballast, its categorical claim calls for further discussion.

Above all, Sinyavsky's book needs a context, for it reads like a lone voice, a voice, moreover, from a distant shore. It needs to be considered not just in the light of anger and disappointment, but in the light of a discussion that acknowledges the problematic image of the intelligentsia and the hazards of both old and new assessments of it. By coincidence *Izvestiya* provided space for such a discussion, actually a forum of opinions about the intelligentsia, on the anniversary of Bastille Day, July 14, 2000.[2] The editors were not surprised that the topic drew a number of responses. They were surprised, however, at the large number of responses and the many sharply worded convictions in them. As a result, they published another forum on this topic in the August third issue. It turned out that both installments took issue with the nature and the role of the intelligentsia, addressing new controversies and reviving old ones. Before looking closely at Sinyavsky's positions, let us briefly consider the opinions in *Izvestia*'s forum regarding the strengths and weaknesses of the intelligentsia and the issue of its leadership in the past and in the present.

Sinyavsky is not alone in condemning the intellectual elite or in juxtaposing it to the old intelligentsia. In fact after considering some of the views of *Izvestia*'s readers, Sinyavsky's attacks seem to be on the same page, expressing, in particular, unqualified reverence for the old intelligentsia and consternation about its current incarnation. *Izvestia*'s respondents, moreover, speak out from different places in society regarding corruption in post-Soviet Russia, demonstrating that dissent is not the property of a particular group with a particular agenda. Out of twelve respondents, only two reject the notion of shifting nineteenth-century responsibilities to the new post-Soviet intelligentsia. Only one suggests that the history of the intelligentsia started with Prince Kurbsky under Ivan the Terrible.[3]

Responding to questions from Yulia Rakhaeva, Yuri Levada, the Director of the All-Russian Polling Center, reminds readers of *Izvestia* about the nature and the evolution of the intelligentsia and the difficulties of defining it. By degrees, he steers the readers to what he ironically calls "the posthumous life of the intelligentsia" after the Bolshevik Revolution, pointing to its revitalization as a white-collar service corps in the mid-thirties and its appearance as a forceful constituency for Gorbachev. Unlike Sinyavsky, Levada attempts to reconcile the theory of the intelligentsia with its record. Although he admires the *intelligent* for standing behind his or her own convictions and actions and for carefully weighing their consequences, he argues that the *intelligent* is capable of dirty tricks (*pakosti*) as well as stupid decisions (8).

German Travin, on the other hand, puts the intelligentsia beyond such capabilities, claiming that this group is determined, above all, by a framework of moral and ethical standards. In fact he argues that the "real *intelligent*" demonstrates the possibility and the necessity of living in a world of the highest moral and ethical standards. Moreover, in Travin's opinion, the "real *intelligent*" reminds us that concepts such as "conscience," "honesty," "unselfishness," and "compassion" are not abstractions (7).

Yuri Chernyshov takes issue with Levada, especially in regard to the intelligentsia's alleged monopoly on benevolence (7). He cannot accept that all forms of rule are indifferent; nor can he accept the use of the term "*intelligent*" to mean the same as "intellectual," for the latter does not necessarily signal ethical qualities. Above all, he is against the widespread notion of the latter-day *intelligent*, who having allegedly fulfilled his or her function, finally takes his or her place as a citizen in a civil society. He does not believe that the intelligentsia becomes a part of a new order, but maintains its primary function, providing "tutors of the spirit." Sinyavsky makes a similar point, but it is buried in other convictions. Arguably, he would agree with Chernyshov's premise that as long as there is Russian culture, the intelligentsia is indispensable. Sergei Magarin also does not question the continued existence of the Russian intelligentsia, but he does not see it as a responsible group. Expecting more than moral and ethical guidance, he reproaches the "brains of the nation" for failing to advance both economic and democratic reforms (7). Outraged by the intelligentsia's eagerness to leave the country, he accuses it of neither fulfilling nor understanding its historical and moral obligations to the people.

Like Sinyavsky, Andrei Bukin and Dmitri Shusharin target especially the intellectual elite and its unhealthy closeness to power under Yeltsin. Making a new case against this elite, they focus on the transition from Yeltsin to Putin, pointing to the "tribal behavior" that comes to the surface when the institutionalization of power threatens to replace a system of patronage (8). They argue that this "tribal behavior" is deeply rooted in the consciousness of the Russian intelligentsia, showing itself specifically in its characterization of the criminal investigation of Media-Most as an attack on free speech. With similar dark inferences, Aleksei Vinokurov enlarges upon the gulf between the intelligentsia and the people, pointing to old as well as new wounds that they have inflicted on one another. In the wounding process he faults the intelligentsia for indulging in abstractions, pessimism, and self-absorption. Today's intelligentsia, he maintains, thinks about itself rather than the people. It originally turned to the people only to keep them from running wild (8).

Mikhail Uspensky, on the other hand, defends today's intelligentsia, underscoring, for some reason, its self-imposed guilt before the people. He suggests that if it is dying of something, that something would be meekness (7). He sees this group pressed between the government and the people, the latter expressing anti-intellectual feelings, the former taking steps to ward off reproaches about the lack of sound social programs. Claiming that the intelligentsia has been victimized, Uspensky argues that the pejorative meaning that was attributed to this group in the first decade after the Bolshevik Revolution is easy to revive. Given the government's fear that the intelligentsia might acquire genuine power, it plays to business circles, hoping to entice educated Russians into the company of entrepreneurs rather than critical thinkers. Echoing this sentiment, German Travin argues that the meek and modest number of voices from the intelligentsia are easily muffled by those in the government who serve the oligarchs.

Leonid Ashkinazi fears that the current circumstances in Russia has produced an epidemic of maniacal-aggressive psychosis among the intelligentsia. He draws the reader's attention to the level of anxiety brought about not only by economic collapse, but also by the bloodshed in Chechnya and the former territories of Yugoslavia which, in his opinion, has caused members of the intelligentsia to suffer amnesia, entirely reversing their positions of what is acceptable and unacceptable, seeing, for example, victims as aggressors and aggressors as victims. Switching from a psychological to sociological window of analysis, he concludes that the Russian *intelligent* is a product of his own or her own era, that is, becoming a dissident when it is fashionable. Hence, the eagerness to become a democrat in a period of democratization.

Merab Mamardashvili poses a leading question about the role of the intelligentsia: "Universal Consciousness or Ideological Engineers?" In reducing the intelligentsia's moral and ethical positions to "cerebral activity" or "enlightened absolutism" he reveals his own answer (8). He goes on to say that Russia is witnessing the resurgence of an intelligentsia that either markets an irrational and apocalyptic social utopia if it cannot make peace with the dominant class, or a technocratic wonderland of social and ideological engineering if it does (8). Taking a parting shot, Mamardashvili says that it is difficult to tell if the intelligentsia is exhibiting a reaction to the vices of a bourgeois society or nostalgia for a lost intellectual monopoly.

In the light of these opinions, Sinyavsky's assault on the intelligentsia lacks a number of important perspectives. Its potential shock value, far from the days of Rozanov, is terribly limited. It would seem that readers would be stunned not so much by Sinyavsky's accusations, but by his failure to show how corruption is rooted in a nebulous layer of society. To readers focused on weak political organizations, oligarchs, gangsters, and the price of oil, the intelligentsia may seem like an abstraction. While there may be, in fact, a link between the decline of Russia and the intelligentsia, Sinyavsky does not flesh out this link.

Casting a wide net, he blames the very group that historically assumed responsibility for the welfare of the Russian people. In fact he seems to favor what is tantamount to a class-action indictment, charging the intelligentsia with greed for power, savage treatment of rivals, and indifference to the plight of the Russian people (*The Russian Intelligentsia* 8, 31, 67). He argues, moreover, that at a time when the promise of a civil society was at hand, the intelligentsia abandoned its critical thinking, supporting Yeltsin's use of force against members of Parliament and the Supreme Soviet, as well as the Chechen separatists. Standing by while the nation was being looted, the intelligentsia, according to Sinyavsky, sold out, abdicating its former role as the conscience of the nation (9). Sinyavsky claims, moreover, that during the Soviet period even well-known writers, who stood apart from the professional and technical intelligentsia, signed their names to the call for the blood of enemies (7, 8). Prepared to initiate a major polemic with his assumptions, Sinyavsky confronts the new intelligentsia with its old responsibilities.

In his classification of the intelligentsia, Sinyavsky uses a broad brush, using little caution with qualifiers such as "classic," "radical," or "technical." [4] At one point he simply divides the post-Soviet intelligentsia into the elite and the poor, the former rallying around Yeltsin, the latter remaining on the side of the people.[5] Making socioeconomic distinctions, he speaks of the poor as "teachers and ordinary people" as opposed to "the privileged part of the intelligentsia," "the court and government intelligentsia, that is, prominent people" (21, 66). At another point he refers to "the intelligentsia in the retinue of the president of Russia," adding that what took place under Yeltsin could not have happened in the United States, France, or Sweden, but in Uganda under President Idi Amin (71).

The personal side of Sinyavsky's misgivings about the intelligentsia should not be overlooked, for it shapes a number of emotionally filled arguments. While sounding the general alarm about panaceas, utopias, father figures, and the evils of nationalism, he expresses deep disappointment in that part of the cultural intelligentsia that was formerly constituted by friends and acquaintances. This disappointment can be sensed in his description of his visit to Moscow in 1994 when he brought Theresa Obrecht's film *To Die in Moscow* to show friends: poets, journalists, and human rights lawyers (33). Consider his surprise when many of them dismissed the seriousness of Russia's situation, blaming the alarmist views of the masses, the disinformation of outsiders, the propaganda of the old Communists, and nostalgia for the welfare programs of the past. Owing to such perceptions, Sinyavsky explains that he stopped listening to friends and started reading newspapers, namely *Vek*, *Izvestia*, *Nezavisimaya gazeta*, *Trud*, *Moskovskii komsomolets*, *Literaturnaya gazeta*, *Obshchaya gazeta*, and *Sobesednik*, to better understand what was taking place in Russia (33).[6]

According to Sinyavsky, newspapers tell another story; such as the one in 1937 when well-known writers such as Olesha, Platonov, Zoshchenko, Yashvili, Babel, Tynyanov, Paustovsky, Antokolsky, Lugovskoi, Marshak, and Shklovsky added their signatures to the call for the blood of enemies (7–8). Recent newspapers, he sadly acknowledges, reveal that ex-dissidents such as Sergei Averintsev, Bella Akhmadulina, Bulat Akudzhava, Marietta Chudakova, Zoya Krakhmalnikova, and Yevgeni Pasternak signed their names in support of Yeltsin's firing on the White House (10, 30). According to Sinyavsky, even Dmitri Likhachev, an enduring symbol of the intelligentsia, signed a letter calling for a ban on all Communist and nationalist parties, fronts, and associations as well as publications such as *Den'*, *Pravda*, *Sovetskaya Rossia,* and *Literaturnaya Rossia* (11).[7]

Earlier, in his *Soviet Civilization: A Cultural History*, Sinyavsky claimed that the intelligentsia also rallied around Gorbachev, welcoming and supporting perestroika (restructuring) (268). He, in fact, reminds us of the eternal divergence between the intelligentsia and the people in the issues of Gorbachev's Russia, pointing out that through the efforts of the intelligentsia, glasnost (openness) won out over bread. Discussing the post-Stalin dissident movement as another manifestation of the Russian intelligentsia, Sinyavsky argues that the individual and his or her rights rather than a sociopolitical category of people became the battle cry of that day. In this movement the intelligentsia did not fight for class interests, land, material privileges, or even democracy (239). Sinyavsky maintains, moreover, that the cultural wing of the intelligentsia spearheaded this movement, going public at great risk, insisting namely on freedom of expression—upon which everything depended. Speaking from personal experience, he explains that after the death of Stalin members of the intelligentsia, who had become prisoners of conscience, made no appeals to the masses, but they did make an unprecedented case for their own existence—an existence rooted in critical thinking and manifested in the power of the word.

In both *The Russian Intelligentsia* and *Soviet Civilization* Sinyavsky acknowledges the ever present distance between the intelligentsia and the people—even in the dissident movement which he had a part in shaping. So how is it possible for him to see this distance in a different way under Yeltsin? Actually he argues that what is different about the intelligentsia under Yeltsin is not so much its distance from the people, but its closeness to the government. Owing to what Sinyavsky calls the post-Soviet intelligentsia's "loyal ecstasy" for the government, he compares it to the intelligentsia of the 1930s (*Intelligentsia* 70). Instead of standing as an intermediary between the people and the authorities, it scrambles to the side of the authorities seeking privileges, participating, according to Sinyavsky, in high corruption, backing policies that undermined the legalization of private property, the initiation of small business, the development of a sound agricultural policy, and opportunities for capital investment. Calling the intelligentsia "subcontractors to the authorities," Sinyavsky cites Andrei Bitov who claims that it is not possible to join forces with authority and still be a part of the intelligentsia (*Literaturnaya gazeta* February 28, 1966, 3). In *Izvestia* Yuri Levada echoes Bitov, claiming that the intelligentsia cannot occupy a position of power, that a philosopher on the throne is no longer a philosopher (8).

On the dust jacket of *The Russian Intelligentsia* Susan Sontag praises Sinyavsky's analysis, calling it "an unflinching, passionate account of what has gone wrong in Russia since the collapse of the Bolshevik system." David Remnick, on the other hand, chides him for not focusing on "the structures of power, property and influence," "the core of crony capitalism" ("How Russia Is Ruled" 14). But neither appraisal accurately addresses the zigzags of Sinyavsky's polemic or the insights that he scatters without warning or development. Besides, Sinyavsky should not be judged as an economist or a political scientist. The gap between his theory and his observations notwithstanding, he, like Levada and Bitov, raises the all-important question about the relationship between authority and what he considers to be a uniquely Russian agency of moral and ethical inquiry—the intelligentsia. In suggesting an answer to this question, Sinyavsky reaffirms his lifelong position regarding ends and means, advocating, once again, agency rather than agenda. In fact he argues that the intelligentsia is the agency that should be occupied with inquiry, with the process and the dissemination of critical thinking (3). For Sinyavsky it is unthinkable for the intelligentsia to both espouse and preside over any agenda. As a result, he maintains that when the members of the intelligentsia sound like the authorities, they devalue the word—which is their only weapon in the struggle for the common good.

Clearly, Sinyavsky's *The Russian Intelligentsia* does not advance his standing as writer or critic any more than *Nov'* (*Virgin Soil*) did for

Turgenev.[8] Although he follows his polemical instincts, he stumbles into a conceptual territory that is filled with land mines. Meanwhile, he reverts to praising and blaming, which has polemical value, but little standing at the substantive end of satire. It follows that having become a critic of Stalin's Russia, Sinyavsky also was to become a critic of Yeltsin's Russia. In fact, in some ways he identifies the problems that illuminate the likenesses and differences of both of these eras. But he puts aside his humor, favoring the language of opprobrium, showing his Juvenalian side, maintaining a stormy discourse of exclamation, sharp addressivity, and accusation.

It is with this project that he concludes a cycle of rather direct social criticism, one that grew over the years during his Paris period. While his views on the Russian intelligentsia belong on the shelf with his other published lectures, that is, with *Ivan-Durak: Ocherk russkoi narodnoi very* (*Ivan the Fool: An Essay on the Beliefs of the Russian People*), "*Opavshie list'ya" V. V. Rozanova: Ocherk russkoi kul'tury* (*V. V. Rozanov's "Fallen Leaves": A Essay on Russian Culture*), and *Soviet Civilization: A Cultural History*, they follow in the path of the prickly inferences of essays such as "*Literaturnyi protsess v Rossii*" ("The Literary Process in Russia"), "*Stilisticheskie raznoglasiya*" ("Stylistic Differences"), "*O kritike*" ("On Criticism"), "*Chtenie v serdtsakh*" ("Reading in a Fit of Temper"), and "*Russkii natsionalizm*" ("Russian Nationalism").

In posing Aleksandr Herzen's question, "Who is to blame" Sinyavsky reveals the context that he imagines for *The Russian Intelligentsia* (59). Moreover, in the framework of this old polemical tradition he admits to setting out to frighten his audience with his revelations (79). But striking fear in the hearts of anyone is not Sinyavsky's forte. The better part of his reputation lies in his ability to summon other emotions. Over the years he has made readers laugh or he has made them angry. What could be more satisfying to a satirist? In fact the strong reactions to his fiction and his nonfiction testify to his success in satire whether attacking, poking fun, or pulling the reader's leg. His irreverence, it seems, took him down a risky path, one that started with polemics and ended with polemics, but which also led to an uncommon world of fiction, of humor and wit, philosophical disputation, and out-and-out fantasy. On this path, filled with more risks than rewards, he ramped up a spotlight to illuminate what was underilluminated, letting readers untangle the laughter from the serious issues in Russian history. Who could better masquerade a treatise in carnival attire or parade the most outrageous idea as an earnest hypothesis? But Sinyavsky drew the line at peddling some kind of truth. In fact he drew our attention to truth peddlers. From the very start of his writing to the very end he flushed them out, whether they spoke for themselves or for institutions. While many epitaphs could pay tribute to Sinyavsky and his work, one of them should read: Truth-Peddlers Beware!

NOTES

1. Sinyavsky delivered three lectures at Columbia University's Harriman Institute in 1996. The following year they were translated by Lynn Visson and published as *The Russian Intelligentsia*. Reviewers immediately recognized Sinyavsky as a spokesman for the intelligentsia; they also recognized that his book fell short of a discussion of Russia's woes in the 1990s. Many reviews were not favorable. Robin Milner-Gulland called it lightweight; David Remnick ("How Russia Is Ruled," 13) claimed that Sinyavsky's analysis was emotional, disoriented, and impaired by omissions and anecdotal information. See also the reviews by Anthony Phillips, Philippe Radley, Derek Offord, Olga Glagoleva, Graeme Gill, and Neil Cornwell.

2. *Izvestia*, July 14, 2000, 8; August 3, 2000, 7.

3. Both Aleksandr Arkhangel'sky and Yuri Levada reject the notion of a post-Soviet intelligentsia with the ideals and expectations of the prerevolutionary intelligentsia. Mark Litvak argues about the origin of the intelligentsia, claiming that its roots predate the late eighteenth century.

4. Martin Malia pays close attention to qualifications for "intelligentsia" in his article "What Is the Intelligentsia" published in Richard Pipes, ed., *The Russian Intelligentsia* (New York: Columbia University Press, 1961); see especially his note on the derivation of "intelligentsia" (18). See also Stuart Ramsay Tompkins, *The Russian Intelligentsia: Makers of the Revolutionary State* and Vladmir C. Nahirny, *The Russian Intelligentsia: From Torment to Silence,* as well as Yulia Vishnevskaya's articles in *Sintaksis* during the 1990s.

5. Aware that readers may jump to conclusions about who is included among the intellectual elite, Sinyavsky pauses to explain that he has no quarrel with "the thousands of highly dedicated intellectuals scattered throughout the schools, plants, libraries and hospitals of the capital, the provinces, towns, cities, villages and settlements" (68).

6. While Sinyavsky expresses a great interest in what was disclosed in newspapers, he senses that the intelligentsia has turned away from them, owing to what they perceive as the devaluation of the word in the absence of censorship (76).

7. *Izvestia* placed Likhachev's picture in the very center of the page devoted to the forum on the Russian intelligentsia, calling him the personification of the intelligentsia—its very "tuning fork" (*kamertona*) (August 3).

8. Like Turgenev's last novel, Sinyavsky's *The Russian Intelligentsia* turned out to be off center.

Selected Bibliography

WORKS BY SINYAVSKY

"L'adieu à Iouli Daniel." *Le Monde*, 3 January 1989, 5.
"Akmeism." In *Kratkaya literaturnaya entsiklopediya*, 1:118–19. Moscow: Sovetskaya entsiklopediya, 1962.
"A. M. Gor'kii." In *Istoriya russkoi sovetskoi literatury*, 1:99–167. Moscow: Akademiya nauk, 1958.
"Andrei Siniavskii," In *The Red Pencil: Artists, Scholars, and Censors in the USSR*, edited by Marianna Tax Choldin and Maurice Friedburg, translated by Maurice Friedberg and Barbara Dash, 94–100. Boston: Unwin Hyman, 1989.
"André Siniavski." *Pourquoi ecrivez-vous*? 400 ecrivains repondent, 199. Paris: Liberation, 1985.
"A. Sinyavskii—ital'yanskomu zhurnalu '*Ekspress*'." *Sintaksis*, no. 31 (1991), 190–91.
"Apofeoz knigi." *Chaiers du Monde russe et sovietique* 29, no. 3–4 (1988): 293–301.
"Bez skidok (o sovremennom nauchno-fantasticheskom romane)." *Voprosy literatury*, no. 1 (1960): 45–59. English translation, "No Discount," in Sinyavsky, *For Freedom of Imagination*, 17–36.
"Chtenie v serdtsakh." *Sintaksis*, no. 17 (1987): 191–205. Reprinted in *Novyi mir*, no. 4 (1992): 204–10.
"Des langages différents." *Le Figaro*, 15 June 1977, 1–2.
"Dissidentstvo kak lichnyi opyt." *Sintaksis*, no. 15 (1986): 131–47. Reprinted in *Yunost'*, no. 5 (1989): 88–91. English translation by Maria-Regina Kecht, "Dissent as Personal Experience," *Yearbook of Comparative and General Literature*, no. 31 (1982): 21–29. Published in *Dissent* 31, no. 2 (Spring 1984): 152–61.
"Dostoevskii i katorga." *Sintaksis*, no. 9 (1981): 108–11.

"Eduard Bagritskii." In *Istoriya russkoi sovetskoi literatury*, 1:397–420. Moscow: Akademiya nauk, 1958.

"Emigré." *Encounter* 51, no. 3 (September 1978): 79–80

"Encounters with the West." *Partisan Review* 50, no. 4 (1983): 517–25.

"Est' takie stikhi. . . ."*Novyi mir*, no. 3 (1965): 244–48. English translation, "There Are Such Verses," in *For Freedom of Imagination*, 92–102.

For Freedom of Imagination. Translated by Laszlo Tikos and Murray Peppard. New York: Holt, Rinehart and Winston, 1971.

"Isaac Babel." *Oeuvres et Opinions*, no. 8 (1964): 157–63. English translation in *Major Soviet Writers: Essays in Criticism*, edited by Edward J. Brown. New York: Oxford University Press, 1973.

Ivan-durak: Ocherk russkoi narodnoi very. Paris: Sintaksis, 1991.

"Izraztsy." *Sintaksis*, no. 18 (1987): 112–37.

"J'ai traversé un cimetière." Translated by Annie Apelboin. In *Culture et pouvoir communiste: l'autre face de "Paris-Moscou*," 157–61. Paris: Recherches, 1979.

"Kafedra Galileya." *Literaturnaya gazeta*, no. 44 (28 October 1992): 6.

"Literatura perioda velikoi otechestvennoi voiny." *Istoriya russkoi sovetskoi literatury*, 3:5–53. Moscow: Akademiya nauk, 1961.

"Literaturnaya maska Alekseya Remizova." *Sintaksis*, no. 14 (1985): 98–114.

"M. A. Voloshin." *Kratkaya literaturnaya entsiklopediya*, 1:1021. Moscow: Sovetskaya entsiklopediya, 1962.

"Mify Mikhaila Zoshchenko." *Sintaksis*, no. 23 (1988): 82–103. Reprinted in *Voprosy literatury*, no. 2 (1989): 50–67.

"Nazyvaya imena (kommentarii)." *Sintaksis*, no. 2 (1978): 48–62. Reprinted in *Zhurnalist*, no. 10 (1991): 27–30.

"N. S. Gumilev." *Kratkaya literaturnaya entsiklopediya*, 11:1962.

"Ne verit"—znat'." *Sintaksis*, no. 34 (1994): 210–20.

"Ob estetike Mayakovskogo." *Vestnik Moskovskogo universiteta*. Seriya obshchestvennykh nauk, no. 1 (1950): 129–39.

"Odin den' s Pasternakom." *Sintaksis*, no. 6 (1980): 131–39. Reprinted in *Yunost'*, no. 2 (1990): 83–85.

"O khudozhestvennoi strukture romana 'Zhizn' Klima Samgina.'" In *Tvorchestvo M. Gor'kogo i voprosy sotsialisticheskogo realizma*, 132–74. Moscow: Akademiya nauk, 1958.

"O kritike." *Sintaksis*, no. 10 (1982): 146–55.

"O novom sbornike stikhov Anatoliya Sofronova." *Novyi mir*, no. 8 (1959): 248–54. English translation, "On a Collection of Verses by Anatoly Sofronov," in Sinyavsky, *For Freedom of Imagination*.

"Opavshie list'ya," V. V. Rozanova. Paris: Sintaksis, 1982. Excerpts reprinted as "Preodolenie literatury: Zhanrovoe svoeobrazie 'Opavshikh list'ev' V. V. Rozanova." *Nashe nasledie*, no. 11 (1989): 84–94; "Iz lektsii o V. Rozanove," *Obshchestvennye nauki*, no. 2 (1990): 174–86; and "Rozanov," in *Ideology in*

Russian Literature, edited by Richard Freeborn and Jane Grayson, 116–33 (London: Macmillan, 1990).
"O sebe." *Inostrannaya literatura*, no. 2 (1989): 241–43.
"Osnovnye printsipy estetiki V. V. Mayakovskogo." *Znamya*, no. 2 (1950): 151–57.
"Otkrytoe pis'mo A Solzhenitsynu." *Sintaksis*, no. 31 (1991): 159–62.
"O. V. Nekrasove." *Znamya*, no. 5 (May 1990): 49–50.
"Pamflet ili paskvil'?" *Novyi mir*, no. 12 (1964): 228–33. English translation, "Pamphlet or Lampoon?" in Sinyavsky, *For Freedom of Imagination*, 78–91.
"'Panorama s vynoskami' Mikhaila Kuzmina." *Sintaksis*, no. 20 (1987): 58–71.
"Poeticheskii sbornik B. Pasternaka." *Novyi mir*, no. 3 (1962): 261–63.
"Poeziya i proza Ol'gi Berggolts." *Novyi mir*, no. 5 (1960): 226–36. English translation, "The Poetry and Prose of Olga Berggolts," in Sinyavsky, *For Freedom of Imagiantion*, 37–62.
"Poeziya Pasternaka." *Stikhotvoreniya i poemy*, by B. Pasternak. Moscow-Leningrad: Sovetskii pisatel', 1965, 9–62. English translations: "Boris Pasternak," in *Pasternak: Modern Judgments*, edited by Donald Davie and Angela Livingstone. London: Macmillan, 1969; "Pasternak's Poetry," in *Pasternak: A Collection of Critical Essays*, edited by Victor Erlich, 68–109. Englewood Cliffs, N.J.: Prentice Hall, 1978; "The Poetry of Pasternak," in Sinyavsky, *For Freedom of Imagination*, 103–66; "The Poetry of Pasternak," in *Major Soviet Writers: Essays in Criticism*, edited by Edward J. Brown, 100–37 (New York: Oxford University Press, 1973).
"Poidem so mnoi . . .'" *Novyi mir*, no. 1 (1964): 260–63. English translation, "Come Walk with Me," in Sinyavsky, *For Freedom of Imagination*, 63–71.
"Pokhvala emigratsii." *Sintaksis*, no. 24 (1988): 39–42. Reprinted in *Stolitsa*, no. 40 (1992): 49–50.
"Prostranstvo prozy." *Sintaksis*, no. 21 (1988): 25–31. English translation, "The Space of Prose," in *The Louisiana Conference on Literature and Perestroika*, 2–4 March 1988, edited by Marta-Lisa Magnusson, translated by John Kendal, 73–80. Esbjerg, Denmark: South Jutland University Press, 1989.
"Qu'est-ce que 'Syntaxis'?" Translated by Annie Sabatier. In *Syntaxis: Réflexion sur le sort de la Russie et de la culture russe*, 9–12. Paris: Albin Michel, 1981.
"Raskovannyi golos (k 75-letiyu A. Akhmatovoi)." *Novyi mir*, no. 6 (1964): 174–76. English translation, "The Unfettered Voice," in Sinyavsky, *For Freedom of Imagination*, 72–77; "The Unshackled Voice: Anna Akhmatova," in *Major Soviet Writers: Essays in Criticism*, edited by Edward J. Brown, 54–57 (New York: Oxford University Press, 1973).
"Realizm fantastiki." *Literaturnaya gazeta*, no. 2 (5 January 1960): 3.
"Reka i pesnya." *Sintaksis*, no. 12 (1984): 121–38.
"Roman M. Gor'kogo 'Mat' —kak rannii obrazets sotsialisticheskogo realizma." *Cahiers du Monde russe et soviétique* 29, no. 1 (1988): 33–40.
"Roman M. Gor'kogo *Zhizn' Klima Samgina* i istoriya russkoi obshchestvennoi mysli kontsa XIX—nachala XX veka." Diss. MGU, 1952.

The Russian Intelligentsia. tr. by Lynn Visson. New York: Columbia University Press, 1997.
"Russkii natsionalizm." *Sintaksis*, no. 26 (1989): 91–110. Reprinted in part in "Iz stat'i 'Russkii natsionalizm'." *Literaturnaya gazeta*, no. 14 (1 April 1992): 3. English translation, "Russian Nationalism," by Dale E. Peterson, *Massachusetts Review* 31, no. 4 (Winter 1990): 475–94.
"Russophobia." *Partisan Review* 57, no. 3 (1990): 339–44.
"S chem sravnivat'?" *Oktyabr'*, no. 9 (1961): 195.
"Sinyavskii o sebe." In *The Third Wave: Russian Literature in Emigration*, edited by Olga Matich with Michael Heim, 107–9. Ann Arbor, Mich.: Ardis, 1984.
"Sinyavsky on Art." *New York Times*, 18 November 1978, 21.
"Sny na pravoslavnuyu Paskhu." *Sintaksis*, no. 8 (1980): 7–14.
"Solzhenitsyn kak ustroitel' novogo edinomyslya." *Sintaksis*, no. 14 (1985): 16–32.
Soviet Civilization: A Cultural History. Translated by Joanne Turnbull with the assistance of Nikolai Formozov. New York: Little, Brown and Company—Arcade, 1990.
"Srez materiala." *Sintaksis*, no. 8 (1980): 180–86.
"Stalin—geroi i khudozhnik stalinskoi epokhi." *Sintaksis*, no. 19 (1987): 106–25.
"The State of Europe: Christmas Eve, 1989." Translated by Michael Glenny. *Granta* 30 (Winter 1990): 151–54.
"Stilisticheskie raznoglasiya." *Iskusstvo kino*, no. 7 (1989): 34–38.
"'Stoyala zima. Dul veter iz stepi . . .' O stikhotvoreniyakh Pasternaka na evangel'skie syuzhety i temy." *Vek Pasternaka: Dos'e: Prilozhenie k 'Literaturnoi gazete'* (February 1990): 22.
"Teatr Galicha." *Vremya i my*, no. 14 (February 1977): 142–50.
"'Temnaya noch'. . . ." *Sintaksis*, no. 1 (1978): 11–22.
"Veseloe remeslo." Introduction to *Rodnaya rech'*, by Petr Vail' and Aleksandr Genis, 5–6. Tenafly, N.J.: Hermitage, 1990.
"V noch' posle bitvy." *Sintaksis*, no. 3 (1979): 41–66.
"V redaktsiyu zhurnala '22.' " *Dvadtsat' dva*, no. 49 (August–September 1986): 221–23.
"V zashchitu piramidy (Zametki o tvorchestve Evgeniya Evtushenko i ego poeme 'Bratskaya GES')." *Grani*, no. 63 (1967): 114–39. English translation, "In Defense of a Pyramid," in Sinyavsky, *For Freedom of Imagination*, 167–95.
"Vse eto bylo: Pochemu ya segodnya protiv El'tsina." *Novoe russkoe slovo*, 1 November 1993, 4.
"Would I Move Back?" Translated by Catharine Theimer Nepomnyashchy. *Time*, 10 April 1989, 129–30, 132.
"Yazyk odinochestva." *Novosti* 1, no. 77 (28 December 1983): 5.
Sinyavskii, A., and A. Men'shutin. "Davaite govorit' professional'no." *Novyi mir*, no. 8 (1961): 248–52.
———. "'Den' russkoi poezii.'" *Novyi mir*, no. 2 (1959): 211–22.

———. *Poeziya pervykh let revolyutsii: 1917–1920*. Moscow: Nauka, 1964.

———. "Za poeticheskuyu aktivnost' (zametki o poezii molodykh)." *Novyi mir*, no. 1 (1961): 224–41.

Sinyavsky, Andrei, and Gunter Grass. "Letters." *Encounter* 43, no. 6 (December 1974), 94–95.

Sinyavskii, Andrei, and Igor' Golomshtok. *Pikasso*. Moscow: Znanie, 1960.

Sinyavskii, A., and M. Rozanova, "Prizhiznennyi nekrolog." Afterword to *Po obe storony okeana. Zapiski zevaki. Saperlipopet ili Esli b da kaby, da vo rtu rosli griby*, by Viktor Nekrasov, 396–99. Moscow: Khudozhestvennaya literatura, 1991.

Sinyavskii, A., V. Maksimov, and P. Egides. "Pod sen' nadezhnuyu zakona . . ." *Nezavisimaya gazeta*, no. 198 (16 October 1993): 1. Reprinted under the same title in *Sintaksis*, no. 34 (1994): 200–202 and under the title "El'tsin—v otstavsku!" in *Novoe russkoe slovo*, 20 October 1993, 5.

Sinyavskii, A., and Yu. Daniel'. "Dialog." *Sintaksis*, no. 24 (1988): 168–73.

WORKS BY TERTS

"Anekdot v anekdote." *Sintaksis*, no. 1 (1978): 77–95. English translation by Olga Matich, "The Joke inside the Joke," *Partisan Review* 51, no. 3 (1984): 356–66.

Chto takoe sotsialisticheskii realizm. Paris: Sintaksis, 1988. Excerpts reprinted in *Dekorativnoe iskusstvo*, no. 5 (1989): 19–20, 29; *Literaturnoe obozrenie*, no. 8 (1989): 89–100; and *Teatr*, no. 5 (1989): 73–83. English translation, *On Socialist Realism*, by George Dennis, introduction by Czeslaw Milosz (New York: Pantheon, 1960). Reprinted in *The Trial Begins* and *On Socialist Realism* (New York: Vintage, 1965; and Berkeley: University of California Press, 1982).

Fantasticheskii mir Abrama Tertsa. Introduction by Boris Filippov. New York: Inter-language Literary Associates, 1967.

Fantasticheskie povesti. Paris: Institut literacki, 1961. English translation by Max Hayward and Ronald Hingley, *Fantastic Stories* (New York: Pantheon, 1963). Reprinted, Evanston, Ill.: Northwestern University Press, 1987.

Golos iz khora. Afterword by Igor' Golomshtok. London: Stenvalley Press, 1973. English translation by Kyril FitzLyon and Max Hayward, *A Voice from the Chorus*, with an introduction by Max Hayward (New York: Farrar, Straus, and Giroux, 1976). Reprinted, New Haven, Conn.: Yale University Press, 1995.

"Gosti." *Sintaksis*, no. 15 (1986): 16–29.

"Iskusstvo i deistvitel'nost'." *Sintaksis*, no. 2 (1978): 111–19. English translation by Catharine Theimer Nepomnyashchy, "Art and Reality," *Formations* 6, no. 1 (Spring 1991): 1–5.

Kroshka Tsores. Paris: Sintaksis, 1980. English translation by Larry P. Joseph and Rachel May, *Little Jinx*, with a foreword by Edward J. Brown (Evanston, Ill.: Northwestern University Press, 1992). English translation of first chapter by Catharine Theimer Nepomnyashchy, "From *Little Tsores*," *Humanities in Society* 7, nos. 3–4 (1984): 173–74.

"Literaturnyi protsess v Rossii." *Kontinent*, no. 1 (1974): 143–90. Reprinted in *Daugava*, no. 5 (May 1990): 95–113. English translaton by Michael Glenny, "The Literary Process in Russia," in *Kontinent*, 77–18 (Garden City, N.Y.: Anchor-Doubleday, 1976).

Lyubimov. Washington, D.C.: B. Filipoff, 1964. Translated into English as *The Makepeace Experiment*, translated and introduced by Manya Harari (New York: Pantheon, 1965). Reprinted by Northwestern University Press, Evanston, Ill., 1989.

"Lyudi i zveri (Po knige G. Vladimova 'Vernyi Ruslan. Istoriya karaul'noi sobaki')." *Kontinent*, no. 5 (1975): 367–404. Reprinted in *Voprosy literatury*, no. 1 (1990): 61–86. Abridged English translation by William E. Harkins, "Beasts and Men" [Review of Georgi Vladimov, *Faithful Ruslan: The Story of a Guard Dog*], *New York Review of Books* 26, nos. 21 and 22 (24 January 1980): 22–24.

Mysli vrasplokh. With an interpretive essay on the literary art of Abram Tertz by Andrew Field. New York: Rausen Publishers, 1966. Excerpts were reprinted as "Mysli vrasplokh. Otryvki iz knigi," *Ogonek*, no. 51 (1991): 14–16; and "Gospod blagoslovil menya togda na etot smekh," *Ogonek*, no. 52 (1991): 29. English translation, "Thought Unaware," *New Leader* 48, no. 15 (19 July 1965): 16–26; and *Unguarded Thoughts*, translated by Manya Harari (London: Collins and Harvill Press, 1972).

"Otechestvo: Blatnaya pesnya . . ." *Sintaksis*, no. 4 (1979): 72–118. Reprinted in *Sel'skaya molodezh'*, no. 9 (1992): 57–60, and no. 10 (1992): 48–52.

"Pamyati pavshikh: Arkadii Belinkov." *Kontinent*, no. 2 (1975): 363–72. English translation, "In Memory of the Fallen: Arkady Belinkov," in *Kontinent* 2 (Garden City, N.Y.: Anchor-Doubleday, 1977): 133–41.

"Posleslovie." *Sintaksis*, no. 7 (1980): 108–9.

Progulki s Pushkinym. London: Overseas Publications Interchange in association with Collins, 1975. Reprinted in Paris; *Sintaksis*, 1989. Reprinted in *Voprosy literatury*, no. 7 (1990): 155–75; no. 8 (1990): 81–111; and no. 9 (1990): 146–78; and in Saint Petersburg: Vsemirnoe slovo, 1993. Excerpts were printed as "Progulki s Pushkinym: Fragment," *Oktyabr'* no. 4 (1989): 192–99; and as "Zolotoe sechenie: Iz knigi 'Progulki s Pushkinym.'" *Mir Pushkina. Dos'e. Prilozhenie k 'Literaturnoi gazete'* (June 1990): 22–23. English translation by Catharine Theimer Nepomnyashchy and Slava I. Yastremski, *Strolls with Pushkin*, introduction by Catharine Theimer Nepomnyashchy, notes by Slava I. Yastremski (New Haven, Conn.: Yale University Press, 1993).

"Puteshestvie na Chernuyu rechku." *Sintaksis*, no. 34 (1994): 3–51.

Sobranie sochinenii v dvukh tomakh. Introduction by Vladimir Novikov. Moscow: SP Start, 1992.

Spokoinoi nochi: Roman. Paris: Sintaksis, 1984. A section of this book was originally published separately as "Ochki," *Sintaksis*, no. 5 (1979): 31–41. Excerpts were reprinted as "Spokoinoi nochi (fragmenty romana)," *Gorizont*, no. 9 (1989): 53–64. English translation by Richard Lourie, *Goodnight!*, with an introduction by Richard Lourie (New York: Penguin, 1989).

Sud Idet. Introduction by Gustav Gerlin: Grudzinskii. *Kultura*. Russian issue (May 1960): 62–130. Published in English as *The Trial Begins*. Translated by Max Hayward. New York: Pantheon, 1960. Reprinted in *The Trial Begins* and *On Socialist Realism*, with an introduction by Czeslaw Milosz (New York: Vintage, 1965; and Berkeley: University of California Press, 1982).

V teni Gogolya. London: Overseas Publications Interchange, in association with Collins, 1975. Reprinted by Sintaksis, Paris, 1981. A chapter was reprinted as "Dva povorota serebryanogo klucha v 'Revizore,'" *Teatr*, no. 10 (1990): 126–46.

"'Ya' i 'oni': O krainikh formakh obshcheniya v usloviyakh odinochestva." *Vremya i my*, no. 13 (January 1977): 169–82. English translation, "'I' and 'They': An Essay on Extreme Forms of Communication under Conditions of Human Isolation," *Survey* 22, nos. 3–4 (Summer–Autumn 1976): 278–87.

"Zolotoi shnurok." *Sintaksis*, no. 18 (1987): 182–87.

INTERVIEWS WITH SINYAVSKY

"André Siniavski." *L'autre Europe*, nos. 7–8 (November 1985): 112–13.

[Arc, Gabriela.] "Bez Dostojevskog se ne ziveti: Odlomak razgovora s Andrejom Sinjavskim." *Knjizenost* 71, nos. 5–6 (May–June 1981): 1189–91.

[Beausang, Michael.] "Exile and Writer." *Mosaic* 8, no. 3 (1975): 15–20.

[Bershin, Efim.] "V Tupikakh svobody." *Literaturnaya gazeta*, no. 14 (1 April 1992): 3.

[Bokov, N.] "Andrei Sinyavsky on Dissidence." *Encounter* 52, no. 4 (April 1979): 91–94.

[Brezna, Irena.] "An Interview with Andrei Sinyavsky." Translated by Kevin Windle. *Australian Slavonic and East European Studies* 3, no. 2 (1989): 51–60.

[Carlisle, Olga.] "Solzhenitsyn and Russian Nationalism: An Interview with Andrei Sinyavsky." *New York Review of Books* 26, no. 18 (22 November 1979): 3–6.

[Daubenton, Annie.] "Andre Siniavski: Certains dissidents veulent remplacer la dictature communiste par une autre." Translated by Lucia Cathala. *Les Nouvelles Littéraires*, no. 2779 (19–26 March 1981): 26.

[Davydova, N., and A. Tarkhanov.] "Kakim ne dolzhen byt' pamyatnik." *Dekorativnoe iskusstvo*, no. 5 (1989): 18.

[Ebanoidze, I.] "Ne bol'she chem pisatel': Interv'iu s Andreem Sinyavskim." *Literaturnoe obozrenie*, no. 10 (1992): 30–33.

[Epelboin, Annie.] "Siniavski: 'La prose: une second poésie.'" *La Quinzaine littéraire*, no. 345 (1–15 April 1981): 7–9.

[Glad, John.] "Antizapadnichestvo v sovremennykh usloviyakh—eto antikultura." *Vremya i my*, no. 88 (1981): 7–9.

[Karaulov, Andrei.] "Vsya zhizn'." *Teatral'naya zhizn'*, no 14 (1989): 28–31.

[Laird, Sally.] "My Life as a Writer." *Index on Censorship* 15, no. 6 (June 1986): 7–10, 14.

[Lur'e, Samuil.] "Abrashka Terts, professor iz Sorbonny." *Literator*, no. 20 (1990): 4–5.

[Maksimov, Maksim.] "Russkaya emigratsiya—eto kolossal'neishee kladbishche . . ." *Smena*, no. 129 (5 June 1990): 2.

[Markish, David.] "Upasi bog ot shovinizma: Interv'yu s Andreem Sinyavskim." *Panorama*, no. 172 (25 July–1 August 1984): 23.

[Medvedev, Feliks.] "Besedy s Andreem Siniavskim i Mariei Rozanovoi o Pushkine, i ne tol'ko o nem." *Knizhnoe obozrenie*, no. 4 (26 January 1990): 8–9.

[Mendzheritskii, I. A.] "Vonnegut i Sinyavskii na fone . . . ukradennoi 'Anzheliki.'" *Knizhnoe obozrenie*, no. 31 (31 July 1992): 3.

[Mogutin, Yaroslav.] "Salman Rushdi russkoi literatury." *Stolitsa*, no. 40 (1992): 48–49.

[Nasaroff, Barbara.] "Andrei Siniavski." *Lire*, no. 161 (February 1989): 26–32, 44.

[Nekhoroshev, Grigorii.] "Tam my schitaemsya krasnymi . . .'" *Knizhnoe obozrenie*, no. 2 (13 January 1989): 3.

[Nepomnyashchy, Catharine Theimer.] "An Interview with Andrei Sinyavsky." *Formations* 6, no. 1 (Spring 1991): 6–23.

[Novikov, Vl.] "Grenobl'skie grezy: Vstrechi s literaturovedami vo Frantsii." *Oktyabr'*, no. 12 (1990): 187–93.

[Platonova, Yelena.] "'Emigration Is a Horrible but Instructive Experience.'" *Moscow News*, no. 2 (15–22 January 1989): 16.

[Pomerantsev, K.] "Sinyavsky: Fiction and Reality." Translated by Michael Glenny. *Times Literary Supplement*, 23 May 1975, 560.

[Putrenko, T.] "Pushkin—nash smeyushchiisya genii." *Literaturnaya gazeta*, no. 32 (8 August 1990): 7.

[Tsitrinyak, G.] "Progulki s professorom Sorbonny." *Nezavisimaya gazeta*, 14 January 1992, 7.

[Uvarova, N.] "Dlya ego pesen nuzhna rossiskaya pochva." *Teatr*, no. 10 (1990): 146–48.

——. "Pisatel'"—tot zhe fokusnik." *Trud*, 27 February 1993, 7.

[Voina, Vladmir.] "Andrey Sinyavsky." *Bostonia* 64, no. 2 (March/April 1990): 34–36.

[Zhavoronkov, G.] "Mozhno li pokayatsya pod dulom pistoleta?" *Moskovskie novosti*, no. 48 (2 December 1990): 15.

[Zinkewych, Osyp.] "An Interview with Andrei Sinyavsky." *Smoloskyp* 1, no. 3 (Spring 1979): 12–13.

WORKS ON SINYAVSKY/TERTS

Abel, Lionel. "Art while Being Ruled: 'Abram Tertz,' Brecht, and Calderon." *Commentary* 39 (May 1960): 405–12.

Adams, Phoebe. "Fiction Here and Abroad." Review of *The Trial Begins*. *Atlantic*, October 1960, 123–24.

———. Review of *The Makepeace Experiment*. *Atlantic*, September 1965, 151.

———. "Potpourri." Review of *The Makepeace Experiment*. *Atlantic*, September 1965, 151.

Adelman, George. Review of *Fantastic Stories*. *Library Journal* 88, no. 9 (1 May 1963): 1905.

"L'Affaire Siniavski-Daniel." *Esprit*, no. 357 (February 1967): 227–310.

Alexandrov, Vladimir E. "Typographical Intrusion and the Transcendent in Bely's *Petersburg* and Sinyavsky's *Lyubimov*." *Slavonic and East European Review* 62, no. 2 (April 1984): 161–79.

Amurskii, Vitalii. "Igra v 'durachka.'" *Novoe russkoe slovo*, 9 March 1993, 11.

Anan'ev, Anatolii. "Kritika ili obvinenie?" *Literaturnaya Rossiya*, no. 35 (1 September 1989): 14–15.

———. "V sekretaiat pravleniya SP SSSR v redaktsiyu 'Literaturnoi gazety.'" *Literaturnaya gazeta*, no. 37 (13 September 1989): 7.

Anan'ev, Anatolii, and Stanislav Lesnevskii. "'O slavyanofilakh, rusofobakh i lyubvi k Rossii . . .'" *Knizhnoe obozrenie*, no. 35 (1 September 1989): 3.

Anninskii, Lev. "A propos." *Soglasie*, nos. 8–9 (August–September 1992): 189–91.

Antonov, M. F., V. M. Klykov, and I. R. Shafarevich. "Pis'mo v sekretariat pravleniya soyuza pisatelei RSFSR." *Literaturnaya Rossiya*, no. 31 (4 August 1989): 4.

Aucouturier, Michel. "Lioubimov." *Esprit*, no. 357 (February 1967): 271–76.

———. "Writer and Text in the Works of Abram Terc (An Ontology of Writing and a Poetics of Prose)." Translated by Alexandre Guerard. In *Fiction and Drama in Eastern and Southeastern Europe: Evolution and Experiment in the Postwar Period*, edited by Henrik Birnbaum and Thomas Eckman, 1–10. Columbus, Ohio: Slavica, 1980.

Azhgikhina, Nadezhda. "Samyi glavnyi dissident." Review of Abram Terts (Andrei Sinyavskii), *Sobranie sochinenii v dvukh tomakh*. *Ogonek*, no. 9 (1993): 17.

———. "Vozvrashchenie Sinyavskogo i Danielya." Review of *Tsena metafory, ili Prestuplenie i nakazanie Sinyavskogo i Danielya*. *Oktyabr'*, no. 8 (August 1990): 203–5.

Bailey, George. "The Trial of Two Soviet Writers: A Special Report on the Failure of Dogma." *Reporter* 34, no. 4 (24 February 1966): 34–38.

Bakhrakh, Aleksandr. "Vechnyi Rozanov." *Literaturnyi kur'er* (Fall 1985): 16–18.

Barrett, William. "Superfluous Man." Review of *On Socialist Realism. Atlantic,* January 1962, 97–98.

Basinskii, Pavel. "Konets Tertsa, ili Andrei Sinyavskii vchera i segodnya." *Literaturnaya gazeta*, no. 4 (27 January 1993): 4.

Batkin, Leonid. "Sinyavskii, Pushkin—i my." *Oktyabr'*, no. 1 (January 1991): 164–93.

Bayley, John. "*Goodnight* by Abram Tertz (Andrei Sinyavsky)." *New York Times Book Review*, 17 December 1989, 1, 26–27.

"'Belaya kniga' o dele Sinyavskogo i Danielya." *Grani*, no. 63 (1967): 204–15.

Bergholz, Stefan. "On Reading Tertz." *Survey*, no. 41 (April 1962): 145–50.

Blake, Patricia. "Soviet Literature Goes West: A Generation of Russian Writers Is Thriving in Exile." *Time* 123, 12 March 1984, 77–79.

Bloch-Michel, Jean. "Siniavski et Daniel." *Preuves*, no. 183 (1965): 76–78.

Blot, Jean. Review of *Goodnight. La Nouvelle revue française*, no. 384 (1 January 1985): 109–11.

Bocharov Sergei. "Obsuzhdenie knigi Abrama Tertsa 'Progulki s Pushkinym.'" *Voprosy literatury*, no. 10 (October 1990); 77–153. English translation of excerpts by Catharine Theimer Nepomnyashchy, "A Discussion of Abram Tertz's Book *Strolls with Pushkin*," *Russian Studies in Literature* 28, no. 1 (Winter 1991–1992): 64–70.

Bogoraz, Larisa. "Dushevnye muki seksota: Otkrytoe pis'mo Aleksandru Voronelyu." *Vremya i my*, no. 93 (1986): 210–14.

Borden, Richard. C. "Andrei Sinyavsky: In Memoriam." *Slavic and East European Journal* 42, no. 3 (1998): 372–76.

Boroff, David. "Message from a New Dimension." Review of *Fantastic Stories. Saturday Review*, 13 April 1963, 28.

Bregel', Yurii. "Ob'yasnenie posle lagerya." *Vremya i my*, no. 91 (1986): 224–29.

"Breve chronologie de l'affaire Siniavski-Daniel." *Esprit*, no. 357 (1967): 235–38.

Brovman, G. "Pisat' pravdivo." *Oktyabr'*, 38, no. 9 (1961): 180–81.

Brown, Clarence. "*A Voice from the Chorus* by Abram Tertz (Andrei Sinyavsky)." *New Republic*, 25 September 1976, 41–43.

Brown, Deming. "The Art of Andrei Sinyavsky." In *Soviet Russian Literature since Stalin*, 331–51. Cambridge: Cambridge University Press, 1978. Reprinted from *Slavic Review* 29, no. 4 (December 1970): 662–81. Also reprinted in *Major Soviet Writers: Essays in Criticism*, edited by Edward J. Brown, 367–87 (New York: Oxford University Press, 1973).

———. "Moscow: The Defense Does Not Rest." *Reporter* 35, no. 4 (22 September 1966): 43–45.

Brown, Edward J. *Russian Literature since the Revolution*. Rev. ed. Cambridge, Mass.: Harvard University Press, 1982.

Brumberg, Abraham. "In Quest of Justice." *Problems of Communism* 17, no. 4 (July–August 1968): 1–5.

———. "'Socialist Legality' on Trial." *Reporter* 34, no. 5 (10 March 1966): 34–36.

———. "Writers in Prison." *Problems of Communism* 15, no. 2 (March–April 1966): 65–78.

Bryan, Catherine. Review of *Soviet Civilization: A Cultural History*. *School Library Journal* 37, no. 1 (January 1991): 123.

Bryden, Ronald. "Nineteen Sixty-Four." Review of *The Trial Begins*. *Spectator*, no. 6878 (29 April 1960): 633–34.

Burg, David. "Molodoe pokolenie sovetskikh pisatelei." *Mosty* 1 (1965): 211–29.

Bushin, V. "Fialki pakhnut ne tem." *Literatura i zhizn'*, no. (17 February 1961): 1–3.

Carlisle, Olga. "A Voice from the Third Russian Emigration." *New York Times Book Review*, 30 October 1977, 15, 50–52.

Carrington, Ildiko de Papp. "Demons, Doubles, and Dinosaurs: *Life before Man, The Origin of Consciousness*, and 'The Icicle.'" *Essays on Canadian Writing*, no. 33 (Fall 1986): 68–88.

Chapple, Richard L. "The Bible and the Zoo in Andrey Sinyavsky's *The Trial Begins*." *Orbis Litterarum: International Review of Literary Studies* 33 (1978): 349–58.

Clardy, J. V. "Andrei Sinyavsky's 'On Socialist Realism': An Analysis." *Cimarron Review*, no. 23 (1973): 29–32.

Clowes, Edith W. "Kafka and Russian Experimental Fiction in the Thaw, 1956–1965." *Modern Language Review* 89, no. 1 (January 1994): 149–65.

Cohen, Gordon, and Donald Fanger. "Abram Tertz: Dissidence, Diffidence, and Russian Literary Tradition," in *Soviet Society and Culture: Essays in Honor of Vera S. Dunham*, edited by Terry L. Thompson and Richard Sheldon, 162–77. Boulder, Colo.: Westview Press, 1988.

Cornwell, Neil. Review of *The Russian Intelligentsia*. *Slavonic and East European Review* 76 (October 1998): 734–35.

Dalton, Margaret. *Andrei Siniavskii and Julii Daniel': Two Soviet "Heretical" Writers*. Wurzburg: Jal-Verlag, 1973.

Davenport, Guy. "Two Straw Men and Gogol's Ghost." Review of *The Makepeace Experiment*. *National Review* 17, no. 34 (24 August 1965): 732, 734–35.

Decker, Robert. Review of *Soviet Civilization: A Cultural History*. *Library Journal* 115, no. 16 (1 October 1990): 102.

Devlin, Kevin. "Echoes of the Tertz Affair." *New Leader* 49, no. 7 (28 March 1966): 17–18.

"Dissent among the Dissidents." *Harper's Magazine* 269 (August 1984): 27.

Dolbier, Maurice. "'The Trial Begins' [Review of *The Trial Begins*]." *New York Herald Tribune*, 12 September 1960, 21.

Dovlatov, Sergei. "Andreyu Sinyavskomu—60 let." *Panorama*, no. 235 (11–18 October 1985): 18.

Downing, John. Review of *Soviet Civilization: A Cultural History*. *Journal of Communication* 42, no. 2 (Spring 1992): 153–62.

Dunham, Vera S. "Serenity: A Note on Sinyavsky's Style." In *The Third Wave: Russian Literature in Emigration*, edited by Olga Matich with Michael Heim, 110–17. Ann Arbor, Mich.: Ardis, 1984.

Durkin, Andrew R. "Narrator, Metaphor, and Theme in Sinjavskij's *Fantastic Tales*." *Slavic and East European Journal* 24, no. 2 (Summer 1980): 133–44.

Eberstadt, Fernando. Review of *Goodnight! Commentary* 89, no. 4 (1990): 34–36.

Efimov, Igor'. "Vymysel demagoga." *Novoe russkoe slovo*, 22 February 1987, 3.

Emerson, Caryl. "Soviet Civilization: Its Discontents, Disasters, Residual Fascinations." *Hudson Review* 44, no. 4 (Winter 1992): 574–84.

———. "Abram Tertz, Literary Critic on Comedic Terrain." *Slavic and East European Journal* 41, no. 3 (1998): 377–80.

Eremin, Dm. "Perevertyshi." *Izvestia*, no. 10 (13 January 1966): 6.

Eremina, L. S., ed. *Tsena metafory ili prestuplenie i nakazanie Sinyavskogo i Danielya*. Moscow: Kniga, 1989.

Etkind, Efim. "Der Doppelganger: Uber Andrej Sinjawskij und seinem Roman 'Gute Nacht.'" *Neue Rundschau* 97, no. 1 (1986): 84–90.

———. "Ispoved' shenapana." *Vremya i my*, no. 91 (1986): 230–36.

Fainsod, Merle. "From the Soviet Literary Underground." Review of *The Trial Begins*. *Herald Tribune Book Review*, 11 September 1960, 7.

Fanger, Donald. "A Change of Venue: Russian Journals of the Emigration." *Times Literary Supplement*, 21 November 1986, 1321–22.

———. "Conflicting Imperatives in the Model of the Russian Writer: The Case of Tertz/Sinyavsky." In *Literature and History: Theoretical Problems and Russian Case Studies*, edited by Gary Saul Morson, 111–24. Stanford, Calif.: Stanford University Press, 1986.

———. "Homo Sovieticus: Utopia and Reality in the Russian Experience." Review of *Soviet Civilization*. *Times Literary Supplement*, 15 March 1991, 5–6.

Fedorov, V. "Vechernyaya vstrecha." *Molodaya gvardiya,* no. 5 (1961): 14–18.

Feifer, George. "Who's Been Spiking the Borscht? [Review of *The Makepeace Experiment*]. *Book Week* [*Washington Post*], 22 August 1965, 4, 15.

Fenander, Sara. "Tertz's Stalin and the Ruse of Charisma." *Russian Review* 58 (April 1999): 286–297.

Feofanov, Yu. "Izoblichenie." *Izvestia*, no. 36 (12 February 1966): 4

———. "Logika padeniya." *Izvestia*, no. 39 (16 February 1966): 4.

———. "Pora otvechat'." *Izvestia*, no. 37 (13 February 1966): 5

———. "Tut tsarit zakon." *Izvestia*, no. 35 (11 February 1966): 4.

Field, Andrew. "Abram Tertz's Ordeal by Mirror." Abram Tertz, *Mysli vrasplokh*. New York: Rausen Publishers, 1966, 7–42. Incorporates "Abram Tertz's Ordeal by Mirror." *New Leader* 48, no. 15 (19 July 1965): 9–15, and "Prisoner in Fantasy," *New Leader* 49, no. 4 (14 February 1966): 17–18.

———. "The Arrest of Andrei Sinyavsky." *New Leader* 48, no. 22 (8 November 1965): 10–11.

———. "The Not So Dissonant Voices in Soviet Literature." *New Leader* 46 (24 December 1962): 15–16.

———. Review of *On Socialist Realism. New Leader* 49 (13 May 1966): 28–29.

Filippov, Boris. "Priroda i tyur'ma." In Tertz, *Fantasticheskii mir Abrama Tertsa*, New York: Inter-language Literary Associates, 1967. Section on Tertz reprinted from "Priroda i tyur'ma. (O tvorchestve Abrama Tertsa i Nikolaya Arzhaka)." *Grani*, no. 60 (1966): 75–93.

Foster, Ludmila A. Review of *Lyubimov* by Abram Terc. *Slavic and East European Journal* 10, no. 1 (1966): 106–7.

Frank, Joseph. "The Triumph of Abram Tertz." *New York Review of Books*, 27 June 1991, 35–43.

———. Review of *Strolls with Pushkin. New Republic* 210, no. 19 (9 May 1994): 30–35.

Frankel, Theodore. "Art, Politics, and the Soviet Writer." *Commentary* 41, no. 5 (May 1966): 52–59.

Frayn, Michael. "Lightning over Moscow." Review of *The Trial Begins. The Guardian*, 29 April 1960, 11.

———. "Writers on Trial: Thoughts on the Sinyavsky-Daniel Case." *Encounter* 30, no. 1 (1968): 80–88.

Fremont-Smith, Eliot. "Serafima Was the Spur." Review of *The Makepeace Experiment. New York Times*, 9 July 1965, 27.

Frioux, Claude. "Siniavskii, Daniel et la conscience publique." *Esprit*, no. 357 (February 1967): 227–34.

Gachev, Georgii. "Andrei Sinyavskii—Abram Terts i ego roman *Spokoinoi nochi* (Ispoved')." *Moskovskii vestnik*, no. 1 (1989): 235–66. English translation of excerpts from this article by Catharine Theimer Nepomnyashchy, "Andrei Siniavskii—Abram Tertz and his Novel *Goodnight!*" *Russian Studies in Literature* 28, no. 1 (Winter 1991–1992): 25–44.

Genis, Aleksandr, and Peter Vail'. "Labardan! Andrei Sinyavskii kak Abram Terts." Chapter in *Sovremennaya russkaya proza*. Ann Arbor, Mich.: Hermitage, 1982, 57–75.

Gifford, Henry. "Andrey Sinyavsky: The Voice and the Chorus." *Encounter* 42, no. 2 (February 1974): 34–39.

Gill, Graeme. Review of *The Russian Intelligentsia. Australian Journal of Politics and History* 45 (March 1999): 139.

Ginzburg, Aleksandr, ed. *Belaya kniga po delu A. Sinyavskogo i Yu. Danielya*. Frankfurt am Main: Posev, 1967.

Glagoleva, Olga E. Review of *The Russian Intelligentsia. Canadian Slavonic Papers* 40 (March–June 1998): 137.

Glenny, Michael. "Sinyavsky and Daniel on Trial." *Survey* 66 (1968): 145–47.

Golomshtok, Igor'. "Posleslovie." *Golos iz khora*. London: Stenvalley Press, 1973, 329–39.

Gorbanevskaya, N. "Kto na chei kryuchok klyunul?" *Russkaya mysl'*, no. 3664 (13 March 1987): 4.

Gul', Roman. "Abram Terts: 'Mysli vrasplokh'." *Novyi zhurnal*, no. 84 (1966): 276–79.

———. "Progulki khama s Pushkinym," *Novyi zhurnal*, no. 124 (1976): 117–29. Exerpted in *Literaturnaya Rossiya*, no. 26 (30 June 1989): 18–19.

Gurvich, I. "Tol'ko li gipoteza?" *Novoe russkoe slovo*, 27 July 1993, 8.

Gusev, Vl. "Kraine Ser'ezno." *Literaturnaya Rossiya*, no. 38 (22 September 1989): 8.

———. "V poslednii raz." *Literaturnaya Rossiya*, no. 45 (11 November 1989): 2–3.

Gusev, Vladimir, and Andrei Turkov. "Nasmeshka gor'kaya . . ." *Literaturnaya gazeta* (31 May 1989): 2.

Haber, Erika. "In Search of the Fantastic in Tertz's Fantastic Realism." *Slavic and East European Journal* 42, no. 2 (Summer 1998): 254–67.

———. "My Personal Strolls with Tertz." *Slavic and East European Journal* 42, no. 3 (1998): 381–84.

Hayward, Max. "Awkward Voices in Russia." *London Times*, 1 Febuary 1966, 11.

———. "The Case of Tertz-Sinyavski." *Dissent*, January–February 1966, 88–91.

———. "The Moscow Trial." *Partisan Review* 33, no. 2 (1966): 227–39.

———. Review of *Voice from the Chorus*. *Books Abroad* 48, no. 3 (1974): 596.

———. "Pushkin, Gogol, and the Devil." In *Writers in Russia, 1917–1978*. Reprinted from *Times Literary Supplement*, 28 May 1976, 630–32.

———. "Sinyavsky's *A Voice from the Chorus*." In *Writers in Russia, 1917–1978*. Edited and with an introduction by Patricia Blake, 265–84. New York: Harcourt Brace Jovanovich Publishers-Harvest/HBJ Book, 1983. Reprinted from introduction to Tertz, *A Voice from the Chorus*. Translated by Kyril Fitzlyon and Max Hayward, vii–xxiii. New York: Farrar, Straus and Giroux, 1976.

———, ed. and trans. *On Trial: The Soviet State versus "Abram Tertz" and "Nikolai Arzhak*." 2nd ed. New York: Harper and Row, 1967.

Hayward, Max, and Leopold Labedz. "Writers and the Police." *Encounter* 26, no. 1 (1966): 84–88.

Hingley, Ronald. "Arresting Episodes." Review of *Spokoinoi nochi*. *Times Literary Supplement*, 15 February 1985, 178.

Holmgren, Beth C. "First-Person Liberties: The Persona in the Work of Witold Gom-Browicz and Abram Terc." Ph.D. diss., Harvard University, 1987.

———. "The Transfiguring of Context in the Work of Abram Terts." *Slavic Review* 50, no. 4 (Winter 1991): 965–77.

Hostowiec, Pavel. "Abram Terc." *Kultura* (Paris), no. 118 (1965): 3–7.
Howe, Irving. "Do Not Go Gentle." Review of *Goodnight! New Republic*, 1 January 1990, 34, 36–37.
———. "Predicaments of Soviet Writing—I [Review of *Fantastic Stories*]." *New Republic*, 11 May 1963, 19–21.
Hugh-Jones, Stephen. "Worm's Eye View." Review of *The Makepeace Experiment*. *Encounter* 25, no. 1 (July 1965): 82–83.
Il'inskii, Oleg. "Neudachnye obobshchenya: Po povodu stat'i A. Tertsa." *Novyi zhurnal*, 118 (1975): 136–43.
Ilyin, M. "Klevetniki." *Sovetskaya Rossiya,* 11 February 1966, 4.
"In Quest of Justice." *Problems of Communism* 17, no. 5 (September–October 1968): 1.
Ivanova, Natal'ya. "Sindrom 'zheleznoi ruki.'" *Ogonek*, no. 37 (September 1989): 21–23.
Ivask, Yurii. "'Golos iz khora' Sinyavskogo: Zametki na polyakh." *Novyi zhurnal*, no. 116 (1974): 95–101.
———. "Rozanov v izobrazhenii Sinyavskogo." *Chast' rechi* 2/3 (1982): 308–13.
Ivsky, Oleg. Review of *The Makepeace Experiment*, *Library Journal* 90, no. 13 (July 1965): 3074.
"Iz pochty *Oktyabrya*. *Oktyabr'*, no. 9 (1989): 204–6.
Jameson, Donald. "What Yevgeny Knew." *New Republic* 196, no. 25 (22 June 1987): 39–41.
Kakutani, Michiko. "A Novel Illuminates a Shocking Soviet Reality." Review of *Goodnight! New York Times*, 13 December 1989, C29.
Kaniewicz, Georges. "Un anonyme." Review of *Fantastic Stories*. *Preuves*, no. 157 (March 1964): 86–88.
Kendrina, Zoya. "Nasledniki Smerdyakova." *Literaturnaya gazeta*, no. 10 (22 January 1966): 2, 4.
Khmel'nitskii, Sergei. "Iz chreva kivota." *Dvadtsat' dva*, no. 48 (June–July 1986): 151–80.
Kleberg, Lars. "Andrey Sinyavsky som litterraturkritiker." *Bonniers litterara magazin* 35, no. 3 (1966): 374–77.
"Klevetniki-perevertyshi." *Izvestia*, no. 4 (18 January 1966): 3.
Kochetov, V. "Skvernoe remeslo." *Oktyabr'*, no. 3 (March 1966): 211–18.
Kolonosky, Walter. "Andrei Siniavskii: The Chorus and the Critic." *Canadian-American Slavic Studies* 9, no. 3 (Fall 1975): 352–60.
———. "Andrej Sinjavskij as a Literary Critic." Ph.D. diss., University of Kansas, 1972.
———. "Inherent and Ulterior Design in Sinjavskij's 'Pxenc'." *Slavic and East European Journal* 26, no. 3 (Fall 1982): 329–37.
———. "Double Talk: Andrei Siniavsky's Dissertation." *Slavic and East European Journal* 39, no. 3 (1995): 396–407.

——. "Andrey Sinyavsky: Puzzle Maker." *Slavic and East European Journal* 42, no. 3 (1998): 385–88.

Kott, Jan. "A Voice from the Chorus." *New York Times Book Review*, 27 June 1976, 1, 25–27.

Kozlovskii, Vladimir. "Vydalo li TsRU Sinyavskogo i Danielya?" *Novoe russkoe slovo*, 10 February 1987, 3–4.

Krist, Gary. Review of *Goodnight! Hudson Review* 43, no. 4 (Winter 1991): 691–98.

Krymov, B. "Sud prodolzhaetsya." *Literaturnaya gazeta*, no. 19 (12 February 1966): 2.

Labedz, Leopold. "The Trial in Moscow." *Encounter* 26, no. 4 (April 1966): 82–91.

Laber, Jeri L. "The Trial Ends . . ." *New Republic*, 19 March 1966, 26–29.

Lamont, Rosette C. Review of *Soviet Civilization: A Cultural History*. *World Literature Today* 66, no. 1 (Winter 1992): 158–59.

Lask, Thomas. "Publishing Sinyavsky." *New York Times*, 17 March 1966, 26–29.

Leatherbarrow, W. J. "The Sense of Purpose and Socialist Realism in Tertz's *The Trial Begins*." *Forum for Modern Language Studies* 11, no. 3 (1975): 268–79.

Lebenson, Ol'ga. "Vizit posle donosa." *Vremya i my*, no. 91 (1986): 229–30.

Lehmann-Haupt, Christopher. Review of *A Voice from the Chorus*. *New York Times*, 2 July 1976, C25.

Leong, Albert. "The Literary Criticism of Abram Tertz." *Proceedings of the Pacific Northwest Conference on Foreign Languages* 28, no. 1 (1977): 118–20.

Levin, Martin. "A Reader's Report." Review of *The Makepeace Experiment*. *New York Times Book Review*, 11 July 1965, 40.

Levitt, Marcus C. "Siniavskii's Alternative Autobiography *A Voice from the Chorus*." *Canadian Slavonic Papers* 33, no. 1 (March 1991): 46–61.

"Litso klevetnikov." *Pravda*, no. 42 (11 Febuary 1966): 6.

Lobanov, Mikhail. "Chelnochnye perestroishchiki." *Moskovskii literator*, no. 7 (10 February 1989): 4.

Lourie, Richard. *Letters to the Future: An Approach to Sinyavsky-Tertz*. Ithaca, N. Y.: Cornell University Press, 1975.

Maguire, Robert A. Review of *On Socialist Realism* and *The Trial Begins*. *Russian Review* 21, no. 2 (1962): 193–95.

Maksudov, S. "Spokoinoi nochi. S dobrym utrom. Priglashenie k chteniyu." *Strana i mir*, no. 10 (1984): 93–96.

Mann, Yu. "Nad bezdnoi Gogolya." Review of *V teni Gogolya*. *Literaturnoe obozrenie*, no. 1/2 (1993): 30–32.

Marchenko, Alla. "Opyt raznomysliya vnutri inakomysliya." *Literaturnoe obozrenie*, no. 8 (1989): 87–88.

[Martynenko, Ol'ga.] "Uvolen za ubezhdeniya." *Moskovskie novosti*, no. 2 (14 January 1990): 4.

Marx, Bill. "Separated at Birth." Review of *Little Jinx* and *Soviet Civilization: A Cultural History*. *The Nation* 255, no. 14 (2 November 1992): 511–13.

Mathewson, Ruth. "Sinyavsky's Mission." Review of *Voice from the Chorus*. *New Leader*, 13 September 1976, 16–17.

Matich, Ol'ga. "*Spokoinoi nochi*: Andrej Sinjavskij's Rebirth as Abram Terc." *Slavic and East European Journal* 33, no. 1 (Spring 1989): 50–63.

———. "Russian Literature in Emigration: A Historical Perspective on the 1970s." In *The Third Wave: Russian Literature in Emigration*, edited by Olga Matich with Michael Heim, 15–20. Ann Arbor, Mich.: Ardis, 1984.

Mayne, Richard. "Technique [Review of *The Makepeace Experiment*]." *New Statesman* 69, no. 1779 (16 April 1965): 619–20.

McLean, Hugh. "Abram Tertz and His Translators." *Slavic and East European Journal* 8, no. 4 (1964): 434–40.

Meerson, Ol'ga. "Progulka s Tertsem." *Forum* 3 (1983): 222–31.

Merkulov, Dmitrii. "Klevetnikam Rossii . . ." *Moskovskii literator*, nos. 30, 31 (15 September 1989): 4

Mikhailov, Mikhailo. *Abram Terts ili begstvo iz retorty*. Frankfurt/Main: Possev-Verlag, 1969. English translation, "Flight from the Test Tube," in *Russian Themes*. New York: Farrar, Straus and Giroux, 1968.

Mikhailov, S. "Klevetniki poluchat svoi zaslugi." *Komsomol'skaya pravda* 15 (February 1966): 3.

Milner-Gulland, Robin. Review of *The Russian Intellingsia*. *Europe-Asia Studies* 50, no. 6 (September 1998): 1101–2.

Monas, Sidney. "Engineers or Martyrs: Dissent and the Intelligentsia." *Problems of Communism* 17, no. 5 (1968): 2–17.

———. "In Defense of Socialist Realism." *Problems of Communism* 16, no. 2 (1967): 4456.

Morsberger, Grace Anne. "'The Icicle' as Allegory." *Odyssey* 4, no. 2 (August 1981): 15–18.

Morson, Gary Saul. Review of *Soviet Civilization: A Cultural History*. *American Scholar* 61, no. 1 (Winter 1992): 132–37.

Muchnic, Helen. "It Happened in Lyubimov." Review of *The Makepeace Experiment*. *New York Review of Books*, 14 October 1965, 33–35.

———. "Light from Above." Review of *A Voice from the Chorus*, by Abram Tertz (Andrei Sinyavsky). *New York Review of Books* 23, no. 13 (5 August 1976), 5, 8.

Muggeridge, Malcolm. "Books: Concerning the BBC TV Reconstruction of the Trial of Sinyavsky and Daniel." *Esquire* 69 (March 1968): 26, 40.

Murav, Harriet. "Sinyavsky's Trial." *Slavic and East European Journal* 42, no. 3 (1998): 389–93.

Nepomnyashchii, Valentin, et al. "Obsuzhdenie knigi Abram Tertsa 'Progulki s Pushkinym.'" *Voprosy literatury*, no. 10 (October 1990): 77–153. English translation of excerpts by Catharine Teimer Nepomnyashchy, "A Discussion of

Abram Tertz's Book *Strolls with Pushkin*," *Russian Studies in Literature* 28, no. 1 (Winter 1991–92): 63–64.

Nepomnyashchy, Catharine Theimer. "Andrei Sinyavsky's 'Return' to the Soviet Union." *Formations* 6, no. 1 (Spring 1991): 24–44.

———. "Andrei Sinyavsky's 'You and I': A Modern Day Fantastic Tale." *Ulbandus Review* 2, no. 2 (1982): 209–30.

———. "Perestroika and the Soviet Creative Unions." In *New Perspectives on Russian and Soviet Artistic Culture: Selected Papers from the Fourth World Congress for Soviet and East European Studies*, Harrogate, 1990, edited by John O. Norman, 131–51. New York: St. Martin's Press, 1994.

———. "The Poetics of Motivation: Time, Narrative, and History in the Works of Solnzhenitsyn, Sinjavskij and Pasternak." Ph.D. diss., Columbia University, 1987.

———. *Abram Tertz and the Poetics of Crime*, New Haven, Conn.: Yale University Press, 1995.

———. "Sinyavsky/Tertz: The Evolution of the Writer in Exile." Special issue of *Humanities in Society* 7, nos. 3–4 (1984): 123–42.

———, ed. "The Return of Abram Tertz: Siniavskii's Reception in Gorbachev's Russia." An issue of *Russian Studies in Literature* 28, no. 1 (Winter 1991–1992).

———. "Andrey Donatovich Sinyavsky (1925–1997)." *Slavic and East European Journal* 42, no. 3 (1998): 367–71.

Nivat, Georges. "André Siniavski: l'écrivain est un assassin." *Magazine littéraire*, nos. 172–73 (May 1981): 92–93.

———. ". . . Chtoby prevozmoch' otchayanie i odinochestvo." Review of *Goodnight. Russkaya mysl'*, no. 3546 (6 December 1984): 10.

———. "Le pistolet de Pouchkine." *Magazine littéraire*, no. 124 (May 1977): 60–63.

"Notes from the Underground." *Time,* 29 October 1965, 37.

Novikov, Vladimir. "*Sinyavskii i Terts*." In Terts, *Sobranie sochinenii v dvukh tomakh* 1:3–12. Moscow: SP Start, 1992.

[Nudel'man, R.] "Dvadtsat' let spustya [Interview with Mark Azbel' and Nina and Aleksandr Voronel]." *Dvadtsat' dva*, no. 46 (January–March 1986): 132–77.

Numano, Mitsuesi. "Iz knigi 'Za odnu ostanovku do vechnosti.' Solzhenitsyn ili Sinyavskii!" *Inostrannaya literatura*, no. 2 (February 1990), 238–41.

Nussbaum, Andrew J. "Literary Selves: The Tertz-Sinyavsky Dialogue." In *Autobiographical Statements in Twentieth-Century Russian Literature*, edited by Jane Gary Harris. 238–59. Princeton, N.J.: Princeton University Press, 1990.

Oberbeck, S. K. "Underground Letters." Review of *The Makepeace Experiment*. *Reporter* 33, no. 7 (21 October 1965): 58–59.

[Obozrevatel']. "Klevetniki v efire." *Izvestia*, no. 88 (14 April 1966): 2.

Offord, Derek. "Review of *The Russian Intelligentsia*. *Journal of European Studies* 28, no. 1–2 (March–June 1998): 209–11.

Ohmann, Richard M. "Soviet and American Literature." Review of *On Socialist Realism*. *Commonweal* 75, no. 15 (5 January 1962): 391–92.

Orekhanova, G. "Posleslovie k replike." *Sovetskaya Rossiya*, 10 October 1989, 4.

"Otkrytoe pis'mo v redaktsiyu gazety 'Izvestya.'" *Izvestia*, no. 45 (23 February 1966): 3.

Parthe, Kathleen. "Sinyavsky on His Way to Tomorrow." *Slavic and East European Journal* 42, no. 3 (1998): 394–98.

Perel'man, Viktor. "Kto obvinyaet Sinyavskogo." *Vremy i my*, no. 91 (1986): 218–22.

"Perestaralis'." *Literaturnaya gazeta*, no. 24 (24 February 1966): 4.

Peterson, Ronald E. "The Writer as Alien in Sinjavskij's 'Pxenc.'" *Wiener Slawistischer Almanach* 12 (1983): 47–53.

Petrov, T. "Prigovor Klevetnikam." *Pravda*, no. 46 (15 February 1966): 4.

Pevear, Richard. "Sinyavsky in Two Worlds: Two Brothers Named Chenier." *Hudson Review* 25 (1972): 375–402.

Phillips, Anthony. Review of *The Russian Intelligentsia*. *Australian Journal of Political Science* 34 (November 1999): 466.

Pine, J. C. Review of *The Trial Begins*. *Library Journal* 85 (1 November 1960): 4008.

Pipes, Richard. "The Soviet Jacobins." *New Leader* 49, no. 9 (25 April 1966): 9–11.

"Pis'ma na odnu temu." *Literaturnaya Rossiya*, no. 37 (15 September 1989): 16.

"Pis'ma na odnu temu." *Literaturnaya Rossiya*, no. 39 (29 September 1989): 20.

Pletnev, R. "O zlom suemudrii knigi Abram Terts." Review of *V teni Gogolya*. *Novyi zhurnal*, no. 121 (1975): 72–80.

Pomerants, G. "Diaspora i Abrashka Terts." *Iskusstvo kino*, no. 2 (1990): 20–26.

Popova, Natal'ya. "Gal'skii petukh i rusofobiya." *Knizhnoe obozrenie*, no. 46 (17 November 1989): 16. English translation by Dobrochna Dyrcz-Freeman, "The Gallic Rooster and Russophobia," *Russian Studies in Literature* 28, no. 1 (Winter 1991–1992): 56–62.

Porte, Joel. "The Laugh's on Us All." Review of *The Makepeace Experiment*. *Christian Science Monitor*, 5 August 1965, 7.

Radley, Philippe. "Reporting the Tertz Affair." *New Leader* 49, no. 1 (3 January 1966): 11–12.

———. Review of *The Russian Intelligentsia*. *World Literature Today* 72, no. 1 (Winter 1998): 164.

Redaktsionnaya kollegiya. "K Chitalelyam." *Oktyabr'*, no. 9 (1089): 207–8.

Redaktsiya "LR." "Provokatsiya." *Literaturnaya Rossiya*, no. 42 (20 October 1989): 2.

Reeve, F. D. "Listen for the Pistol Shot." Review of *Fantastic Stories*. *Kenyon Review* 25, no. 4 (Autumn 1963): 743–47.

Renshaw, John. "The Elusive 'Abram Tertz.'" *New York Times Magazine*, 31 October 1965, 52–53.

Remnick, David. Review of *The Russian Intelligentsia*. *New York Review of Books* 45, no. 6 (9 April 1998): 10–13.

Roberts, Henry L. "Capitalize P in Purpose." Review of *On Socialist Realism*. *New York Times Book Review*, 26 November 1961, 10.

"Rossiiskie dokumenty po delu A. Sinyavskogo i Yu. Danielya." *Grani*, no. 62 (1966).

Rozanova, Mariya. "Abram da Mar'ya." *Nezavisimaya gazeta*, 12 January 1993, 5 and 13 January 1993; Reprinted in *Sintaksis*, no. 34 (1994), 125–51.

——. "Fantasticheskii realizm." *Dekorativnoe iskusstvo* 3 (1967).

——. "K istorii i geografii etoi knigi." *Voprosy literatury*, no. 10 (October 1990), 154–61. Reprinted in Abram Terts, *Progulki s Pushkinym*, 147–59 (Saint Petersburg: Vsemirnoe slovo, 1993). English translation by Catharine Theimer Nepomnyashchy, "On the History and Geography of This Book," *Russian Studies in Literature* 28, no. 1 (Winter 1991–1992): 89–98.

——. "Kto za kogo reshaet." *Moskovskie novosti*, no. 3 (28 January–2 February 1990): 6. English translation, "Who Decides for Whom?" *Moscow News*, no. 3 (28 January–2 February 1990): 3.

Rubinshtein, Natal'ya. "Abram Terts i Aleksandr Pushkin." *Vremya i my*, no. 9 (July 1976): 118–33.

Rumens, Carol. "*Goodnight!*: A novel by Abram Tertz." *The New Statesman & Society* 3, no. 98 (27 April 1990): 35.

Runin, B. "Logika spora i logika iskusstva." *Novyi mir* 37, no. 8 (1960): 236–48.

——. "Spor neobkhodimo prodolzhit." *Novyi mir* no. 11 (1960): 195–220.

[Russian Writers' Union]. *Losing the Battle of Stalingrad. The Economist* 313, no. 7632, 9 December 1989, 97.

Ryurikov, B. "Sotsialisticheskii realizm i ego nisprovergateli." *Inostrannaya literatura,* no. 1 (1962): 191–200.

Salisbury, Harrison E. "Russian Dissenters." Review of *Fantastic Stories*. *New York Times Book Review*, 5 May 1963, 35.

Sandler, Stephanie. "Sex, Death and Nation in the *Strolls with Pushkin* Controversy." *Slavic Review* 51, no. 2 (Summer 1992): 294–308.

Scammell, Michael. "Speculations of a Captive Monk." Review of *A Voice from the Chorus*. *Times Literary Supplement*, 20 May 1977, 626–27.

Schwartz, Harry. "Globov, Marina, and Seryozha of the Soviet New Class." Review of *The Trial Begins*. *New York Times Book Review*, 16 October 1960, 4.

——. "Man-Centered Theology." Review of *On Socialist Realism*. *Saturday Review*, 11 November 1961, 26.

Sekretariat pravleniya Soyuza pisatelei SSSR. "Otkrytoe pis'mo v redaktsiyu 'Literaturnoi gezety.'" *Literaturnaya gazeta*, no. 22 (19 February 1966): 1.

"Ser'eznye nedostatki." *Literatura i zhizn'*, 29 July 1962, 3.

Sh., I. "Pozitsiya izdatelya. Po stranitsam zhurnalov '22' i 'Sintaksis.'" *Vremya i my*, no. 91 (1986): 181–93.

Shafarevich, I. "Fenomen emigratsii." *Literaturnaya Rossiya*, no. 36 (8 September 1989): 4–5. English translation by Dobrocha Dyrcz-Freeman, "The Emigration Phenomenon," *Russian Studies in Literature* 28, no. 1 (Winter 1991–1992): 45–55.

———. "Rusofobiya." *Nash sovremennik*, no. 6 (1989): 167–92, and no. 11 (1989): 162–72. Reprinted from *Veche*, no. 32 (December 1988): 9–75, and no. 33 (March 1989), 5–54.

Sheppard, R. Z. "Notes from the Underground." Review of *Goodnight! Time, 25* December 1989, 76.

"VI plenum pravleniya SP RSFSR." *Literaturnaya Rossiya*, no. 48 (1 December 1989): 2–13.

Shturman, Dora. "Spokoinoi nochi . . . ." *Novoe russkoe slovo*, 2 July 1993, 21.

Simmons, Ernest J. "The Trial Begins for Soviet Literature." *Massachusetts Review* 7, no. 4 (Autumn 1966): 714–24.

Simonov, Vladimir. "Vid iz okna." *Moskovskie novosti*, no. 8 (22 February 1987): 3.

Singer, Herman. "Fugitive from Socialist Realism." Review of *The Trial Begins. New Republic*, 5 December 1960, 19–20.

Sinyavskii i Daniel' na skam'e podsudimykh. New York: Inter-language Literary Associates, 1966.

Smirnov, I. "Rozhdennaya revolyutsiei." *Russkaya literatura* 7, no. 1 (1965): 203–7.

———. "Metnulo! Replika dvum kritikam." *Ogonek*, no. 9 (1961): 29.

"Socialist Surrealism." Review of *The Trial Begins*. *Time*, 3 October 1960, 84–85.

Solov'ev, B. "Legkii nesesser i tyazhelaya klad'." *Oktyabr'*, no. 6 (1961): 179–93; no. 7 (1961): 186–93.

[Solov'eva, Yu.] "Monologi." [Interview with Mariya Rozanova]. *Sovetskii tsirk*, no. 22 (31 May 1990): 14, and no. 23 (7 June 1990): 14–15.

Solzhenitsyn, Aleksandr. ". . . Koleblet tvoi trenozhnik." *Vestnik russkogo khristianskogo dvizheniya*, no. 142 (1984): 133–52. Reprinted in *Novyi mir*, no. 5 (1991): 148–59.

———. "Otvetnoe slovo na prisuzhdenie literaturnoi nagrady amerikanskogo natsional'nogo kluba iskusstv, N'yu-Iork, 19 yanvarya 1993." *Novyi mir*, no. 4 (1993): 3–6. English translation, "The Relentless Cult of Novelty and How It Wrecked the Century," *New York Times Book Review*, 7 February 1993, 3, 17.

———. "Nashi plyuralisty." *Vestnik russkogo khristianskogo dvizheniya*, no. 139 (1983): 133–60. Reprinted in *Novyi mir*, no. 4 (1992): 211–25. English translation, "Our Pluralists." *Survey: A Journal of East and West Studies* 29, no. 2/125 (Summer 1985): 1–28.

Spector, Ivar. Review of *The Trial Begins*. *Saturday Review* 43, 5 November 1960, 32.

Starikov, D. "Sporit' po sushchestvu." *Literatura i Zhizn'*, 24 February 1961, 1–3.

Steinberg, Sybil. Review of *Goodnight! Publishers Weekly* 236, no. 14, 6 October 1989, 82.

Steinman, Maxiene. Review of "Fantastic Stories" by Abram Tertz. *East Europe* 13, no. 10 (October 1964): 54–56.

Stuttaford, Genevieve. Review of *Soviet Civilization: A Cultural History*. *Publishers Weekly* 237, no. 34 (24 August 1990): 49.

"Sud nad A.D. Sinyavskim I Ju. M. Danielem." *Grani*, no. 60 (1966): 94–116.

Tatarinov, Aleksei. "Andrei Sinyavskii i Abram Terts." Review of *Spokoinoi nochi*. *Strelets*, no. 11 (November 1985): 20–22.

"Témoignage pour Siniavski." *Le Monde*, 23 November 1965, 6.

Ternovskii, E. "V neyasnom i nereshennom mire Rozanova (O knige Sinyavskogo 'Opavshie list'ya' V. V. Rozanova)." *Russkaya mysl'*, no. 3429 (9 September 1982): 11.

Tikos, Laszlo M. "On Abram Tertz's *A Voice from the Choir*." *International Fiction Review* 2, no. 2 (July 1975): 168–73.

Todd, William Mills, III. "Tertz's 'Strolls with Pushkin' in Leningrad: A Personal Reminiscence." *Slavic and East European Journal* 42, no. 3 (1998): 399–401.

Tsyurupa, Aleksei. "Ne sotvori sebe kumina (Pochti vavilonskaya istoriya)." *Kamchatskii komsomolets*, 12 December 1989, 6.

Tvardovskii, A. "Po sluchayu yubileya." *Novyi mir*, no. 1 (January 1965): 3–18.

——. "Ot redaksii." *Novyi mir*, no. 8 (1961): 253–57.

Updike, John. "The Lament of Abrashka Tertz." *New Leader* 49, no. 2 (1966): 3.

Urnov, Dmitrii. "Obsuzhdenie knigi Abrama Tertsa 'Progulki s Pushkinym.' *Voprosy literatury*, no. 10 (October 1990): 77–153. English translation of excerpts by Catharine Theimer Nepomnyashchy, "A Discussion of Abram Tertz's Book *Strolls with Pushkin*," *Russian Studies in Literature* 28, no. 1 (Winter 1991–92): 80–87.

Viereck, John. "World Power through Witchcraft." Review of *The Makepeace Experiment*. *Saturday Review*, 24 July 1965, 45–46.

Vinogradov, Igor'. "Osobyi put' . . . ?" *Moskovskie novosti*, no. 38 (17 September 1989): 16.

Vlasenko, A. "Opisatel 'nym metodom." *Oktyabr'* 38, no. 9 (1961): 184–85.

Volker, Levin. *Das Groteske in M. Bulgakov's Proza. Mit einem Exkurs zu A. Sinjavsky*. Munich: Sanger, 1975.

Voronel', Aleksandr. "Pravo byt' uslyshannym . . ." *Dvadtsat' dva*, no. 48 (June–July 1986): 145–51.

Vozdvizhenskii, Vyacheslav, "Progulki s Shafarevichem i bez . . ." *Strana i mir*, no. 6 (1989): 166–71.

"V sekretariate moskovskoi pisatel'skoi organizatsii." *Literaturnaya gazeta*, no. 23 (22 February 1966): 4.

"Vse zaedino: stseny VI plenuma pravleniya Soyuza pisatelei RSFSR 13–14 noyabrya 1989 goda." *Ogonek*, no. 48 (November 1989): 6–8, 31.

Weiner, Stephen. "Socialist Legality on Trial." *Problems of Communism* 17, no. 4 (1968): 6–12.

West, Anthony. "Books: Inside the Wrong Skin." Review of *Fantastic Stories*. *New Yorker*, 21 September 1963, 181–88.

West, Paul. "New Novels." Review of *The Trial Begins*. *New Statesman* 59, no. 1520 (30 April 1960): 642–43.

Williams, A. M. "Ces contes d'Abram Tertz sont-ils des faux ou de nouveau 'Kafka'?" *Le Figaro Litéraire*, no. 7 (April 1962): 2.

Woronzoff, Alexander. "The Writer as Artist and Critic: The Case of Andrej Sinjavskij." *Russian Language Journal* 37, nos. 126–27 (1983): 139–45.

Yevtushenko, Evgeny. "Kontramarka na protsess." *Ogonek*, no. 19 (May 1989): 19. Abridged English translation, "A Pass to See the Trial," *Soviet Life*, February 1990, 58–59.

——. "A Poet's View of Glasnost." *Time*, 9 February 1987, 32–33.

Young, Cathy. Review of *Soviet Civilization: A Cultural History*. *Reason* 23, no. 2 (June 1991): 55–57.

Zamoyska, Helene. "Andrey Sinyavsky Arrives in Paris." *Encounter*, no. 41 (November 1973): 63–65.

——. "Pis'mo Elen Zamoyska (Pel'te) Andreu Sinyavskomu." *Vremya i my*, no. 91 (1986): 222–23.

——. "Quelques souvenirs sur André Siniavski." *Esprit*, no. 357 (February 1967): 258–70.

——. "Siniavski et sa patrie." *Le Monde*, 17–18 April 1966, 1, 3.

GENERAL REFERENCES

Alter, Robert. *Partial Magic: The Novel as a Self-Conscious Genre*. Berkeley: University of California Press, 1975.

Bakhtin, M. M. *The Dialogic Imagination*. edited by Michael Holquist, translated by Caryl Emerson and Michael Holquist. Austin: University of Texas Press, 1981.

——. *Problemy poetiki Dostoevskogo*. 2nd edition, Moscow: Sovetskii Pisatel', 1963.

Booker, M. Keith, and Dubravka Juraga. *Bakhtin, Stalin, and Modern Russian Fiction: Carnival, Dialogism, and History*. Westport, Conn.: Greenwood Press, 1995.

Burger, Peter. *Theory of the Avant-Garde*. Translated from the German by Michael Shaw, foreword by Jochem Schulte-Sasse. *Theory and History of Literature*, vol. 4. Minneapolis: University of Minnesota Press, 1984.

Caute, David, ed. *Essential Writings of Karl Marx*. London: MacGibbon & Kee, 1967.

Cornforth, Maurice. *The Open Philosophy and The Open Society: A Reply to Dr. Karl Popper's Refutations of Marxism*. London: Lawrence and Wishart, 1968.

Cowan, Louise, ed. *The Terrain of Comedy*. Introduction by Louise Cowan. Dallas: Institute of Humanities and Culture, 1982.

Dostoevsky, M. F. *Prestuplenie i nakazanie* in *Polnoe sobranie sochinenii v tridtsatikh tomakh*. 10: Leningrad: Nauka, 1974.

———. *Besy* in *Polnoe sobranie sochinenii v tridtsatikh tomakh*. 11: Leningrad: Nauka, 1974.

Draitser, Emil A. *Techniques of Satire: The Case of Saltykov-Shchedrin*. Berlin: Mouton de Gruyter, 1994.

Elkin, P. K. *The Augustan Defence of Satire*. Oxford: Oxford University Press, 1973.

Elliott, Robert C. *The Power of Satire: Magic, Ritual, Art*. Princeton, N.J.: Princeton University Press, 1960.

Ershov, L. F. *Satira i sovremennost'*. Moscow: "Sovremennik," 1978.

Fitzpatrick, Sheila. "The Problem of Class Identity in NEP Society." In *Russia in the Era of NEP*, edited by Sheila Fitzpatrick, Alexander Rabinowitch, and Richard Stites, 12–33. Bloomington: Indiana University Press, 1991.

Fletcher, Angus John Stewart. *Allegory: The Theory of a Symbolic Mode*. Ithaca, N.Y.: Cornell University Press, 1964.

Frank, Joseph. *Through the Russian Prism: Essays on Literature and Culture*. Princeton, N.J.: Princeton University Press, 1990.

Frye, Northrop. *Anatomy of Criticism*. New York: Atheneum, 1967.

Garrard, John, and Carol Garrard. *Inside the Writers' Union*. New York: The Free Press, 1990.

Gogol', N. V. *Mertvye dushi* in *Polnoe sobranie sochinenii*, 3. Moscow: Akademiya nauk, 1951.

Gor'kii, Maksim. *Zhizn' Klima Samgina*. 1. Moscow: Sov. Pisatel', 1938.

———. *Pis'ma o Literature*. Sostav. A. I. Ovcharenko, Moscow: Sov. pis., 1957.

Griffin, Dustin. *Satire: A Critical Reintroduction*. Lexington: University Press of Kentucky, 1994.

Groys, Boris. Translated by Charles Rougle. *The Total Art of Stalinism: Avant-Garde, Aesthetic Dictatorship, and Beyond*. Princeton, N.J.: Princeton University Press, 1992.

Guilhamet, Leon. *Satire and the Transformation of Genre*. Philadelphia: University of Pennsylvania Press, 1987.

Heller, Michael, and Aleksandr Nekrich. *Utopia in Power: The History of the Soviet Union from 1917 to the Present*. Translated by Phyllis B. Carlos. New York: Simon & Schuster, 1986.

Hirschop, Ken, and David Shepherd eds. *Bakhtin and Cultural Theory*. Manchester: Manchester University Press, 1989.

Hutcheon, Linda. *A Poetics of Postmodernism: History, Theory, Fiction*. London: Routledge, 1988.

Huyssen, Andreas. *After the Great Divide: Modernism, Mass Culture, Postmodernism*. Bloomington: Indiana University Press, 1986.

Lermontov, M. Yu. *Geroi nashego vremeni* in *Sobranie sochinenii v chetyrekh tomakh*. 4: Moscow: Khudozhestvennaya literatura, 1976.

Lunacharsky, A. *On Literature and Art*. Edited by A. Lebeder. Moscow: Foreign Languages Publishing House, 1965.

——. "Samgin." *Stati o Gor'kom*. Moscow: Sov. Pisatel', 1938.

Marsh, Rosalind. *Images of Dictatorship: Portraits of Stalin in Literature*. New York: Routledge, 1989.

Mayakovsky, Vladimir. *Klop* in *Polnoe sobranie sochinenii v trinadtsati tomakh*. 11. Moscow: Khudozhestvennoi literatury, 1958.

Muravina, Nina. *Vstrechi s Pasternakom*. Tenafly, N.J.: Hermitage, 1990.

Nabokov, Vladimir. *Speak, Memory*. New York: Vintage, 1989.

Nahirny, Vladimir C. *The Russian Intelligentsia: From Torment to Silence*. New Brunswick, N.J.: Transaction Books, 1983.

Narodnye russkie skazki A.I. Afanas'eva. 3. Moscow: 1957.

Nash, Walter. *The Language of Humour*. Foreword by Randolph Quirk. London: Longman, 1985.

Paulson, Ronald. *The Fictions of Satire*. Baltimore: Johns Hopkins University Press, 1967.

Pipes, Richard, ed. *The Russian Intelligentsia*. New York: Columbia University Press, 1961.

Plett, Heinrich F., ed. *Intertextuality. Research in Text Theory.* Berlin: Walter de Gruyter, 1991.

Riasanovsky, Nicholas V. *A History Of Russia*. 4th ed. New York: Oxford University Press, 1984.

Rozanov, Vasilii. *Izbrannoe*. Munich: Neimanis, 1970.

Shcherbina, E. "'Zhizn' Klima Samgina' M. Gor'kogo." *Oktyabr'* 20, no. 11 (1936).

Slonim, Marc. *Soviet Rusian Literature: Writers and Problems 1917–1967*. New York: Oxford University Press, 1969.

Stahlberger, Lawrence L. *The Symbolic System of Majakovskij*. The Hague: Mouton & Co., 1964.

Struve, Gleb. *Russian Literature under Lenin and Stalin: 1917–1953*. Norman: University of Oklahoma Press, 1971.

Tompkins, Stuart Ramsay. *The Russian Intelligentsia*. Westport, Conn.: Greenwood Press, 1976.

Vekhi: Landmarks. Translated and edited by Marshall S. Shats and Judith E. Zimmerman. Amonk, N.Y.: M.E. Sharpe, 1994.

Wachtel, Andrew B. *An Obsession with History: Russian Writers Confront the Past*. Stanford, Calif.: Stanford University Press, 1994.

Waugh, Patricia. *Metafiction: The Theory and Practice of Self-Conscious Fiction*. London: Routledge, 1984.

Index

About the Author

Walter F. Kolonosky teaches Russian at Kansas State University. He earned his undergraduate degree from Lycoming College and his graduate degrees from the University of Pennsylvania and the University of Kansas. In addition to receiving numerous awards for teaching and research, he has been selected to participate in IREX Summer Teacher Exchanges and NEH Summer Seminars and Institutes. An advocate of international education, he established an office of study abroad at Kansas State, coordinating study-travel programs and exchanges for students in the College of Arts and Sciences. His interest in Russian led him to research in Russian literature of the twentieth century and literary theory, the results of which he has published in the *Slavic and East European Journal*, *Canadian-American Slavic Studies*, *Modern Fiction Studies*, and the *Russian Literature Triquarterly*. He is currently writing a book on the history of Russian students who have studied abroad since the time of Boris Godunov.